Pro Data Backup and Recovery

Steven Nelson

Apress®

Pro Data Backup and Recovery

ISBN-13 (pbk): 978-1-4302-2662-8

ISBN-13 (electronic): 978-1-4302-2663-5

Printed and bound in the United States of America (POD)

Trademarked names, logos, and images may appear in this book. Rather than use a trademark symbol with every occurrence of a trademarked name, logo, or image we use the names, logos, and images only in an editorial fashion and to the benefit of the trademark owner, with no intention of infringement of the trademark.

The use in this publication of trade names, trademarks, service marks, and similar terms, even if they are not identified as such, is not to be taken as an expression of opinion as to whether or not they are subject to proprietary rights.

Publisher and President: Paul Manning
Lead Editors: Frank Pohlmann and Michelle Lowman
Technical Reviewer: Russell Brown
Editorial Board: Steve Anglin, Mark Beckner, Ewan Buckingham, Gary Cornell, Jonathan Gennick, Jonathan Hassell, Michelle Lowman, Matthew Moodie, Jeff Olson, Jeffrey Pepper, Frank Pohlmann, Douglas Pundick, Ben Renow-Clarke, Dominic Shakeshaft, Matt Wade, Tom Welsh
Coordinating Editor: Mary Tobin
Copy Editor: Nancy Sixsmith
Compositor: MacPS, LLC
Indexer: Carol Burbo
Artist: April Milne
Cover Designer: Anna Ishchenko

Distributed to the book trade worldwide by Springer Science+Business Media, LLC., 233 Spring Street, 6th Floor, New York, NY 10013. Phone 1-800-SPRINGER, fax 201-348-4505, e-mail orders-ny@springer-sbm.com, or visit www.springeronline.com.

For information on translations, please e-mail rights@apress.com, or visit www.apress.com.

Apress and friends of ED books may be purchased in bulk for academic, corporate, or promotional use. eBook versions and licenses are also available for most titles. For more information, reference our Special Bulk Sales–eBook Licensing web page at www.apress.com/info/bulksales.

The information in this book is distributed on an "as is" basis, without warranty. Although every precaution has been taken in the preparation of this work, neither the author(s) nor Apress shall have any liability to any person or entity with respect to any loss or damage caused or alleged to be caused directly or indirectly by the information contained in this work.

To Elena, Christopher, and Tommy

Contents at a Glance

Contents

About the Author

 **Steven Nelson** has almost 20 years of experience in all areas of System Administration, spanning both *NIX and Microsoft Windows operating systems, but he has spent the last 10 years focusing on backup, recovery, and storage architecture and administration. He has worked for major manufacturing, online retail, and financial services companies, as well as working as a consultant to leading cellular telecom and industry-leading storage manufacturers. Steven is currently heading up the design and deployment of global backup, recovery, and storage services for the Research and Development division of a large software developer.

About the Technical Reviewer

 **Russell Brown** is a graduate of Texas A&M University, where he earned a B.S. degree in Agricultural Engineering, and the University of Colorado, where he earned a Masters degree in Business Administration. His work experience includes time as a Backup & Recovery Systems Administrator for a computer system manufacturer in Austin, Texas and a major entertainment studio in Burbank, California. Between systems administration roles, Russell spent four years flying around the United States while working as a Denver, Colorado-based professional services consultant specializing in backup and recovery. During the past five years, Russell has worked in a backup and recovery-focused systems engineering role in Los Angeles, California and Sydney, Australia. When Russell isn't working on backup and recovery, he enjoys travel, live music, automotive maintenance, and walking his dog along Sydney's northern beaches.

Acknowledgments

There is a myth about being an author: you sit at a computer, write an entire book, send it in, and *voila!* a book is published. Nothing could be further from the truth—writing a book, especially a technical book, is a team effort. There are many people involved in this process and all of them have played a vital role in getting the book completed.

To the team at Apress: Frank, you took a chance on an unproven author with an offbeat idea for a book, and who was working in environments where time was limited. Thank you for giving me the opportunity and pushing me to get things done. Mary and Michelle, my editors, you guys were great about giving me feedback and helping me along where you could. I appreciate all the support in writing this book.

A technical book is not possible without a great technical reviewer. Russell Brown, I could not have chosen a better TR. I cannot tell you how I appreciate all the time and effort you put into someone else's project and helped it to be so much better than it started. Thank you is not enough to say. When you decide to embark on this journey, I hope I can be as much help to you as you were to me.

Finally, I could not have done this without the support of my family. Chris and Tommy, I know that there have been lots of times when you guys wanted to do stuff with your dad and I was "working on the book." You guys have been really patient and understanding, and I love you more than you can know. Thank you for being the best sons a dad could ever ask for.

Elena, my lovely wife, you pushed me when I thought that I would never complete this, you supported me when I was down and celebrated with me on my accomplishments. You once told me that I would be very proud of myself when I finished this project. You were right. I love you with all my heart and cannot tell you how much I appreciate all the sacrifices you made for me over the years that allowed me to reach this point in my career and in my life.

CHAPTER 1

■ ■ ■

Introduction to Backup and Recovery

Who Should Read this Book?

Pro Data Backup and Recovery has come from the many views of people that I have interacted with during my career as a systems administrator, systems engineer, and consultant. This book is primarily geared toward the systems engineers and architects within an organization, but it will also be useful for the day-to-day functions of systems administrators and line managers of both teams. System administrators will find it useful for understanding the issues that are involved in protecting the data that they are responsible for providing on their systems, as well as helping to fashion systems and methods that will help protect that data against inevitable systems failures. Systems administrators can also use the information in this book to influence users of their systems to protect their data, create data structures that are easy to back up, and identify data that is most critical to be backed up and how it should be protected.

Line managers will find this book useful for understanding some of the technical trade-offs in data protection, helping them make better decisions regarding the recommendations that their systems engineers are making and system administrators are implementing for backup and recovery. The book will also help these line managers interact with the various vendors of backup products, giving the manager help to ask the hard questions and be able to answer them when their team asks them.

Backup systems have several characteristics:

- They are not inexpensive over the life cycle of the backup solution

- Large amounts of resources can be consumed in terms of:

    - People time

    - Operational and capital expenses

Additionally, the value of backup systems is difficult to express in terms of direct organizational mission contribution. This book will help the line manager show that the organization's data is being protected based on the criticality of the data, the cost of the backup platform, and the availability of the data for recovery.

Pro Data Backup and Recovery is primarily for systems engineers and architects (and administrators, in many cases) who are responsible for the design, implementation, and operation of backup and recovery systems. Backup is the one of those "invisible" jobs in systems—if people know who you are it is because bad things have happened. The main goal of this book is to help those who are in this sometimes thankless role to design, modify, and optimize your backup systems; to make those times where you are visible as short as possible; and to give you the tools to help make the recoveries successful. Within the pages of this book, you will find various configurations of both hardware and

1

software that will allow you to build or upgrade backup systems to grow and meet the changing needs of your organization. Although these configurations can be applied to many different brands of backup software, this book focuses only on the two major backup vendors: Symantec NetBackup and CommVault Simpana. These two vendors represent similar approaches to performing backups, but for different customer organizational sizes.

What this book is not is a tutorial on the specific commands and day-to-day operational functions that are executed directly by system administrators. I make some assumptions about the familiarity of engineers and/or architects with the backup software being used with regard to commands and options. This book is more concerned with the "why" of using various components as well as the "how" of putting them together, but not with specific command sets used to do it. There are command examples within this book as necessary to illustrate particular use cases, but there is an assumption that the commands used will already be familiar to the reader.

Backup and Recovery Concepts

Backup and recovery is a topic that might seem basic at first glance, but it seems to be a little confusing to many people. Backups and archives tend to be used interchangeably, representing some type of data protection that spans a period of time. Adding to the confusion is the fact that many organizations group the functions together in a single group, with the emphasis more on the data backup side, thus giving the illusion of being a single function. Let's look at this in a little more detail to get a common language and understanding of the functions and roles of both backups and archives.

▓ **Note** Where the difference between backups and archives gets particularly confusing is when backups are stored for long periods of time, on the order of years. Such backups can be mistakenly referred to as *archives* because the data the backup contains might indeed be the only copy of the data in existence at any particular point in time. This is particularly common in organizations that contain both open systems (UNIX/Linux and Windows) and mainframe environments because of terminology differences between the two platforms.

Backups

Backups are snapshot copies of data taken at a particular point in time, stored in a globally common format, and tracked over some period of usefulness, with each subsequent copy of the data being maintained independently of the first. Multiple levels of backups can be created. *Full backups* represent a complete snapshot of the data that is intended to be protected. Full backups provide the baseline for all other levels of backup.

In addition, two different levels of backups capture changes relative to the full backup. The *differential backup*, also known as the *cumulative incremental backup*, captures backups that have occurred since the last full backup. This type of backup is typically used in environments that do not have a lot of change.

The differential backup (see Figure 1–1) must be used with care because it can grow quickly to match or exceed the size of the original full backup. Consider the following: An environment has 20 TB of data to back up. Each day 5 percent or 1 TB of data changes in the environment. Assuming that this is a traditional backup environment, if a differential backup methodology is used, the first day 1TB of data is backed up (the first day's change rate against the previous full backup). The second day, 2 TB is backed up, and so on. By the end of 5 days, 5 TB of data is being backed up; by the end of 10 days, 10 TB might be being backed up; in 20 days, it could be a backup of 20 TB.

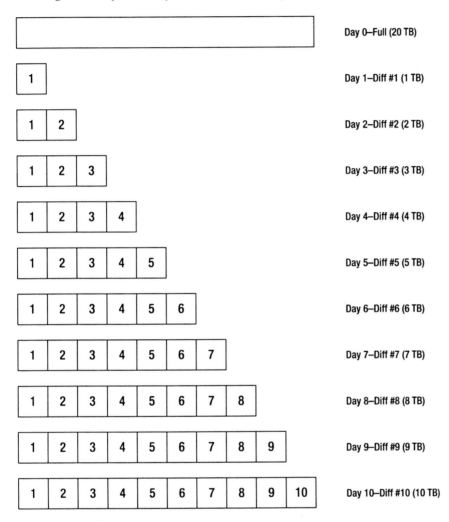

Figure 1–1. Differential backups

However, this 20 TB is not necessarily representative of a full backup. If the change rate represents a mixture of new files added to the respective clients as well as changes to existing data, the cumulative data backed up will not capture data that has not changed, even though the total amount of a full backup would still only incrementally change in size.

The advantage of using differential backups, especially during a restore, is the number of backup images required to perform the restore. A differential restore requires only the full backup plus the latest differential backup to complete the restore of any file in the backup image. Because there are only a limited number of images required, the probability of both images being lost, corrupted, or offsite is decreased significantly.

The second level of backup that captures images relative to the full backup is the *incremental backup* (see Figure 1–2). This backup captures changes that have occurred since the last backup of any type. Traditionally this is the most utilized form of backup in combination with a full backup. The incremental backup will contain the smallest amount of data required during a backup cycle, reducing the amount of data moved, and in general, the time required for a backup. Take the previous example of the 20 TB full backup. The first day after the full backup, the backup size would be 1 TB, the second day, 1 TB, and so on. The quantity of data backed up is only dependent on the difference between the previous backup and the current one, so the size (and proportionally the time required) for the backup is relatively consistent.

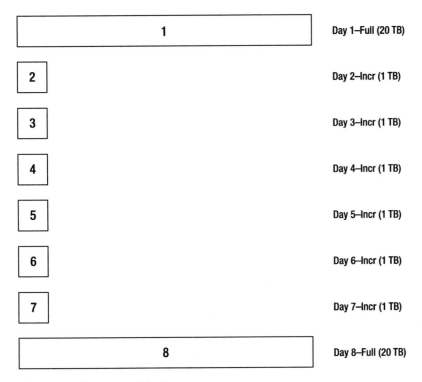

Figure 1–2. Incremental backups

There are some downsides to incremental backups. If you are recovering a set of files from a set of full and incremental backups, you will likely require more than two different backup images to complete the restore.

Suppose that four files need to be recovered: one has not changed since the full backup, one changed the first day, one changed the second day, and one changed the third day. To complete this restore, four images—the full backup and three different incremental images—are required to retrieve all the files needed (see Figure 1–3). In addition, because the images are relative to each other, some pieces of backup software will not allow parallel restores from the related sets of backup images, so the file recovers have to occur in serial fashion, each loading and unloading its own set of images for the restore. This can have a large impact on the time required for a restore.

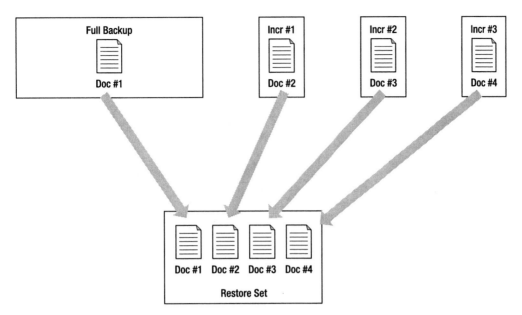

***Figure 1–3.** Multiple file incremental restore*

Also, because incremental backups capture the changes since the last full backup, the full set of backups can contain multiple copies of individual files. This can present problems during restore because it is too easy to select a copy of a file that shouldn't be restored.

Let's look at an example to illustrate this situation. Suppose that you have a file that contains the inventory for a particular division. This file gets updated on a daily basis, so it gets backed up daily. Three weeks later, a copy of the file needs to be restored, but now there are 21 copies to choose from. Which file is the one you want? Why 21 copies? Because the file gets updated each day, a new copy gets added to the backup index each day for 3 weeks or 21 days—thus 21 copies.

Another potential issue is the probability of loss or corruption. In many types of less sophisticated backup software, if a single incremental is corrupted or not available for recovery, the entire recovery will fail, even if the file is not located on that particular piece of media.

An alternate type of incremental backup is called the *level backup*. Each backup session is assigned a number, usually 0–9, with level 0 representing a full backup. Backups are executed relative to the number assigned, and a difference is taken against the next highest level of backup that was previously executed. Sound confusing? It can be, but it is a very powerful method of managing backups.

Consider the 20 TB example once again (see Figure 1–4). This time, a level 0 backup is executed against the 20 TB data set, capturing all 20 TB of data. The next backup executed is a level 1, which captures 1 TB of backup, representing the change since level 0 (the full backup). Now the next backup is a level 2 backup, which captures only the differences between the level 1 and the current backup—likely much smaller than a comparable level 1 backup. If another level 2 backup is executed as the next backup, the differences between the current data set and the last level 1 backup are captured. This type of backup can be much smaller than a comparable set of traditional incremental backups, resulting in short backup windows. However, the weaknesses of the incremental backup are also present in the level backup and need to be taken into consideration.

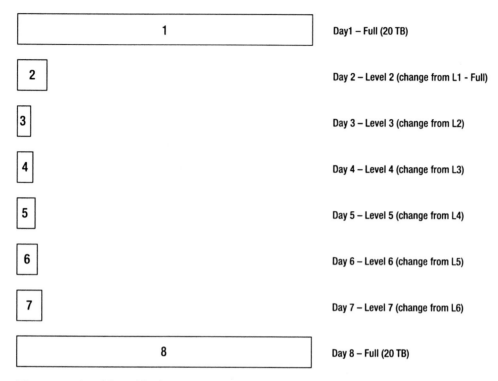

Figure 1–4. Level-based backups

Given the variety of backup levels, it is easy to see that multiple versions of individual data sets can exist within a particular set of backups. This feature allows for recovery of data to a particular point in time, complete with any changes in the specific data being recovered. This function exists because the backup software takes a complete copy of the data at the point of backup, regardless of the contents, usually based upon static information such as file names.

■ **Note** Many disk array vendors claim that the simple act of creating either a snapshot or clone of data using a piece of secondary storage constitutes a backup. However, this is not the case. Although single or even multiple copies of data can be made using these types of technologies, backups require tracking individual data sets. Technically, if the array- or file-based snapshots are identified by date of creation, and a manual record maintained all data sets and contents of the data sets that are protected, the set of snapshots could be considered backups. Pieces of backup software do maintain snapshot tracking, which then can be used as the recovery source—effectively making the snapshot a backup. EMC NetWorker is one example of backup software that has this capability.

Backups also quickly grow in total storage required. Take the 20 TB example you have been using and assume that there is a requirement to hold on to the backups for some period of time so that the data can be recovered at some point in the future. The period of time that the backups are required to be available is called the *backup retention period*. As the 20 TB data is repeatedly backed up with a combination of full and incremental backups, the total amount of data retained grows very quickly. This is not because of the addition of data to the system being backed up overall; it is strictly due to the number of copies of the same data that is stored repeatedly by both full and incremental backups.

To illustrate this, we will say that the organization has to keep a copy of this 20 TB of files and be able to retrieve a file that is 4 weeks old, relative to the current date—the backups must have 4 week retention. Also, assuming that weekly full and daily incremental backups are taken of this data, a minimum of 150 TB of backup storage media must be available to meet the four week requirement (see Figure 1–5).

	Full	Incr	Incr	Incr	Incr	Incr	Incr	
Wk 1	20	1	1	1	1	1	1	
Wk 2	20	1	1	1	1	1	1	
Wk 3	20	1	1	1	1	1	1	
Wk 4	20	1	1	1	1	1	1	
Wk 5	20	1	1	1	1	1	1	
Wk 6	20							
	120	5	5	5	5	5	5	150

Totals for the required retention for a 4 week retention cycle.

Figure 1–5. Required storage for a 20 TB backup

■ **Note** A common mistake is to simply count the number of weeks to meet a retention requirement. For instance, retaining four weeks of full backups to meet a four-week retention requirement does not satisfy the requirement. Why not? Because the fourth week's backup has expired on week four, making it ineligible (or potentially unavailable) for recovery by the backup software. The fifth week is required to ensure that if the requirement is to go back four weeks, the oldest week will still be available, with the sixth week's full backup needed to fully release the first week and provide a full four weeks (see Figure 1–6).

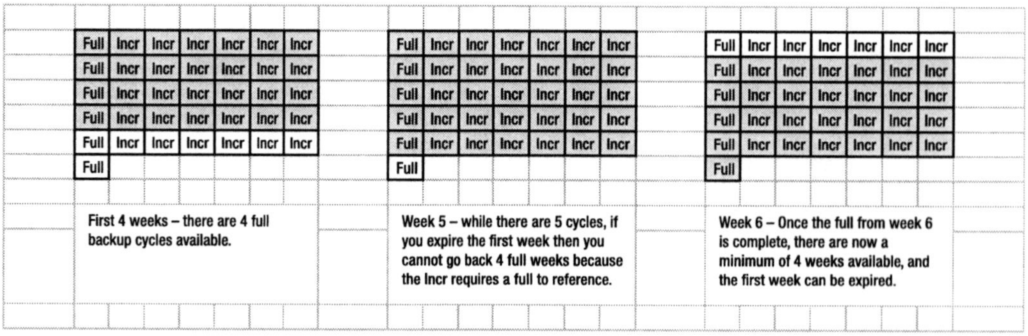

Figure 1–6. Backup pattern for four week retention

Note that the driving force of the total size of the backup is not the backup size itself, but the number of copies of the same data, made repeatedly. This is particularly marked in backups of relatively static data (for example, government records such as U.S. Census statistics). These files are static once they are completed, but are backed up each time there is a full backup. So if the particular record is 10 TB in size, even if there are only 10 full backups retained, the single record represents 100 TB, not including any other records that are also in the set of records. The vast majority of data stored has not changed in these types of environments and has been copied in exactly the same form repeatedly, taking up unnecessary space and backup resources. Because of this tendency to grow quickly and without bounds, backups should be intended for short- or medium-term storage and used for long-term storage only when absolutely required—backups are intended to be restored.

A backup that has been stored for a very long time, on the scale of years, is probably not usable. Why not? Changes in hardware, operating systems, application software, database systems, and even backup software can make recovery exceedingly difficult, if not impossible in some cases. Backups should truly be considered for storage options only for no longer than three years. Beyond this point, changes in one or all of the variables discussed previously will most likely render the backup useless and/or unrecoverable. In order for data to be recovered over longer periods of time, the data must be put into a format that is universal and onto media that has a higher probability of accessibility in the future. This is the purpose and design of archives.

Archives

Let's postulate that an organization needs to maintain a copy of data for ten years and selects a backup to store the data. Let's also assume that the data is static—it will not change over the lifetime of the data—and that traditional full/weekly incremental backups are taken on the data. What has happened: there are now 520 copies of exactly the same data stored in a very large set of backups.

Archives, on the other hand, are not copies of the data; they are the actual original data that has moved from one location to another. This movement is based on criteria assigned to the data such as age, value, criticality, and so on. Archived data is tracked over time, much like backup data, but the data is unchanging and therefore only a single copy of the data exists at any one point in time. If data within the archive is modified, the archive can either treat the new data as a new entry in the archive or replace the existing entry, depending on the capabilities of the archive system and the data-protection policies assigned to the archive. Archives are intended to allow for long-term storage of data to media that are resistant to degradation over time.

Examples of the type of data that might have this type of general protection requirement are criminal records. These types of records need to be maintained indefinitely because they contain information that might assist law enforcement with solving additional crimes, provide clues to individual behavior, and so on. As such, these records are important to protect. However, simply backing them up, over and over, is a waste of resources and ultimately does not provide a long-term method of storage and recovery. An archive would remove the criminal data from primary storage and place it on storage specifically designed for static data. The archive could be either offline or nearline, depending on the requirements.

Although the focus of this book is not on archiving, it does warrant mention. Why? Archives are a powerful tool in reducing the amount of data that is backed up, thus an effective tool in reducing the backup windows required to perform a backup of a particular environment.

To understand this, let's expand the 20 TB example (see Figure 1–7). Within the 20 TB, assume that 5 TB of data is static and a candidate for archiving. An initial archive copy of the data is created on some piece of archive media, (disk storage, in this case). Once the 5 TB of data has been removed from the original 20 TB, the next time the backup occurs it will have to move only 15 TB of data in the same period of time. Assuming that the overall data transfer performance of the backup does not change, the backup will take only 75 percent of the time previously required to accomplish the original 20 TB backup.

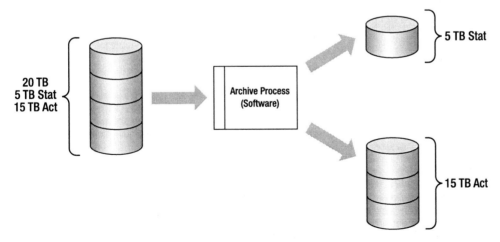

Figure 1–7. Data reduction in an archive

9

The original data can be referenced in one of two ways, depending on the method of creating the archive. The first method creates a copy of the data on static media and removes the original copy. Recalls of data are made through specific requests to the software that performed the archive, which is then recalled from the storage media and placed back on primary storage. This is what is known as an *offline archive* (the data is not directly accessible and is said to be offline), as shown in Figure 1–8. The offline archive typically removes the data completely from the original storage, requiring operational intervention to restore the data. Offline archives usually operate strictly on a file system basis, by archiving a particular file, set of files, or entire directory structures, regardless of other factors. Data is almost exclusively migrated to static media types, such as tape or optical platters. In order to access the archived data, end users must specifically request the data to be retrieved from the static media and replaced back on the original file system or into an alternate location.

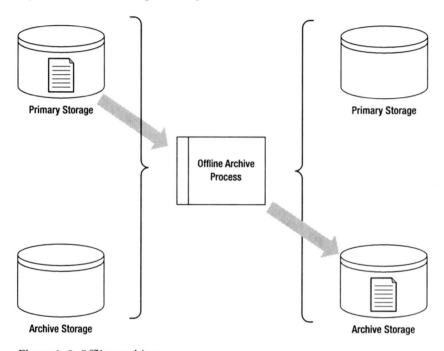

Figure 1–8. Offline archives

The offline archive system is most often included with backup software products and is part of both CommVault Simpana and Symantic NetBackup. As such, offline archives have a direct impact on both the size and performance of backups that are made of file systems that have data archived. Because the data has been physically removed and placed onto a separate piece of media, it no longer exists in the context of the backup. Thus, the amount of data backed up as well as the number of files per file system required to be processed are reduced. Although this might appear to solve the problem briefly stated previously, the removal of the data requires that all access requests be operationally satisfied, thus placing a great burden on backup operations staff to constantly retrieve data files.

The *active archive* (or *nearline archive*) differs from the offline archive by providing an archive of data, with the fact of the archive's existence transparent to the end user of the data. Active archives typically interact dynamically with the file systems or data structures that are being managed, typically will migrate data to various types of media, both static and dynamic (for example, disk-based), and leave markers, or *stubs*, behind on the file systems that represent the actual data migrated. Data is migrated based on metadata, such as the age, size, access time, owner of the data, or some combination thereof. The active archive product, typically a piece of software installed on individual file servers, migrates data on an automated, policy basis, using these metadata markers, leaving the stubs behind in its wake.

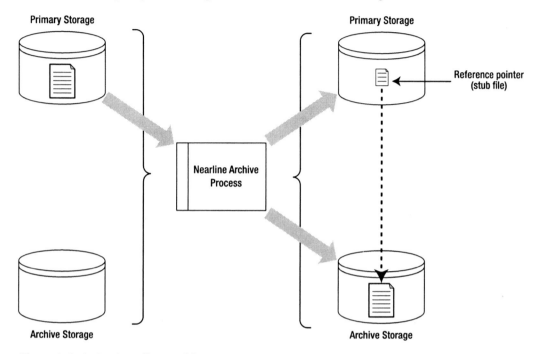

Figure 1–9. Active (nearline) archive

When the end user accesses the data in an active archive, the archiving software or hardware intercepts the request (typically an open(2) call to a particular file), preventing the operating system from immediately and directly satisfying the request. The archiving product then identifies whether the file in question is currently managed and whether the data has been archived to a secondary piece of media. If so, the archiving product recalls the data back to the original source and then allows the operating system to satisfy the request for the data to the end user. Note that the end user does not have to be a human user; it can be an automated application that is performing some type of access on data to satisfy a higher-level request. This could be anything from a virus scanner to a process that puts the contents of the file into a database.

Active archives are typically separate from backup software and have an indirect impact on the overall size and performance of the backup of the data source. Although the active archive removes data from the backup stream, it still leaves some data behind in the form of the stub. The stub can vary from 4 K to 8 K in size, depending on the original data type, and (in the case of a large number of files) can still represent a significant amount of data. One of the issues that will be addressed in Chapter 8 is the high density file system (HDFS). An HDFS is a file system with a very large number of files out of proportion to the size of a normal file system—typically one with more than 2 million files per terabyte. Although an active archive might reduce the amount of data backed up, the backup software will still need to process the stubs left behind on the file system. In the case of an HDFS, process can represent a substantial amount of time in the backup, outside of the data transfer.

Does the creation of an archive, whether active or offline, mean the data placed in the archive is never backed up again? No, to the contrary—it is doubly important that the archive is protected because the archive copy represents the only valid copy of the data. Depending on the type of media on which the archive is stored, it might mean that the archive will still require a backup of some type. This backup will not be as frequent, however, and there will be far fewer copies of the archive retained.

If the data were archived to unprotected static media such as a disk, an additional backup of the 5 TB of data in the archive would be required to ensure the survival of the archive in the event of a hardware or logical failure. The backup of the archive would be required only as frequently as new data is added to the archive, or as frequently as required to satisfy organizational or regulatory requirements that ensure the validity of data that is backed up.

Using our 5 TB archive example, suppose that the organization requires that backups older than one month need to be refreshed to ensure that the backup is valid and readable. For simplicity, also assume that no new data is added to the archive, making it static over the lifetime of the archive. To ensure that the 5 TB of data is recoverable, a backup is taken every month of the archive, with the backup having one month retention. How many copies of the data are required to be maintained at any time to ensure the recoverability of the archive? Two: the retention of any one backup copy will not exceed twice the period in which the archive is backed up—in the same way backups required additional weeks to achieve desired retention periods. To satisfy the rules of retention, both the current month and the previous month must be retained to have one month retention. On the third month, the first month's backup copy can be retired, leaving only the two most recent copies of the archive. Thus, only two copies are required at any one time to ensure the survival of the archive, as long as the retention period of the complete set of copies meets the requirements of the business or organization.

Although both backups and archives are copies of data, there is a fundamental difference in what they do with the copies. Backups simply make a copy of the existing data, place it into a specified format, and store the result on some type of media. Archives, on the other hand, make a copy of the data on a separate storage media and then remove the original copy, leaving only the copy as the representative of the original data. Even though the archive location is tracked, there will always only be a single piece of data within an archive situation, regardless of age.

Backups are typically intended to protect against an immediate threat: accidental deletion, system failure, disaster recovery, and so on. Archives are generally created for two reasons:

- To move inactive data from primary storage to lower-cost, longer-term storage

- To provide storage of data required to be stored for long periods of time in a static format

Backups and archives are not mutually exclusive. As discussed previously, the use of archives prior to executing backups can significantly enhance the performance of the backups by reducing the amount of data required to be backed up at any particular point in time.

Unfortunately, backups in many organizations tend to be used as long-term, "archive-like" storage of data and are typically used to satisfy internal or regulatory requirements. They are typically held for periods of more than 5 years and are stored in offsite locations under controlled conditions. As noted previously, backups should not be considered as long-term archives for a number of reasons. First of all is the problem of recoverability. Although the media itself might still be readable (some media has rated static life spans of more than 30 years under controlled conditions), the devices that are needed to actually read the tapes will most likely be gone well before that time.

One example is the videocassette recorder (VCR). When VCRs were first introduced to consumers, there were two competing formats: VHS and BetaMAX. For various reasons, VHS won. Because the two formats were fundamentally incompatible, that meant that anyone with a Beta videocassette was out of luck using it because the players disappeared. Now the same thing is happening to VHS because of DVDs—it is increasingly difficult to find a VHS player to read those tapes. Even the media is degrading—most original VHS tapes are virtually unreadable only 5–10 years after they are created.

Even if the devices are available and the backup software used to create the backup to the media can still read the backup, the application that was originally used to create the data will almost certainly not exist or function on existing hardware or operating systems even short time spans removed from the date of the backup creation. This typically becomes an issue with backups of database systems, but can also affect all types of software applications.

When architecting backup systems, it is important to consider data to be backed up as well as data that will be archived or stored for long periods. Although backups and archives are related, they are distinctly different in character. Backups should be used to provide short- and medium-term protection of data for purposes of restoration in the event of data loss, whereas archives provide long-term storage of data in immutable formats, on static or protected media. The data classification is critical for the proper design of backup systems needed to provide the level of protection required by the organization.

Service and Recovery Objectives: Definitions

When designing a backup solution, there are three key measures that will be the primary governors of the design with regard to any particular set of data:

- Recovery Time Objective (RTO)

- Recovery Point Objective (RPO)

- Service Level Agreement (SLA) associated with the data set

As such, these measures deserve a substantial review of their meaning and impact on design.

There are many different definitions of the SLA that are available. It can refer to the quality of service provided to a customer, the responsiveness of operational personnel to requests, and/or many other factors, but the measure that will be the focus of this discussion is the window in which backups of a particular data set are accomplished. The identification of what constitutes a backup window can be particularly difficult because different stakeholders in the completion of the backup will have differing views of when the window should start and end, and the length of the window. This definition of the SLA must be well-documented and agreed-upon by all parties so that there is no confusion regarding how the SLA is to be interpreted. The proper performance expectations of all parties should be set well before the SLA is in force.

The RTO represents the maximum amount of time that can elapse between the arbitrary start of the recovery and the release of the recovered data to the end user. Although this seems like a simple definition, there can be a great many vagaries embedded into this measure if you look closely (see Figure 1–10). The first is the definition of when the recovery starts. Depending on who you are in relation to the data being recovered, it can mean different things. If you are the end user of the data, this window might start at the point of failure: "I have lost data and I need to access it again within the next 'X' hours." If you are the systems administrator responsible for where the data resides, it might start at the point at which the system is ready to receive the restoration: "The system is up and I need the data back on the system in 'X' hours." Finally, as the backup administrator, you are concerned with the amount of time that it takes from the initiation of the restore to the end of the restore, including identification of data to be restored—"I need to find data 'ABC', start the restore, and have the restore finish in 'X' hours."

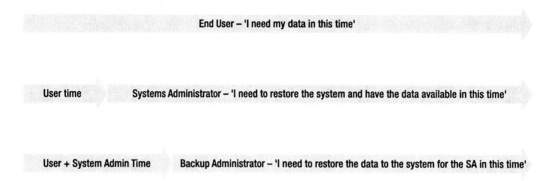

Figure 1–10. Relative views of RTO

Note that each of these viewpoints also contains an implied definition of the end time, or the time at which the data is released to the end user. For the purposes of this book, the RTO will refer strictly to the point at which the data has been identified and the restore initiated and measured to the point at which the restore has completed—Backup Administrator time in Figure 1–10. Although this is a narrow view of the RTO, it provides a point at which the design can be coherent against the variables that can be controlled by the backup infrastructure designer. However, any design must take into account all considerations, and might require significant modification to meet the other stakeholder needs.

The RPO on the other hand, represents the maximum amount of data that can be lost from the point of the last data protection event (see Figure 1–11). Note that a "data protection event" need not be a backup, *per se*, but can represent other types of transient data protection, such as snapshots, log dumps, or replications. Although these events can be controlled by many methods, selecting backup software that integrates the control of these events will simplify any design. The RPO, like the RTO, can be measured from a number of different perspectives. For the backup administrator, it will represent the largest amount of time that can elapse between backups (or controlled snapshots) in order to ensure that the data age is appropriately protected: "I need to complete a backup every 4 hours to ensure that only 3 hours of data is lost".

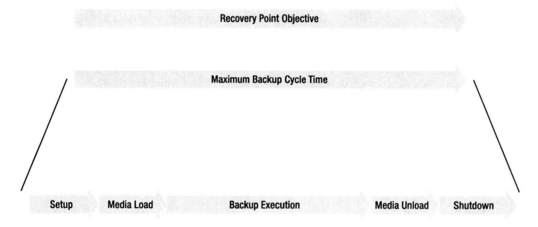

Figure 1–11. RPO activities

From the perspective of the data owner, this might represent a number of transactions, an amount of data that can be lost, or a particular age of data that can be regenerated: "The organization can afford to lose only the last 30 transactions".

The primary issue with establishing the RPO is the translation between time and data. A good way to illustrate this is to look at the two requirement statements in the previous paragraph. The first one, from the backup administrator, talks in terms of time between backups. For the backup administrator, the only way to measure RPO is in terms of time—it is the only variable into which any backup software has visibility. However, the requirement statement from the organization does not have a direct temporal component; it deals in transactions. The amount of time that a number of transactions represent depends on any number of factors, including the type of application receiving/generating the transactions. Online transaction processing (OLTP) database applications might measure this in committed record/row changes; data warehouse applications might measure this in the time between extract/transform/load (ETL) executions; graphical applications might measure this in the number of graphic files imported. The key factors in determining an estimated time-based RPO using data transactions are the time bound transaction rate and the number of transactions. The resulting time between required data protection events is simply the number of transactions required to be protected, divided by the number of transactions per unit time. For instance, if a particular database generates an average of 100 transactions per minute, and the required RPO is to protect the last 10,000 transactions, the data needs to be protected, at a minimum, every 100 minutes.

The other issue with RPO is that when designing solutions to meet particular RPO requirements, not only does the data rate need to be taken into account but the time for the backup setup and data writing also needs to be taken. In the previous example, if there is a requirement to protect the data every 8 hours, but it takes 8.5 hours to back up the data, including media loads and other overhead, the RPO has not been met because there would be 30 minutes of data in the overlap that would not necessarily be protected. This actually accelerates as time progresses. Again with the example, if on the first backup, it takes 110 minutes to perform the backup, the backup cycle is 30 minutes out of sync; the next time it will be 1 hour, and so on. If the extra time is not accounted for, within a week the backup process will be 8 hours out of sync, resulting in an actual recovery point of 16 hours.

If the cause of the offset is simply setup time, the frequency of the backups would simply need to be adjusted to meet the RPO requirement. So, let's say that it takes 30 minutes to set up and 8 hours to back up the data. In order to meet the stated RPO, backups would need to happen every 7.5 hours (at a minimum) to ensure that the right number of transactions are performed.

However, if simply changing the backup schedule does not solve the problem, there are other methods that can be used to help mitigate the overlap, creating array-based snapshots or clones. Then performing the backups might be able to help increase the backup speed by offloading the backups from the primary storage. Other techniques such as using data replication, either application- or array-based, can also provide ways to provide data protection within specified RTO windows. The point is to ensure that the data that is the focus of the RTO specification is at least provided initial protection within the RTO window, including any setup/breakdown processes that are necessary to complete the protection process.

■ **Note** So are the RTO and RPO related? Technically, they are not coupled—you can have a set of transactions that must be protected within a certain period (RPO), but are not required to be immediately or even quickly recovered (RTO). In practice, this tends not to be the case—RTOs tend to be proportionally as short as RPOs. Put another way, if the data is important enough to define an RPO, the RTO will tend to be as short as or shorter than the RPO:

```
RPO <= RTO
```

Although this is not always the case, it is a generalization to keep in mind if an RPO is specified, but an RTO is not.

Summary

When talking about designs of backup solutions, it is important that all people involved in the design have the same vocabulary. This chapter establishes a baseline vocabulary to allow for the communication of design elements between disparate types of backups and backup software, as well as to clarify some elements that tend to be confusing. In the following chapters, the terms defined here will be applied to designs of backup environments that cover the two largest commercial backup software products: CommVault Simpana and Symantec NetBackup. However, the concepts contained within these chapters can also be applied to a number of products with similar architectural components, such as EMC NetWorker, Symantec BackupExec, and others.

CHAPTER 2

▪ ▪ ▪

Backup Software

Software: CommVault Simpana

History and Background

Now that we have established some basic definitions in the previous chapter, we can delve into the specifics of how to build out architectures that provide solid, scalable backups for the organization. The most important component of any backup architecture is the backup software selected for use. We will address the specific subject software packages individually, beginning with CommVault Simpana.

CommVault Simpana started as a project within AT&T Labs back in 1987. Originally known as Automated Backup and Automated Recovery and Archive Software, CommVault was the internal backup software used by AT&T Labs until the division was split off as Lucent Technologies. As part of the divestiture of Lucent from AT&T, Automated Backup was relaunched as CommVault backup. Later renamed as Galaxy, and currently as Simpana, CommVault is relatively unique among backup software because it uses a Microsoft SQL database instance as the information repository for backup information. The use of a standard database (SQL Server) allows for validation of the referential integrity of the data within the catalog and provides for known ways to tune the database for performance in large deployments. This does, however, require that the CommVault server (called the CommServe) be installed on a Microsoft Windows-based system.

Terminology

Some notes regarding CommVault terminology: Backup software is in many ways similar to operating systems particularly in the way that the terminology for functions that are common between pieces of backup software is specific to the application. CommVault Simpana is no exception.

There are three general types of storage media within CommVault:

- *Magnetic libraries (MagLib)*: Backup targets that reside on disk storage.

- *Tape*: Tape targets are any type of magnetic tape drives, whether they are in a tape library or stand-alone tape drives.

- *Single Instance Library Option (SILO)*: SILOs actually represent more of a policy of migration than storage type. SILO media is simply the process of migration of backups from MagLib to external media. However, CommVault refers to SILO as media (this will be explained later in the chapter[1]).

---

[1] Dahlmeier, Mike. *Common Technology Engine*. CommVault: 2009, p 323.

The most basic element within a CommVault is the CommCell, which contains all clients and data that are to be protected and tracked, as well as resources that are to be used to store the media. A CommCell contains at least one CommServe—the brains of the operation that schedules backups, tracks media, and is responsible for the overall operation of the CommCell. A basic CommCell is shown in Figure 2–1.

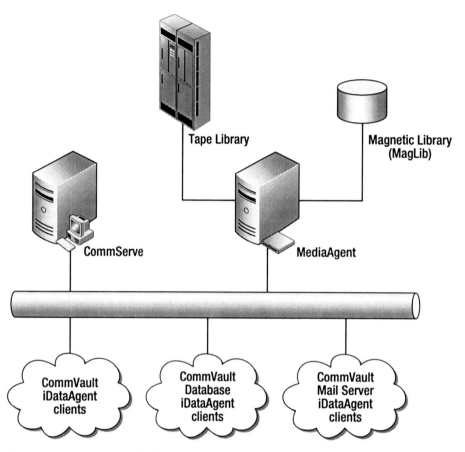

Figure 2–1. *Basic CommVault CommCell*

At its core, the CommCell contains three basic types of servers: the Client, the CommServe, and the MediaAgent. The CommServe acts as the brains of the operation, directing the execution of backups; the MediaAgent is the muscle—transporting data from the LAN connections to the backup media; and the Client is the customer—providing the data that needs to be protected.

Clients

Clients are the devices that contain the data that requires protection from loss. Clients can be traditional servers; Windows, UNIX/Linux, and NAS devices; virtual servers as provided by VMware or other virtualization methods found on the various OS platforms; and even nontraditional platforms such as OpenVMS. The client software within CommVault consists of a package of binaries that are loaded on the target platform and set to start at boot time. CommVault is unique in its capability to automate configuration of the client at installation time. By default, client installation requires a running, fully resolvable CommServe to verify the data path for the backup and to activate the client software. When the installation package or scripts are executed, part of the process "registers" the client with the CommServe, placing the client into the default client configuration. This allows clients to be immediately backed up once the client software is installed, providing for quick protection of clients.

However, unlike most types of backup software, client software in CommVault is built on a series of components that build upon each other. Instead of having a "base" client that all others are built on, CommVault provides iDataAgents (iDAs) that provide specific client functionality, based on the type of data that is to be protected. What would be thought of as a standard backup is actually a File System iDA (FSiDA)—an iDA that provides protection *only* for the file system (data files). This has both advantages and disadvantages. On the positive side, only code that is needed is applied to the client, however, if it is necessary to provide both application-level and file system–level protection, both iDAs must be applied—potentially creating an explosion of individual agents running independently on a single client.

In addition, CommVault also introduces the concept of "subclients," which are simply subsets of the data to be protected on the physical client—they are logical clients, not physical clients. CommVault iDAs are available for a number of different applications, including all major Microsoft products, SQL Server, Exchange, SharePoint; Oracle, SAP, and others. CommVault utilizes native snapshot technologies where possible on the operating systems supported, notably VSS on Microsoft platforms and SnapMirror on NetApp ONTAP filer appliances.

CommVault CommServer

Where the Client is the beginning point of the backup, the CommVault CommServe is the end point. The CommServe provides the control functionality needed for all operations within the CommCell, and is responsible for a number of different functions:

- Maintaining backup schedules and executing backups on schedule

- Managing backup media devices and media inventory/capacity

- Managing backup media and allocating media resources to backups

- Monitoring backup completion and providing basic notifications of errors

- Tracking both the backup and media ages and comparing them against retention, expiring backups and media as necessary

- Tracking the movement of backup data between pieces of media as well as copies of backup data

- Protecting the metadata associated with the CommCell for which it is responsible

In addition, the CommServe can, and frequently does, receive data from the client and writes it to media.

In the performance of these tasks, CommServe uses an approach that has been adopted by only a few software providers: the use of a relational database as the primary tracking mechanism for metadata. CommVault also provides the ability to recover data directly from media without the use of full CommServe software by also storing a copy of all metadata generated by a backup session locally with the backup itself.

When constructing backup environments, it is important to know how the data flows from the client to the backup medium. This information allows the designer to identify potential bottlenecks and to mitigate them where possible.

Before moving on to the specifics of data flow, there is a simple but critical concept to understand. CommVault establishes a three-way relationship between CommServe, MediaAgent, and Client, as shown in Figure 2–2.

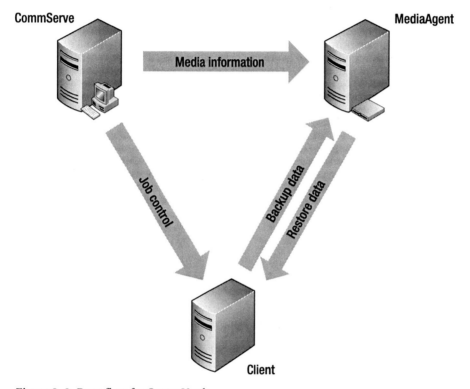

Figure 2–2. Data flow for CommVault

Using the illustration in the figure, the process for backups within a CommVault CommCell is as follows:

1.   The CommServe requests the Client to initiate a backup.

2.   The CommServe identifies media to use, based on the client Storage Policy, and informs the MediaAgent. Metadata regarding the subclients and the media are stored in the CommServe database.

3.   The Client initiates the requested backup and passes all data and metadata regarding the backup to the MediaAgent.

4. The MediaAgent stores metadata on both the media and in the local cache regarding the media as subclients are being written.

The tracking of backups and media is one of the most important jobs that a CommServe completes as part of a CommCell. As backups are completed, backup data is sent to the storage media, and metadata is sent to the CommServe. On the CommServe, this data is stored within a SQL Server database that acts as a repository for the metadata (see Figure 2–3).

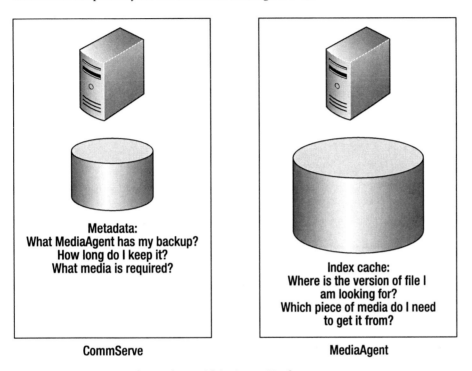

Figure 2–3. *Locations of metadata within CommVault*

However, the metadata contained in the SQL database is only a *backup* copy of the metadata regarding the actual backup of the client. CommVault utilizes a pointer base structure to quickly locate and redirect clients to particular pieces of media by maintaining local copies of metadata associated with particular pieces of backup media.

How does this work? The client pushes data to both the CommServe and the MediaAgent. The CommServe stores pointers to where the backups are stored, both in terms of the media they are stored on and the MediaAgent that performed the backup. The CommServe only knows what clients were backed up and when, along with which subclients were protected. The MediaAgent, however, has all the information regarding what files are in each backup and particular media that the backups are stored on. This information is stored in what is called the local cache. The local cache allows for accelerated restores over other products as particular files from specific backups can be quickly located and the restore process initiated. (See Figure 2–4.)

21

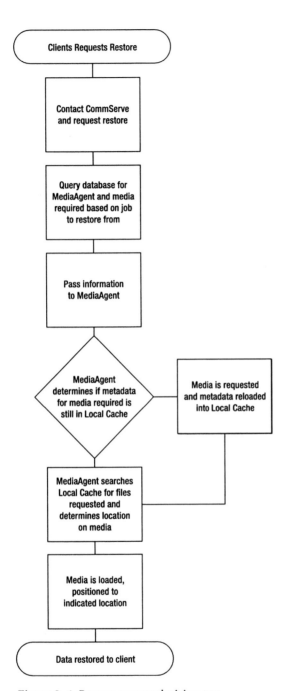

Figure 2–4. Restore process decision tree

The way that this works is that a restore is requested for a particular client to the CommServe. The CommServe identifies which MediaAgent contains the backup needed and directs the restore to the MediaAgent. The MediaAgent then searches the local cache and identifies the media and location of the items to be restored. If the information has been purged from the local cache to save space, as happens periodically, based on a set of configurable parameters, the cache is refreshed from the media and the file location process occurs again. As stated, the advantage is that recoveries of data can execute very quickly if the metadata is in the local cache; however, if the metadata has to be recovered from the media, recovery times are significantly affected.

Because the MediaAgent stores the bulk of the information regarding the backup information, the amount of metadata stored by the CommServe is relatively small. However, the CommServe uses a Microsoft SQL Server backend for this data. To maximize performance of the CommServe, high-speed, locally attached, protected storage is strongly recommended. For very large environments, the SQL Server can be migrated to a separate server that is specifically tuned for database performance, thus gaining backup performance for full maximization. By using specifically tuned servers within a SQL Server farm, you can take advantage of standard SQL perf tuning techniques and gain performance out of the CommServe.

Separating the SQL database backend of the CommServe also provides the additional benefit of giving the CommServe some resiliency. This separation allows the database to be protected with standard SQL utilities, such as log shipping or database replication, independent from the functions running on the CommServe. By replicating the database in this way, an alternate site can be established for the CommServe, and with the appropriate licensing, a "warm" CommServe, available for use in the event of a disaster at the primary site. While under normal operations there is one-to-one correlation between a CommCell and CommServe, warm recovery, disaster-tolerant configurations allow for a second standby CommServe to be present within the CommCell. The SQL replication is fully integrated into the CommServe, with all the necessary replication scheduled as a scheduled task. This configuration allows for a rapid switchover between CommServes in a single CommCell and allows for an easy method to provide protection of the CommCell over distance. However, this feature is not included by default and requires a license to enable it, and it can be completely implemented without any additional consulting. (See Figure 2–5.)

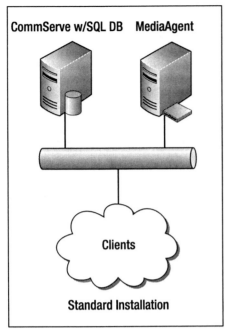
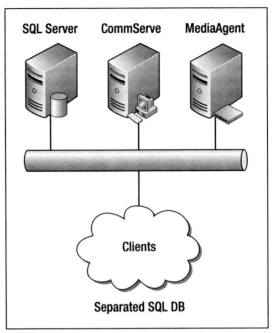
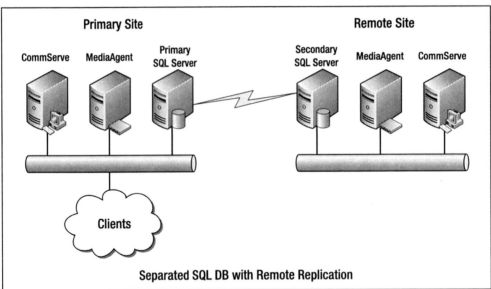

Figure 2–5. CommVault database options

MediaAgents

While the CommServe controls the overall operation of the CommCell, the MediaAgent provides the portal for all backup operations. However, unlike other backup software, the MediaAgent also provides another critical function—the storage of a local cache of backup metadata that it has put onto backup media. As was described in the preceding CommServe section, the MediaAgent is the point at which clients obtain detailed backup information for restoration purposes. A MediaAgent (MA) in its simplest form takes the backup stream and associated metadata and writes to storage media. MediaAgents also can take on more complex roles, such as target-based, software de-duplication and NDMP tape servers.

CommVault also takes a novel approach to managing where clients back up and how the media is managed. Instead of having the CommServe assign a particular MediaAgent dynamically, the MediaAgent is defined using what is called a Storage Policy. The Storage Policy provides a complete definition of the life cycle of a backup, including which MediaAgent is used to write a particular piece of media. While this may seem to introduce overhead to the management of the CommCell, it actually provides a defined way to ensure that backups are balanced and managed across all available resources.

However, this storage of metadata adds a requirement on the MediaAgent that is not typically found on similar types of systems in other applications. The local cache requires high speed storage to host the cache, as the overall performance of both backups and restores are dependent on the performance of the cache. Backup performance is dependent on the performance of the cache in depositing the metadata within the local cache. Restore performance, as described previously, is completely dependent on the ability to retrieve data from the local cache, with the location and media that contains the requested backup.

MediaAgents can also be grouped together using a technology called Gridstor. Gridstor provides the ability to define set rules that govern the way different data paths, basically the complete paths of a backup from the client through the media, are used—including how multiple MediaAgents can be used for parallel backups of particular hosts. Gridstor allows different subclients of a particular host to use different paths as part of a Gridstor configuration. This can be for load balancing or failover reasons, and provides a method of load distribution that is unique. Figure 2–6 shows an example Gridstor configuration. The Exchange server is configured to have three separate subclients, all using the same storage policy. The storage policy has been configured to use three different storage paths to three different MediaAgents. In this case, the storage policy will round robin each of the subclients between the storage paths, thus creating a load balanced configuration.

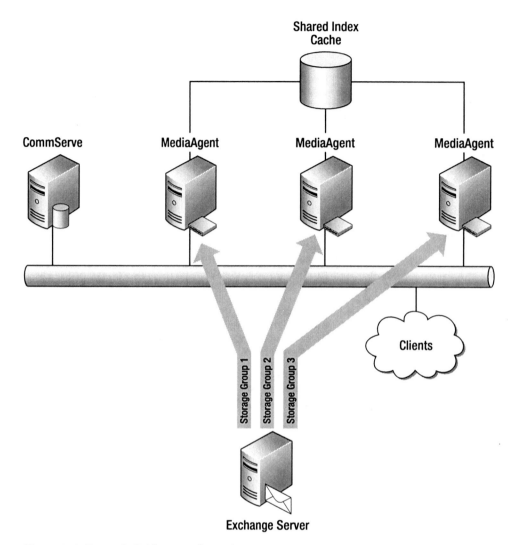

Figure 2–6. Example Gridstor configuration

MediaAgents can serve any type of supported backup targets: tape, disk, and virtual. While the CommServe can (and is required to for local backups of the CommCell database), MediaAgents also provide a level of resiliency within the CommCell by allowing clients to back up to, or recover from, MediaAgent(s) that have been defined within their storage policy configuration. Should the primary MediaAgent that a client normally uses fail, the backup can be shunted to a surviving MediaAgent for continued operation. (See Figure 2–7.)

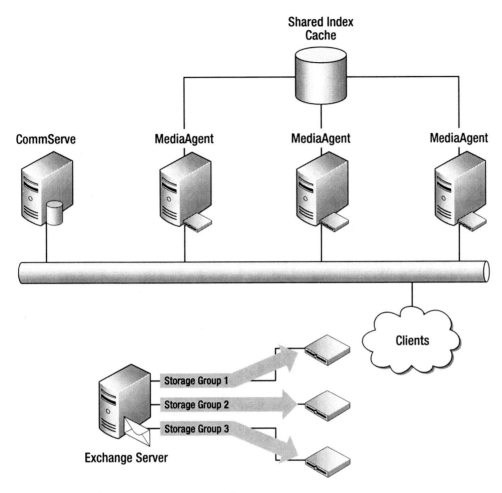

Figure 2–7. Dedicated MediaAgent w/Gridstor

The MediaAgent functionality also can assist with backing up large clients. One of the issues that will be addressed in later chapters is that of moving large amounts of data in as small an amount of time as possible. By making a Client also function as a MediaAgent, the Client can back up the data directly to the target media, without traversing any backup network to do so. In the diagram above, we take the previous example of the Exchange server being backed to multiple MediaAgents with Gridstor. If the Exchange server becomes too large to back up reliably over a network connection, it can be converted into a MediaAgent, as well as an Exchange server, potentially providing more speed for use by the backup. In this example, we have also applied the Gridstor licensing to allow for parallel use of resources, in just the same way as the regular MediaAgents had used Gridstor in the previous example.

Symantec NetBackup

History and Background

Symantec NetBackup is currently the holder of the largest market share of the backup software environment. It too has had a long history and many changes along the way.

Originally, NetBackup was two separate products: BackupPlus and Media Manager. BackupPlus was developed by Control Data for Chrysler to perform backups of servers within the Chrysler environment. Control Data began to deploy the software to other customers who liked the functionality that it provided. Later, Control Data was acquired by a company called OpenVision who added the Media Manager portion of the product. Eventually the company became Veritas and was later acquired by the current owner Symantec. As with EMC NetWorker, legacies of its heritage can be found in the software (the 'bp' prefix comes from the BackupPlus days and the default base install path '/usr/openv' from OpenVision).[2]

The architecture of NetWorker and NetBackup are very similar. Whereas in a NetWorker environment the collection of servers and other managed devices under a single NetWorker Server is called a *DataZone*, within NetBackup the same collection of devices and servers is known as a *backup domain*. A basic backup domain is pictured in Figure 2–8.

Just as with NetWorker, NetBackup contains three basic elements: the NetBackup Master Server, Media Server, and Client. The Master Server contains all the management and tracking mechanisms for the backup domain; the Client is the source of the backup data; and the Media Server provides several services, including moving data from the Client to the target media and providing the method of scalability within the environment.

---

[2] Wikipedia contributors, "NetBackup," *Wikipedia, The Free Encyclopedia*, http://en.wikipedia.org/w/index.php?title=NetBackup&oldid=299910524 (accessed July 2, 2009).

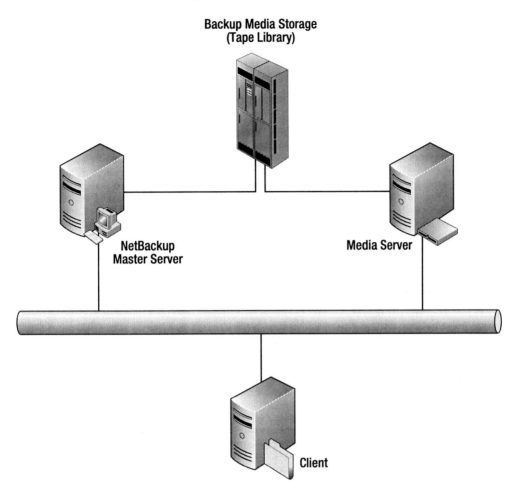

**Backup Media Storage
(Tape Library)**

**NetBackup
Master Server**

Media Server

Client

Figure 2–8. Basic NetBackup backup domain

NetBackup Master Servers

The NetBackup Master Server provides all the management of the Clients, Media Servers, and backup media within the backup domain. The Master Server has a number of responsibilities within the backup domain for various functions:

- Maintains backup schedules and executing backups on schedule

- Manages backup media devices and status, and media inventory/capacity

- Manages backup media and allocates media resources to backups

- Monitors backup completion and provides basic notifications of errors

- Track the backup and media ages and compares them against retention, expiring backups, and media as necessary

- Tracks the movement of backup data between pieces of media and copies of backup data

- Protects the metadata associated with the backup domain for which it is responsible

The Master Server can optionally receive data from Clients for writing to backup media, but this is not as common in NetBackup as in CommVault, for reasons that will be discussed later in this chapter.

The Master Server stores information about client backups and media in two locations: metadata regarding Client backups is stored within the Catalog, and media tracking information is stored within Media Manager. The NetBackup Catalog consists of a number of structured directories into which each Client's metadata regarding all backups is stored. The data is stored in a structure series of packed binary files that allow for efficient storage of the file metadata associated with a particular backup. Each collection of data backed up for a particular Client, at a particular time is referred to as a *backup image.* Unlike NetWorker, the entire collection of backup images is stored within the NetBackup catalog, making it the most important component of a NetBackup server. Because of this structure, the Catalog can grow to be very large, with the size dependent on the total number of files, combined with long retention periods. As the Catalog grows, performance of both restores and backups will tend to decrease because of the necessity of the Master Server to scan the Catalog during backup operations in order to determine if a) a file has already been backed up as part of a previous backup image, and b) if so, where to insert the new version of the file into the index. Restores are similarly affected because the restore has to scan the images included that can be part of a restore of a file in order to identify all versions that are available for restore. To ensure that the Master, and therefore all the other functions of the DataZone, are operating at their best performance, the layout of the Master Server is a critical item that needs to be addressed. The second function that the Master Server provides is that of Media Management. Over the years, the way that NetBackup managed media has changed. In the beginning, media was tracked using a catalog system that was similar to that of the Catalog used for the client information, known as the *volDB.* The volDB was maintained on any server that provided media services such as the Master Server and any Media Servers that were in the backup domain. Each volDB had to be synchronized back with the Master Server within the particular backup domain to ensure the integrity of the Media Manager. If this synchronization process failed, manual steps had to be carried out to resynchronize the domain, frequently with downtime of the domain being required.

However, as of NetBackup 6, a new method for tracking media information was substituted that utilizes an ASA-based database for media tracking, known as the Enterprise Media Manager (EMM). This upgrade provided a more efficient method of media tracking as well as better consistency of media reporting and management. While the volDB still remained as a remnant of the previous functionality, it now serves as little more than a lock and timing file that provides information regarding the last contact with the Master Server. The function of the database has been further enhanced in the NetBackup 6.5 series to extend the capabilities of the database. (See Figure 2–9.)

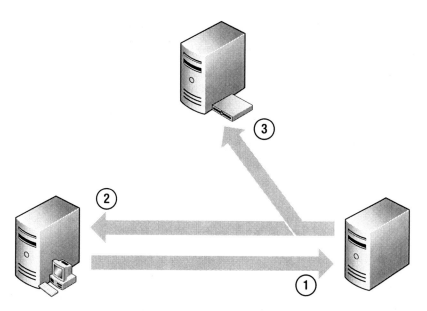

- (1) Master initiates backup and intructs client to begin the backup

- (2) Client sends metadata to Catalog on Master

- (3) Client sends backup data to media on Media Server

Figure 2–9. NetBackup data/metadata flow

When NetBackup initiates a client backup, the NetBackup server builds a list of work to accomplish and allocates resources to the job. Once all resources are allocated, the media is ready and all setup tasks are completed, the Master Server sends the request to the Client to begin sending data to the assigned server that will receive the backup image. The client splits the data flow so that the metadata regarding the backup is sent to the Master Server, and the data itself is sent to the server storing the data. As the metadata is received, it is stored within the NetBackup Catalog and contains all the information regarding the files backed up, the time, and the associated media list on which the backup image is stored. Each time a backup is executed, a separate set of files is created within the Catalog that contains all information regarding the particular backup image.

As a result, the NetBackup Catalog can grow extremely large. There are two reasons for this. First, each image file set contains information regarding all files that have been backed up as part of that image. For systems that have an extremely large number of files, this means that these individual files can be very large. Second, these files are the only direct reference into what data is available for restore at any particular point in time and must be maintained on the Master Server until the backup expires. Because there is no way to prune off images that may contain backups that are still required to be maintained, but not operationally useful, the storage on the Master Server for the Catalog will grow without bound. For this reason, it is important to allocate storage for the Catalog that is well oversized for the initial requirements to allow for the growth of the Catalog and to ensure that the storage is well optimized for large block, random access. This is particularly true of Windows environments, as dynamically growing NTFS file systems can be a difficult process. In addition, this storage must be protected storage—storage in a RAID configuration, such as RAID-5 or RAID-10 because the Catalog represents the sole source of information regarding the contents of the backup images available for a particular client.

At the same time, the media information is being stored within the EMM database. The EMM is receiving data from the Master Server regarding the allocation of backup media to the various backups. It is also receiving data regarding the volumes themselves from the servers that actually are streaming data to the backup media regarding the backup images being created on the media, and which media are active at any one time. An advantage of the EMM database is that because it is an actual database, and not a flat file catalog, it can be relocated to a server separate from the Master Server itself. If the EMM database is on the same server as the Catalog, it is important to create a separate set of storage to ensure that the performance characteristics of the database are not affected by that of the Catalog, and vice versa.

Media Servers

While NetBackup Master Servers can, and frequently do, act as backup targets for the Clients, the method of scaling capacity within growing NetBackup backup domains has not been to simply add more Master Servers to the environment and split out Clients. The primary method of growing the backup potential of a backup domain within a NetBackup environment is the use of Media Servers. Media Servers also provide the ability to extend backups to isolated network areas where the transport of backup data is either impractical or restricted, by providing a backup media target that is "local" to the isolated clients.

A Media Server is simply a server that has specialty NetBackup software installed that enables it to receive data from a Client, send that backup data to backup media, and report back the media status to the Master and the EMM database server (if it is not located on the Master). Although in some of the original versions of NetBackup, media metadata and catalogs were maintained on each Media Server, that functionality has been effectively eliminated in versions greater that NetBackup 4.5 and replaced with a fully consolidated media database, as described previously.

The basic Media Server simply sits on the network and waits for connections from both the Master Server and Clients. At some point, however, Clients become too large or have too stringent backup requirements to move their backup images over the LAN to a general purpose Media Server. Just as with NetWorker, NetBackup supports the installation of Media Server software on large clients to assist with just this issue. When configured in this way, the large client can perform backups of data to local resources, without the necessity of moving data across the LAN to a separate target.

Clients

NetBackup clients have the same functionality as NetWorker clients. Clients within NetBackup can be UNIX/Linux, Windows, NAS platforms, and virtualization platforms. NetBackup also has clients for data warehouse platforms such as Teradata and others. Client software, also known as *agents*, is installed on each platform and consists of a number of binaries that provide the functionality needed to execute backups on the particular server.

NetBackup provides additional client components, called *extensions*, which allow for integrating the basic NetBackup client into specific applications to allow for complete end-to-end management of backups with a minimum of user interaction. NetBackup has client extensions for databases, such as Oracle, SQL, Informix, and DB2; Microsoft applications such as Exchange and SharePoint; and specialty applications such as SAP and Lotus Notes. NetBackup also provides support for NDMP-based backups of NAS file servers and other NDMP stream providers, as well as providing for support of VMWare Consolidated Backup (VCB) backups.

In addition, NetBackup provides a rich set of options. An option is add-on client functionality that provides services above and beyond that of the base client. There are options for such things as Bare Metal Recovery, Encryption, the use of shared SAN disk as a backup target, or the use of snapshots for backups.

Data Flow within the NetBackup Environments

Just as with CommVault, it is important to understand how data flows within NetBackup environments in order to ensure that bottlenecks are not created as a result of basic architecture design (see Figure 2–10).

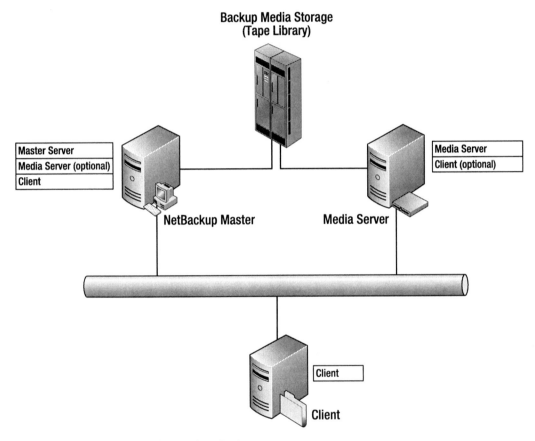

Figure 2–10. NetBackup software distribution

Within NetBackup, each server type only has to be the type designated. Put another way, if you want a Media Server to be *only* a Media Server and not a client, NetBackup will treat that platform *only* as a Media Server and never as a client. Software has to be explicitly loaded and configured on each platform type to make that platform function. Functions can be layered, as indicated. However, this is not to say that when a Media Server is built, that the Client software is not loaded; just that the definition of the

33

Media Server within NetBackup does not necessarily imply that the Media Server is also a client; it is simply a Media Server with a single function in life.

What this means when creating a design is that the flow of data, in particular metadata changes, depends on the functionality that is loaded on to a particular platform. The process and metadata flow is much more complex than that within CommVault (see Figure 2–11) and needs to be taken into consideration when performing the design.

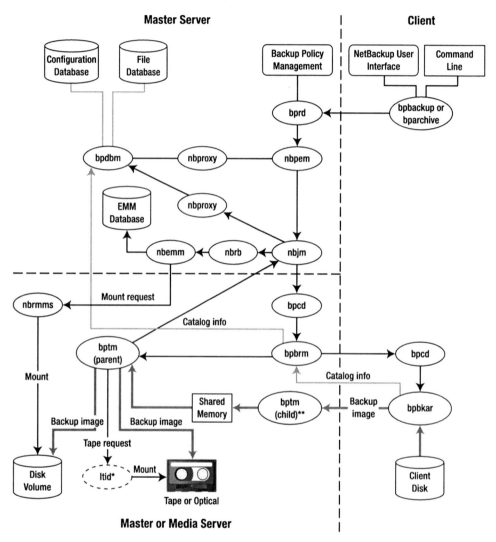

Figure 2–11. *NetBackup process flow[3]*

---

[3] Various authors, *Troubleshooting Guide, Symantec NetBackup, Release 6.5,* copyright 2007, pg. 591.

Figure 2–11 is a very complex but accurate representation of the process flow within NetBackup. It is important to understand that there is a large number of processes that run as a result of adding functionally, such as that provided by a Media Server. The more processes required, the more CPU and RAM are required on the particular server to ensure that the function runs efficiently. It also illustrates why all NetBackup functions can run on a single server, but in doing so, that server quickly becomes overwhelmed. Consider running a single NetBackup Master as a Master and Media Server. When the amount of data to be protected is low, the single server (with all the associated processes), may be able to handle the load placed on it by the initial backup. However, as the amount of data increases and the relative demands placed on the single server increase, the overall load on the single server will increase to the point where it can no longer can efficiently or adequately perform necessary tasks. This subject will be addressed in much more detail later on.

Summary

This chapter was designed to provide a brief overview of both CommVault and NetBackup server types and software components. NetWorker and NetBackup both have very similar architectures when looking at the overall design of backup environments. However, as we have illustrated, there are some distinct differences that should be taken into account when performing the basic implementation of the environment; in particular when looking at the CommServe or the NetBackup Master Server disk characteristics.

One core concept that is important to understand as a basis for all backup designs is that the performance of the backup server will ultimately govern the capability of any design to complete backups in a timely manner.

For more detail regarding specific process flow and execution relationships, it is important to consult the administration and troubleshooting guides for the version of CommVault/NetBackup that is used within the environment. These guides provide detailed information about these processes that is beyond the scope of this book and can provide valuable insight into the details of each piece of backup software.

CHAPTER 3

■■■

Physical Backup Media

Chapter 2 discussed the two main pieces of backup software. In this chapter, we will discuss the most common pieces of hardware that are used as backup targets.

In general, backup media can be broken up into two major categories: physical and virtual. The difference is how the underlying hardware is addressed. *Physical media* do not have any abstraction layer that presents the hardware in a format or manner other than its native format. *Virtual media* do the same thing as physical hardware, but use a combination of software and hardware to make disk storage look like physical tape hardware.

There are advantages and disadvantages to each approach. Physical media types have the advantage of not requiring any special hardware emulation or having any translation layer that might inhibit performance. Physical media types typically are granular in nature—in other words, physical media types represent the most basic level of media targets and generally cannot be aggregated or managed as anything other than individual elements. There are two common types of physical backup media: tape and disk.

Tape

Traditionally, magnetic tape cartridges are the media of choice as backup targets. As the original backup type, magnetic tape has a long history of use and is the most mature backup media available. *Magnetic tape*, or just *tape*, is a cartridge-based component that is typically made of some type of rigid plastic. It contains one or more reels of flexible plastic that has been impregnated with a material that will hold a magnetic signature.

Tape cartridges are made in various formats. Each format has different characteristics that meet different physical and backup storage needs, both in terms of the amount of data stored, lifetime of the storage media, cost, and physical profile. Tape formats commonly in use are the following:

- DLT/SDLT
- LTO
- AIT
- STK 9840/9940/T10000
- IBM 3490/3590

Each cartridge has distinct capacities and characteristics regarding differing speeds. They are ever-changing as technology advances, so listing them here is an exercise in futility because whatever is published here will be out of date. However, three of the formats are the most common and have particular characteristics that will be described here as examples of architectural elements of design:

DLT, LTO, and STK T10000. The remaining formats, although common, are typically used for niche environments such as archiving and nearline storage.

Digital Linear Tape (DLT)

Digital Linear Tape (DLT) is the oldest and most mature of the products. Originally designed and implemented by DEC in 1984, and then acquired by Quantum and redistributed in 1994[1], DLT provided the first real compact tape cartridge for open systems backups in the enterprise. While other media types were in use (such as half-inch, 4mm/8mm, and others), DLT provided the best balance of all factors due to its size, capacity, speed, and relative reliability. DLT was licensed for production by many vendors, which helped spread the format into many customer sites through distribution by various manufactures of both drives and cartridges. DLT connectivity, however, is limited to the traditional SCSI, and is limited to 300 GB of native storage capacity and 160 MB/sec transfer rate (SDLT600). Other variants were available, but never generally deployed. Today, DLT is typically found as legacy backup media targets in environments or in smaller environments that do not require larger capacities.

Linear Tape Open (LTO)

Linear Tape Open (LTO) was designed and devised as an evolution and alternative to DLT and other more proprietary formats, and was intended to provide a common platform for tape backups. Seagate, HP, and IBM were the original initiators of the LTO Consortium, which performed the initial development and maintains the technology licensing and certification process.[2]

In theory, this should have produced a standard format of tape and drives that all participating manufacturers could follow and market with their own additional features and functions. Although this is largely true today, the original LTO-1 and LTO-2 formats had compatibility issues. These problems ranged from simple tape jams when using media acquired from two different vendors to the inability for an LTO drive from one manufacturer to read data written on a cartridge from another. The initial LTO-1 provided 100 GB of native storage and 15 MB/sec, with current LTO-4 systems providing 400 GB of native storage at 160 MB/sec. LTO-5, just recently released, provides 800 G of native storage capacity, at the same 160 MB/sec.

Sun/StorageTek T10000 (T10k)

The Sun/StorageTek T10000 (T10k) represents a leader in proprietary tape storage technology in terms of capacity. The T10k is a proprietary format only produced by StorageTek and is typically found in environments where previous STK technologies (9840/9940) have been deployed either for open systems or mainframe. The T10k is rated to hold 500 GB of native storage at 120 MB/sec.

Tape Storage Characteristics

Although all these statistics represent interesting performance numbers, all tape devices share similar performance characteristics that must be taken into account when designing backup environments. The

---

[1] Wikipedia contributors, "Digital Linear Tape," Wikipedia, The Free Encyclopedia, http://en.wikipedia.org/w/index.php?title=Digital_Linear_Tape&oldid=304862101 (accessed July 29, 2009).

[2] Wikipedia contributors, "Linear Tape-Open," Wikipedia, The Free Encyclopedia, http://en.wikipedia.org/w/index.php?title=Linear_Tape-Open&oldid=307951652 (accessed August 14, 2009).

first and most important of these is the fact that all tape drives are serial media environments. Disk devices have a number of writing devices, or *heads*, that move to various points on the rotating disk to put data in an optimal fashion. This allows disk devices to read any piece of data as requested. Because disks have multiple heads to return data blocks in a parallel fashion, multiple systems can access a disk at the same time.

Unlike disk devices, tape devices write data blocks in a linear fashion, one after another. Tape drives only have a single writing head that writes data a block at a time onto the tape as the tape media moves by. Reading the data off is the reverse process: The tape must rewind to the beginning of the tape, forward to the block that is needed, and return the block of data. And because only a single piece of data can be read at a time, tape devices cannot be shared in parallel between systems, without a mechanism to hand off control between systems that utilize the tape device. Figure 3–1 shows the difference between the two.

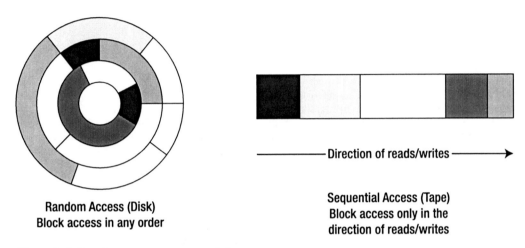

Direction of reads/writes ⟶

Random Access (Disk)
Block access in any order

Sequential Access (Tape)
Block access only in the
direction of reads/writes

Figure 3–1. Random access vs. sequential access

Connectivity types also have an effect on the utilization of tape devices. Tape drives depend on a direct connection to the host for data transport. Again, this is due to the fact that tape drives are serial devices—they only accept a single connection at a time. Although many tape drives have dual connections, they have uses that do not involve multiple connections to multiple hosts.

Many vendors and manufacturers attempt to advertise dual connectivity as dual path, but they are different. *Dual connectivity* allows the ability to have a secondary path to the device available in case the primary is not available or to have a secondary path that can be used to provide connectivity to another host. *Dual path* is the ability to use both paths simultaneously in order to provide more simultaneous bandwidth than would be available with a single path. Serial devices cannot operate with multiple simultaneous connections because there is no way to determine which path would write on which block during any point in time.

Traditionally, tape devices are connected to hosts via wired SCSI connections. SCSI connections consist of a single wide cable that runs between the host and the device being connected. The connection is very limited in distance—25m (~75ft) being the longest that reliable SCSI connections could be made. Also, because this type of connection is a point-to-point connection, there is generally a one-to-one ratio of connections to drives. These would typically be Fast-Wide SCSI connections that allow the maximum speed available to the tape drive. SCSI devices can be "daisy-chained" together into a string of devices on a single SCSI connection (see Figure 3–2).

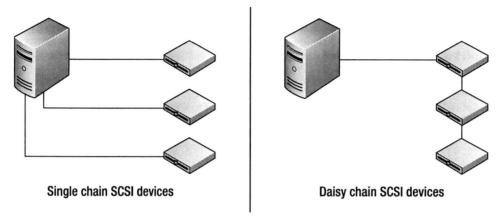

Figure 3–2. *SCSI chaining configurations*

In such a configuration, the maximum performance of any single device will be governed by the maximum speed of the SCSI connection, minus the speed being used by other operations. In other words, the bandwidth is shared between all devices on the chain. Daisy-chained devices will either use a Y-cable to make the connection to the next device or have a second SCSI port on the device being attached to allow for a point connection to the next device in the chain. There are also many other limits on SCSI connections, as shown in Table 3–1.

Table 3–1. *SCSI Connection Specifications[3]*

Interface	Width (bits)	Bandwidth (MB/s)	Length (single ended)	Length LVD	Length HVD	Devices
SCSI-1	8	5 MB/s	6m	NA	25m	8
Fast SCSI	8	10 MB/s	3m	NA	25m	8
Fast-Wide SCSI	16	20 MB/s	3m	NA	25m	16
Ultra SCSI	8	20 MB/s	1.5m	NA	25m	8
Ultra SCSI	8	20 MB/s	3 m	NA	NA	4
Ultra Wide SCSI	16	40 MB/s	NA	NA	25m	16
Ultra Wide	16	40 MB/s	1.5 m	NA	NA	8

[3] Wikipedia contributors, "SCSI," *Wikipedia, The Free Encyclopedia,* 16 August 2010, http://en.wikipedia.org/w/index.php?title=SCSI&oldid=379237549 (accessed 22 August 2010)

Interface	Width (bits)	Bandwidth (MB/s)	Length (single ended)	Length LVD	Length HVD	Devices
SCSI						
Ultra Wide SCSI	16	40 MB/s	3 m	NA	NA	4
Ultra2 SCSI	8	40 MB/s	NA	12m	25m	8
Ultra2 Wide SCSI	16	80 MB/s	NA	12m	25m	16
Ultra3 SCSI	16	160 MB/s	NA	12m	NA	16
Ultra-320 SCSI	16	320 MB/s	NA	12m	NA	16

The table illustrates a number of significant limitations with the use of SCSI. Connectivity is the largest issue. SCSI devices typically can be connected to either one or two hosts at any one time. A chain can contain only 15 devices, and only a maximum of 2 servers can access the devices. If there is a requirement to grow beyond this number of devices for a number of reasons, an additional controller must be added to the servers and additional devices physically added to the new controller. For a large number of servers requiring backup, the number of devices and their distribution can rapidly grow to unmanageable proportions.

Reliability is a huge issue. In an SCSI environment, the end of the chain (even if the chain size is exactly one) has to be physically ended with a special cable end (or *terminated*, as it is known), or else the SCSI protocol does not function. If any member of the chain fails, the entire chain will have to be taken offline to replace the failed member. Additionally, the cables themselves, consisting of a large number of individual pins, make a mechanical connection to other receptors in the chain. Any type of mechanical connection, especially involving a large number of small connections, is susceptible to mechanical and connection failure, thus reducing the reliability of the overall solution.

The distance limitation of SCSI also presents a problem. Because maximum distances are relatively short, servers that need to access the devices must be clustered near the tape drives or the tape drives must be individually distributed to each server. Either solution presents significant problems. If the servers needing access to the tape drive have to be nearby, attaching those servers to other devices, such as external disk drives or additional tape drives, becomes problematic because the distance limitations for SCSI tape also apply to SCSI disk. If you reverse the problem, there is a proliferation of devices to individual servers that require backup, presenting a management and maintenance problem as the number of devices grows to meet demand.

Historically, with all its limitations, SCSI was the only option. As technology progressed, both in signaling and media connectivity, other options became available. One of the first alternatives to SCSI developed was Fibre Channel. *Fibre Channel (FC)* is a network protocol solution that allows for the integration of devices into networks of target storage devices, both disk and tape. FC is typically run over optical cable; however, there are specific purpose-built implementations of FC that utilize standard copper connectivity, but typically not for host connectivity to FC devices or infrastructure. Devices no longer had to be chained together because FC switches (similar to those used for LAN connectivity) were developed to allow a many-to-many relationship between devices. Distance limitations were also effectively eliminated because FC has distance limitations on the order of hundreds of meters, depending on the media type being used—some implementations can run for over 1km natively.

Additionally, because FC is a network protocol, other higher level protocols can run on FC—such as SCSI. This is the core piece of technology that allows FC to be extremely useful in backup applications.

By running SCSI over FC, standard tape devices were quickly adapted for use. This allowed tape devices to be centralized into large libraries that were accessible by multiple servers. Servers could be distributed where needed and still have connectivity back to the tape drives as needed. Because connectivity is either by standard optical or 8 pin copper Ethernet, mechanical connectivity reliability is significantly increased. In addition, all of the operating system tape drivers required very little modification because the exact same protocol (SCSI) and command set was used to control the FC based tape drives as was used for the direct connected SCSI tape drives.

FC is a network protocol that allows many-to-many relationships, multiple connections to a single tape resource could be effectively and economically affected to allow for maximum utilization of the centralized tape resource by multiple servers. However, the even with this ability, the single connectivity limitation of tape drives still applies. In order to get around this limitation, both CommVault and NetBackup include tape drive sharing options. These options, Dynamic Drive Sharing (DDS) for CommVault and Shared Storage Option (SSO) for NetBackup, allow the backup application to "schedule" the use of a tape drive resource between different servers. This scheduling ability allows for the assignment of idle tape drives to servers that require tape services, without dedicating a particular resource to a particular server. However, this does require that all servers that will participate in the sharing mechanism be able to access all of the possible devices that would be shared. This is not typically an issue when using FC as the connection media because it is a simple matter to present multiple devices, or *targets*, to multiple servers, or *initiators* (see Figure 3–3).

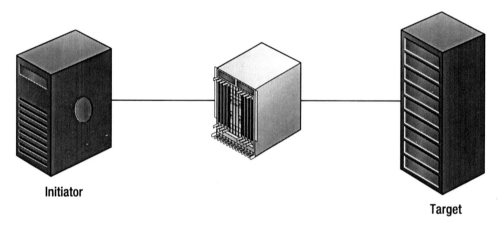

Initiator

Target

Figure 3–3. FC initiators and targets

FC does not place any limitations on the number of connections to a particular target and leaves the management of the actual connections and data flow to the initiators and targets involved in the device relationship (see Figure 3–4).

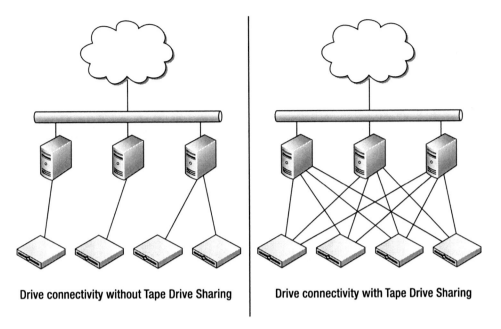

Drive connectivity without Tape Drive Sharing | **Drive connectivity with Tape Drive Sharing**

Figure 3–4. Drive allocation examples

To enforce this type of connectivity, storage area networks (SANs) use software in the switches to establish logical, point-to-point connections between targets and initiators to ensure that only data from particular servers goes to the designated target devices. This software function within the FC switch is called zoning (see Figure 3–5). *Zoning* uses each connected device's unique identifier, called a World Wide Name (WWN), to create the virtual connection. The zone matches the WWN of the initiator with the WWN, or WWNs, of the targets that the initiator should see. Any target WWN that is not included in the virtual connection is invisible to the initiator.

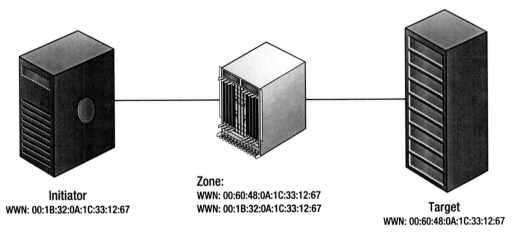

Initiator
WWN: 00:1B:32:0A:1C:33:12:67

Zone:
WWN: 00:60:48:0A:1C:33:12:67
WWN: 00:1B:32:0A:1C:33:12:67

Target
WWN: 00:60:48:0A:1C:33:12:67

Figure 3–5. FC zoning example

Both DDS and SSO operate in a similar fashion: The server that wants to perform a backup requests a tape device from the CommServe/Master Server. The server then allocates the resource and places a "reservation" on the particular resource for that server. Media are loaded in the normal fashion, and notification is passed to the requesting server to indicate that the media have been loaded. The server maintains the reservation on the tape device until it is done. Once the job is complete, the resource is released back to the server for reallocation to another job. In this way, the tape resource is used as much as possible by reducing idle time as much as possible.

Tape drives also have another important characteristic. In order to maximize the throughput to the tape media, move the tape as fast as possible across the tape heads. However, this assumes that the data rate is fast enough to write data effectively at the speed of the tape transport across the tape head. In practice, however, the data rate to the tape drive is less than the required transport rate, forcing the tape drive to slow the tape transport.

At some point, depending on the drive type in use, the transport cannot be effectively slowed, and the tape must stop. When this happens, once the tape drive receives enough data in the memory buffer to begin writing again, the drive must reposition the tape back before the end of the data stream, get the tape transport up to the physical speed required, and then start sending data once the end of the last tape block is reached. If the data buffer is not replenished with enough data to keep the transport moving, the whole process starts again. When using LTO tape drives, there are five transport speeds, each of which represents a point at which the data rate has been reduced to the point where the tape transport must slow. This stopping and starting of the tape transport is known as *shoe-shining*. This shoe-shining of the tape media takes a great deal of time relative to the time required to write the data on tape and significantly reduces the amount of data that can be written in a given period of time—the definition of throughput. The only way to avoid this effect is to ensure that the maximum amount of data is sent to a tape drive to keep it streaming at a rate above the minimum required to keep the tape transport moving.

Fortunately, both CommVault and NetBackup have mechanisms to assist with ensuring that the tape transport is fed as much data as possible through the use of multiplexing (see Figure 3–6). *Multiplexing* is the ability to interleave backup streams from multiple clients onto a single device. Each client sends the backup stream to the backup server, in which it is broken up into blocks of data within a data buffer. The blocks are placed into a queue for writing to the tape, with each block tracked by the backup software as to which backup it belongs to. In theory, this will create a constant stream of data to be received by the tape drive and prevent shoe-shining. This is due to the cumulative effect of multiple clients pushing data in parallel to a serial device. Although a single client might not be able to generate enough data in unit time to prevent shoe-shining, multiple clients generating multiple data streams will typically generate enough data to keep the tape drive running at optimal speeds. This functionality will be addressed in more detail in later chapters.

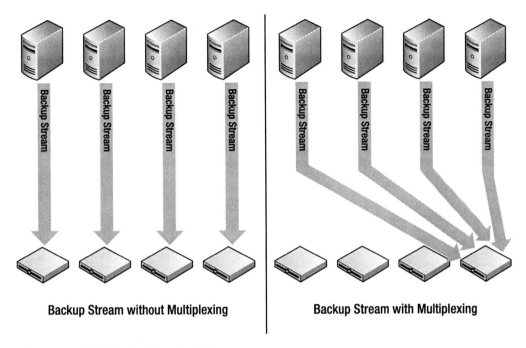

Figure 3–6. Multiplexing functionality

Finally, the physical presentation of the tape drives to the operating system will also have a large impact on the overall performance of the backup environment as a whole. Regardless of which connectivity option is utilized, there is a fixed maximum transmission rate, or bandwidth, that can be achieved via the particular connection type. For direct SCSI connections, this rate is limited to 160 MB/sec using SCSI-3 type connections (the most common type of SCSI connection utilizing traditional cabling). For FC connections, the current industry standard connection rate per port is 4 GB/sec or approximately 400 MB/sec. This is maximum aggregated bandwidth; put another way, the sum of the bandwidth of all parallel active devices on a single connection should not exceed the total available bandwidth. Let's illustrate this with an example. If you have a single 4 GB FC connection, want to connect the highest number of LTO-4 tape drives (rated data bandwidth: 120 MB/sec) to the connection, and you want to utilize as much of the available bandwidth as possible without exceeding the maximum FC speed, how many tape drives could you theoretically attach? You can use this formula to estimate the number drives per given bandwidth to determine the answer:

$$N_d = (B_c * (1 - P)) / B_d$$

Where:

N_d = Number of devices to attach
B_c = Connection Bandwidth, in MB/sec
P = Performance overhead (OS, RAID controller inefficiencies, and so on), as a % reduction
B_d = Rated Device Bandwidth, in MB/sec

Although the connection has a reduction in performance, the device bandwidth does not. Most inconsistencies in device performance are found at the source of the data flow (i.e., the server sending the data), not at the target. Because of this, and to ensure both a conservative and consistent design method across similar targets, a performance reduction metric should not be applied to the target devices.

Given the equation, and assuming that the maximum performance of the FC connection is reduced by 20 percent, the maximum number of drives that should be assigned in this case is as follows:

$$N_d = (400 * (1 - .2))/120$$
$$N_d = (400 * .8)/120$$
$$N_d = 320/120$$
$$N_d \approx 3$$

So an approximate maximum of 3 (actually 2.6) LTO-4 drives should be attached to a single FC 4 GB connection to ensure that the bandwidth is not exceeded, as illustrated in Figure 3–7.

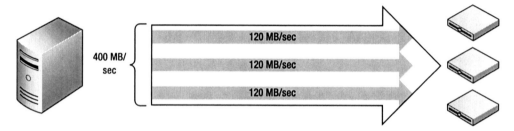

Figure 3–7. Full subscription of connections

The figure shows that the full 120 MB/sec is always being pushed from the server to the tape drive at the other end, fully utilizing the bandwidth available on the connection—in this case, 400 MB/sec. However, this assumes that the server will push, and the drives will always receive the full 120 MB/sec that they are rated at, even with the overhead introduce by the server. This is not generally the case because other variables affect the actual utilization of the devices, such as the amount of data that is actually received per second by the server and the amount of shoe-shining that is introduced by the data performance.

Given these factors, the designer can choose to add more devices to the connection than would be physically supported—a concept called *oversubscription*. When a device or set of devices is oversubscribed, the apparent amount of data that would be sent to the connection would exceed the available bandwidth. To illustrate, let's take the previous example and expand on it.

If instead of assuming that the full bandwidth of the device can be used, let's assume that the clients can only move data at a cumulative rate of 60 MB/sec. Instead of using the full 120 MB/sec of the tape drive performance in the previous analysis, we use the 60 MB/sec instead. We can do this because the cumulative rate does not exceed the rated ingest rate of the device.

When we substitute this value, the number of drives changes, as follows:

$$N_d = (400 * (1 - .2)) / 60$$
$$N_d = (400 * .8) / 60$$
$$N_d = 320 / 60$$
$$N_d \approx 6$$

So the resulting assignment of drives increases from 3 to 6, allowing more data drives to be utilized down a given connection (see Figure 3–8).

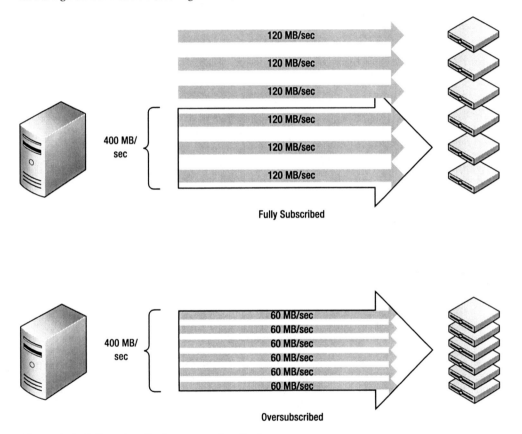

Figure 3–8. Fully subscribed vs. oversubscribed

But there is a limit to the number of drives. As discussed previously, once the drive drops below a certain point with regard to the ingest rate, it must stop the tape mechanism and wait until sufficient data is built back up in the buffer for the mechanism to start again. This threshold varies by drive type. Although it will increase the number of drives that can be used down a particular connection, it becomes costly to simply increase the number of drives (tape drives can cost a great deal of money). So, both in terms of efficiencies of use and efficient cost, simply adding more drives is not the way to go. Given this, we can change our formula slightly to reflect the variables in determining the number of drives that can be used:

$$N_d = (B_c * (1 - P))/ B_d$$

Where:
N_d = Number of devices to attach
B_c = Connection Bandwidth, in MB/sec
P = Performance overhead (OS, RAID controller inefficiencies, and so on) as a percentage reduction
B_d = Data flow to device, in MB/sec
And:
$B_{min} < B_d <= B_{max}$

With:
B_{min} = Minimum amount of data rate to sustain drive speed
B_{max} = Maximum rated data rate to device

Although tape is perceived as old-fashioned and out of date, it still has some significant advantages over other types of backup media. First, it is portable. Tape cartridges can easily be moved from one location to another because they are small, lightweight, and are constructed to industry standards to ensure that tapes generated by one manufacturer and written to on a particular tape drive will be able to be used on tape drives of any other manufacturer of the same format. Second, tape storage can grow without bound, without the addition of hardware for the storage. Cartridges can be stored outside of the tape library in any number and simply recalled as necessary for use. Finally, tape systems are typically initially less expensive to acquire. Tape drives are fixed pieces of hardware into which low-cost pieces of storage media are inserted. For a relatively small initial cost, tape still represents a good way to provide inexpensive storage of backups, simply based on a measurement of $/TB stored, as compared with other types of media.

But many of these advantages are also disadvantages of tape systems over other types of backup media. Take tape's portability, for instance. Because tape is so portable and easy to transport and read, it also makes it easy to illicitly acquire and read. Traditional tape systems do not provide a built-in means to protect against unauthorized access, although newer tape drives, such as the LTO-4 and T10000, have the ability to encrypt data using standard encryption techniques that prevent decoding of the data on the tape without the key used to encrypt the data.

Also, although tape storage can grow without bound, in doing so large amounts of space with carefully controlled environmental conditions must be provided for storage. Tapes do not do well simply stuffed into the proverbial closet—they must be stored in a climate-controlled environment in order to ensure that both the mechanical and magnetic health of the cartridges is maintained. Conditions such as high humidity can ruin the mechanics and magnetic heads of tape drives, dust jams the mechanisms of both drives and cartridges, and vibration or shock can render either useless, sometimes even in the smallest amounts. And even though tape systems and cartridges are relatively inexpensive to acquire, over time the cost of an ever-growing tape environment—including the space, storage racks and additional cartridges—will generally exceed most other forms of storage for a given amount of space.

But tape's biggest disadvantage lies in the reliability of the media and drives. Tape drives and media are highly complex, high-precision pieces of equipment. Tape drives are masters of mechanical complexity, with motors that move tape across spinning heads at very precise rates of speed, can stop near instantaneously, and then restart move tape media back to high speed within very short periods of time. On the other end the cartridge is a very precisely formed piece of plastic, with a long stream of flexible magnetic impregnated media that is easily stretched and/or broken. Combine these two pieces of equipment, and you have a complex set of mechanisms subject to unpredictable breakdown, with a larger probability of error than most other types of media. Additionally, a typical repair is a replacement exercise, adding additional complexity and outage time that exacerbates the reliability problem.

An additional factor to take into consideration when looking at tape reliability is the mechanism used to insert tapes into the tape drives within a library: the robot. The robotic arm in a library is yet another piece of highly complex equipment, in some ways even more so than the tape drive. This mechanism must be able to read the barcodes (using an optical scanner), grab the tape just hard enough to pull it from the slot (too softly and the tape drops to the ground; too hard and the cartridge or robot can be damaged), and move to the tape drive, center up on the drive itself, and then, finally insert the cartridge into the drive. Between the mechanisms of the arm and all the potential alignment problems that can happen, it is a wonder of modern engineering that libraries work at all. But work they do.

When breakdowns do occur, however, they are costly, both in terms of productivity and availability. In large environments, generating hundreds of tapes a day, long outages due to robotic failures can represent a loss of protection of an entire day's worth of data. So given all these disadvantages, why use tape?

Tape, once written and stored properly, provides an inexpensive method of keeping large quantities of data for a long period of time. Tape storage costs around $.02/GB for the acquisition cost of tape, and storage costs can be much less than that. Compare this with the cost of disk storage—typically on the order of three or four times the acquisition costs, coupled with ongoing power/space/cooling costs. So tape is a very attractive long-term medium. This makes tape an excellent candidate for secondary or tertiary media storage. This level of storage would be appropriate for backups that are infrequently used and are maintained strictly for offsite recoveries or for regulatory or corporate governance requirements.

Table 3–2 summarizes the advantages and disadvantages of implementing a tape-based backup solution. Tape is still the cheapest backup medium for small quantities of data, and is good for small sites that do not have stringent backup and recovery requirement for data. Sites that do not have the infrastructure required for other types of media, do not have a need to keep backups for more than one or two weeks, or simply need a quick way to provide backups without worrying about retentions or other offsite requirements should still consider tape as a primary backup medium.

Table 3–2. Tape Advantages/Disadvantages

Tape Targets

Advantage	Disadvantage
Inexpensive media	Media sensitive to environmental conditions
Well known, mature technology	Mechanically complex; reliability issues
Simple to grow storage size	Expensive to grow performance (add more tape drives)
Media portable between sites	Difficult to share drive resources between servers

Tape has frequently been characterized as a dying backup medium. However, although its uses as a primary media target are rapidly diminishing, the use as a secondary medium for transportation and long-term storage of backups will remain for the foreseeable future.

Disk

With all the issues with tape, administrators looked toward the medium that would allow for quick access to backups and provide a way to have fast and reliable storage: disk. Disk backup targets are simply file systems that have been set aside for use by the backup software as a media target. Although this sounds simple, the implementation and management of disk-based solutions can be a complex operation.

When thinking about disk-based solutions, it is important to understand how disk systems are put together and their characteristics and limitations. When presenting disk storage to systems, especially for backup applications, the disks that are presented to the OS are typically not individual disks. When disks are presented individually, whether for backup or other purposes, the type of presentation is referred to as *just a bunch of disks (JBOD)*. When storage is presented in this way, the data on each disk is not protected in any way. If an individual disk fails, all the data stored on that particular disk is lost. Additionally, presenting storage in this way does not allow for an easy way to balance workload across disks—one disk might be busy, although another is idle.

Needless to say, using JBOD for backups is less than optimal and is not recommended. Typically, storage that is presented for any type of modern operating system and backup system is presented as a Logical Units or LUN. LUN actually stands for logical unit number, but common usage is to refer to any discrete device as a LUN that is presented to the operating system, regardless of back-end configuration. The back-end storage is grouped together using specialized disk controllers in to *redundant array of inexpensive disks (RAID)* groups. RAID controllers take individual JBOD disks and create a low-level relationship between the disks, presenting them up the chain as a single disk.

There are different methods of presenting storage using RAID, each with its own characteristics. The typical RAID levels in use for backup systems are the following:

- RAID 10

- RAID 5

- RAID 6

There are other RAID levels that are defined, but they are not often seen in backup applications.

RAID 10

RAID 10 disk groupings take a set of disks and create what is called a *mirrored stripe*. Disks in this RAID type or level are constructed by creating a pair of disks that contain a matched set of block between them—this is the mirror. These mirrored sets are then grouped together in such a way as when data is written, the data blocks are written in streams, or stripes, across all the mirrored pairs in the RAID set (see Figure 3–9). RAID 10 groups can consist of as few as four disks, and always must have an even number of disks participating in the RAID group. RAID 10 configurations can tolerate disk failures without loss of performance or availability. This is due to the fact that if a disk fails within the set, the disk's partner will have the same data that the failed disk contained. Once the disk is replaced, the data is written back from the surviving disk to the new disk, thus re-creating the protection scheme. RAID 10 also has the best performance characteristics of the RAID levels, balancing both read and write performance with the highest level of protection. However, this comes at a price—the RAID level requires a doubling of storage acquired in order to provide the amount of storage needed. Because each disk requires a matched pair, the amount of usable storage is only half of what the raw installed storage is—thus the requirement for double the storage.

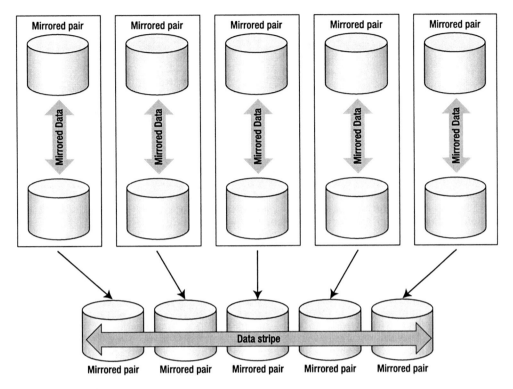

Figure 3–9. RAID 10

RAID 5

The RAID 5 level takes a different approach to protecting data (see Figure 3–10). Instead of the brute force method of writing every piece of data twice, the RAID 5 method striped the data across a single set of disks, but then calculates a data stripe signature called *parity*, which is then also written across the set of disks participating in the RAID level. Using this parity method, a RAID 5 set can tolerate exactly one disk failure at a time without loss of data. Performance of the RAID 5 set is also significantly decreased during a failure, as well as after the replacement of the failed disk. When a RAID 5 set experiences a disk failure, the data is no longer available in that section of the stripe and must be regenerated *in flight* when requested through a complex calculation of what the data should look like based on the information contained in the parity stripe. This performance hit continues for a time after the failed disk is replaced. Once the replacement is inserted back into the RAID group, the data on the disk must be completely re-created from the parity calculations. This not only imposes a large write penalty due to the newly calculated data being written during normal operations but also imposes a large read penalty due to the parity reads from the surviving disks. Additionally, as the RAID 5 set gets larger, the time to rebuild any data on a particular volume gets longer because more parity has to be read and processed to reconstruct the data drive.

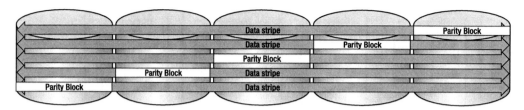

Figure 3–10. RAID 5

RAID 5 sets present at least 75 percent of the raw disk storage used in the set—a significant advantage over the RAID 10 set. However, RAID 5 does have some disadvantages. Write performance is typically much slower than that afforded by a RAID 10 set. The reason for this is twofold. When data is written to the stripe, a new set of parity must be calculated for that new data in the stripe. This new parity must now also be written to the disk set, in addition to the actual data. Both the calculation of the parity and the additional writes required contribute to the performance differential over RAID 10.

RAID 6

RAID 6 is a relatively new RAID level for backup applications. In a RAID 5 set, the loss of more than a single disk in the RAID set is catastrophic for the entire set, resulting in a complete loss of all data stored on the RAID set. This is typically seen during the rebuild process of a RAID 5 set following as described previously. RAID 6 helps avoid this issue by providing a dual-parity model in which parity for a single stripe is stored on two different disks within the RAID set. This allows for a second disk failure during the rebuild process of the first failed disk, without loss of data. However, the same penalties still apply to RAID 6 sets as they do to RAID 5 sets, with write performance penalties increasing due to the second parity calculation that has to take place during the data write process. RAID 6 also reduces the amount of usable storage over RAID 5—again storage space that is needed for the secondary parity calculation.

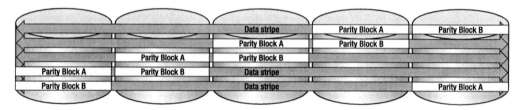

Figure 3–11. RAID 6

RAID Implementation and Disk Performance

A note must be made here regarding the hardware implementation of the RAID sets and presentation to the operating system. Write performance of the parity-based RAID sets is significantly increased through the use of a memory buffer, or write cache, to receive the I/O intended for the disk, acknowledge the write back to the operating system, and then schedule the write to the physical disk in the background. This allows some of the inefficiencies introduced by the parity calculation to be masked by the write cache, thus increasing performance. The amount of performance increase is largely governed by several factors: the amount of cache space available for the writes, the rate at which data is being written into and flushed out of the cache, and the efficiency of the cache management firmware built into the RAID controller or array. Typical internal RAID controllers have small amounts of cache relative to the amount of disk, and can be overrun by the large I/O requirements of backup operations. External arrays typically have much larger amounts of cache and can handle the data rates necessary for backup operations.

RAID sets can also be implemented via software on the operating system. Software vendors such as Symantec, or OEM UNIX and Linux implementations, offer methods of combining individual disks at the operating system and managing those disks in RAID groups, in exactly the same fashion as would have been implemented within hardware. However, this comes with several important implications.

First, all calculations are performed at the OS layer, adding significant amounts of overhead to the system as a whole, and potentially driving down the overall performance of the RAID group. Second, because CPUs within servers are general-purpose devices, they do not contain the specific hardware and firmware optimizations to efficiently calculate the parity needed to perform write operations, adding additional overhead beyond that described previously. Lastly, because the OS exposes the RAID calculations as a kernel thread, or at worst a discrete process, it is subject to both malicious and unintentional corruption and destruction, potentially resulting in data loss. Although the software is very stable and mature as a product, a great deal of thought should be used when considering the use of OS-based, software RAID within backup systems.

Performance on disk systems can be measured in methods similar to those used for tape units. However, there are a number of characteristics that allow for better overall instrumentation of backup performance. Because disk-based backups are typically written to LUNs that consist of more than one disk, there are benefits from the aggregation of disks that are realized. Disk performance is not only measured based on transfer rates, but on the number of IOPS or I/O Operations Per Second. This is a measure of how much data can be moved during a given period of time, not just the rate of transfer, and standardizes the performance metrics of dissimilar disks. Measurements of bandwidth are useful in determining the *rate* at which data can transfer, but IOPS ultimately determine the total quantity of data that can be transferred because IOPS measures in terms of blocks of data, which can vary from platform to platform, and even from version to version of particular operating systems, and is much more granular than overall bandwidth, which is in gross MB/sec.

Another factor to consider when assessing the performance of disk based backups is how the storage is presented to the operating system for management, and the number of devices that are presented for a particular purpose. Unlike tape, where there is a nice simple way of determining the number of devices that should be connected for a given set of parameters, finding the number of disk devices requires a more in depth analysis of the environment. When trying to determine the number of devices that is optimal for a given backup set, start with the connection bandwidth, just a with the tape analysis. The connections are the same: 160 MB/sec for SCSI-3 and 400 MB/sec for 4 GB FC. But here is the twist: because disks are parallel devices, they can have more than one path to them, effectively increasing the available bandwidth to a particular device. In addition, disks do not suffer from any type of shoe-shining, so there is no minimum speed. The difference between disk and tape media targets can be summed up in this maxim:

Tape operates at the speed of the slowest client, whereas disk operates at the speed of the fastest client up to the speed of the disk itself.

What does this mean? As you saw previously, tape must maintain a transfer rate above a specific threshold in order to maintain efficient throughput. If the throughput falls below this threshold, the tape drive must stop and wait until the data can be pushed to the tape. Even with multiplexing, the aggregated stream is simply the weighted average of the speed of all the data streams feeding in to the multiplex. If the aggregate is below one of the stepdown thresholds, the performance of the tape drive is artificially reduced to below what is actually possible. Individual streams are limited by both the aggregation of the data and the stepdown speed of the tape drive. In a disk-based environment, although the individual streams might not perform any better, the overall aggregate of the streams is almost exactly the weighted average of all the streams feeding the disk, and any individual stream will operate independently of all other streams with regard to transfer rate. In fact, the disk will accept data as fast as the client will push data, up to the limit of the IOPS of the particular RAID group. Additionally, there is not a measurable time lag (at least as far as backup applications are concerned) that occurs when data rates increase. This means that disk can easily absorb varying data rates with almost no effect on the overall performance of the backup as a whole.

In the discussions regarding RAID groups, we talked about the fact that RAID groups, in addition to providing protection of the data from disk failure, also provide improved performance characteristics over drives of equivalent size. Typically the number of I/Os that a given disk can handle is relatively small—on the order of 190 IOPS. When disks are combined together in RAID groups, the number of IOPS is increased based on specific formulas. This is because the IOPS of individual drives have a cumulative affect over that of a single drive—the more drives, the more IOPS available—up to a point, of course. For the purposes of this discussion, it is not important to know exactly how to calculate IOPS for a given set of disks, just to know that RAID groups of disks have higher IOPS capacities than individual disks. In Figure 3–12, the aggregate IOPS of the 4 x 500 GB drives far exceeds that presented by the 2 TB drive, even with the loss of some of the IOPS per drive within the aggregation to RAID overhead.

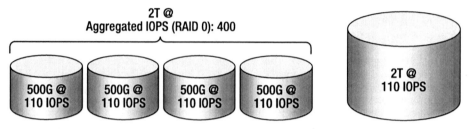

Figure 3–12. IOPS effects of RAID groups

The measurement of bandwidth that is available is highly dependent on the total number of IOPS that can be received or generated by the set of drives within the RAID group, as well as the performance of the RAID controller. Assessing bandwidth when looking at disk backup media tells only part of the story: the number of IOPS that are available based on the number and type of disk drives participating in the back-end storage, the overhead introduced by the RAID/array controllers, and the presence of any memory buffer (cache) on the RAID controller will be a far better determinant of backup performance than raw bandwidth numbers.

RAID controllers typically also have the ability to present the disk device down multiple paths. This allows the operating system the ability to protect access to the device against a single connection failure, but also provides the added benefit of distributing I/Os between multiple channels. Why do this? Adding paths will not add IOPS because that is controlled by the RAID groups/controllers, but does allow more I/Os to potentially flow by providing multiple paths to the same set of disks, thus removing a potential bottleneck to data flow through a single point.

Additionally, multiple paths also provide redundancy and guard against the failure of any one path to the disks by enforcing dynamic path access from the operating system to the target storage. Multiple paths should initially be added for redundancy and to *prevent* I/O bottlenecks at the server, but should not necessarily be added to solve performance issues because flowing more I/O to IOPS limited drives might make performance worse and not better.

This concept of expanding backup performance by adding disks to RAID groups has an important implication. The number of IOPS that a disk can handle is independent of the actual size of the disk. IOPS depends on the amount of time required to position the head to the right spot on the disk and write the data so that it can be efficiently read back off when requested. This time is called *latency*—and there are two types: rotational and seek. Typically, the high speed disks (in RPMs) have lower latency values and thus can have more IOPS. Seek latency is optimized by a combination of factors within the disk drive that reduces the amount of time the disk head has to spend moving back and forth across the disk.

What this all means is that in order to get the maximum performance out of a particular set of drives, space might have to be wasted on those drives. Why? If the number of IOPS required exceeds the total amount of IOPS that are available, regardless of the capacity of the drives, the overall performance of the disk drive will drop in relation to the amount of excess IOPS that are attempted to be requested. Because IOPS are independent of the size of the disk, if the performance requirements of a particular backup or set of backups exceed the maximum IOPS of the RAID group or disk set, the backup will actually decrease in performance. There is actually a practice called *short stroking* that does this on a per-drive basis. The concept is that the outer part of the drive is the fastest because the heads have to travel the shortest amount due to the physics of how data is written on the drive. The amount of space that can be used to achieve a short stroke area is typically only 20-30 percent of the space, and must be explicitly defined through formatting to achieve this. Short stroking is typically only done for very high IOPS requirements and is discussed here to illustrate the ability to gain more IOPS through a reduction in the overall drive utilization.

So, given all this, how do you determine what you need to implement a disk backup solution?

1. Determine average sustained throughput required. This is a relatively simple calculation. Take the amount of data required to be backed up and divide it by the time in which the backup needs to be completed:

$$R = D / T_b$$

R—Data rate required
D—Data (in GB) to be backed up to the device
T_b—Time in which the backup needs to complete

2. Determine the amount of space required to store the backup for the required amount of time. This will require looking at some details regarding how much data is being stored in a backup of a particular type. You can get a very rough estimate by taking the amount of data that is on the clients that you are backing up and multiplying the result by 2.2 (two full backups, plus daily incremental backups of 10 percent of the data).

$$S_{T(est)} = S_c * 2.6$$

S_t—Total backup size over the backup period
S_c—Size of single client full backup

3. Determine the number of channels required based on the throughput calculated in Step 1. For a 4 GB FC channel, this is about 400 MB/sec of total throughput. However, in real life, this limit will not be reached, so put an estimated overhead factor in—for FC you can typically get to around 80 percent of the rated performance, depending on the type of servers that are driving the FC and the efficiency of the operating system. For the purposes of this step, use the 80 percent.

$$C = R / (B_c * P_f)$$

C—Number of channels (rounded to the next highest even number)
R—Data rate (from step 1)
B_c—Rated data rate of an individual channel
P_f—Performance reduction factor, expressed as a percentage of the bandwidth available after overhead is taken into account

If the number of channels is an odd number or a fraction of an even number such as 2.3, round up to the next even number. If you have a single channel requirement, round to two channels. This will account for a dual path connection to the backup device that will provide two benefits. First, protection against path failure—most modern operating systems and arrays allow the utilization of multiple paths to a single device. In the event that a single path fails, operations can still go forward on the surviving path. Second, using two paths allows the I/O generated to be balanced across the controller inputs, thus potentially increasing performance, depending on the RAID type and quantities of RAID groups presented to the server from the array.

4. Determine the storage configuration taking into account the results in steps 1 and 2.

Work with your storage administrator on this—there are tools that can calculate the number of disks for a given I/O requirement. Once the number of disks is determined to meet the I/O requirement within a given RAID configuration, see if that configuration will satisfy the amount of storage required from step 2. If so, you are done. However, if more storage is required, determine the amount of additional storage required to satisfy the shortfall. If the amount of additional space required is less than 50 percent of the total amount of storage required for the backup, work with your storage administrator to see whether the RAID configuration can be changed to meet the space need, without sacrificing IOPS. If the configuration will reduce the overall IOPS or the amount of additional storage is more than 50 percent of the total, have your storage administrator create additional RAID groups that split the storage into equal parts, with each RAID group having maximal and equivalent IOPS characteristics. If you have to add RAID groups in this manner to acquire the required space, see if the storage administrator can create a logical grouping of the RAID groups that presents all groups to the server as a single LUN. If this is not possible or practical, it is time to consider the use of software RAID to create the appropriate LUN for use by the backup. Remember the discussion of RAID 10 earlier? The RAID 0 component of this is simply the stripe component. A RAID 0 stripe has no parity protection and therefore can take full advantage of the performance offered by the multiple physical LUNs presented. The parity is not needed, because the protection from loss based on an individual disk failure is handled by the RAID controller presenting the original disk configuration.

There are many ways to balance both the size of the LUNs and the performance with no real silver bullet, and the requirements and performance characteristic of the backup will change over time. Do not expect to get this exactly correct and have the optimal performing disk backup target. The number of variables that go into simply determining the number of IOPS for a given workload will guarantee that the disk target will perform well under most workloads but will not perform as well under others. The previous steps will give you the best chance of determining a configuration that will perform well for 80–90 percent of the workload, with the remaining backups performing (not badly, but simply less optimally).

In addition to having different storage and performance characteristics, disk backup media also has a number of different connectivity options that are not available to tape devices. In general, there are two different major connectivity options for disk-based backups: direct and LAN attachment. The *direct* attachment of storage for backup is accomplished through the use of the same connections used for tape: FC and direct attach storage (DAS). All the characteristics described previously for the use of both FC and DAS (in this case, SCSI) apply for disk. However, when using FC as the method of attachment, a large number of LUNs of various configurations are available for attachment to the system being used for the backup server. However, one area is different: storage sharing. When using tape, both NetBackup and CommVault provide a method (by using Shared Storage Option [SSO] or Dynamic Drive Sharing [DDS], respectively) to share tape drives between servers to help ensure the maximal utilization of the resource. However, this is not possible with disk storage when direct attached. Why not?

When backup software writes backups to disk-based solutions, they write the backup as a series of files. These files are a proprietary compilation of the data being backed up and are stored in a specific format that can only be readable by the backup software. However, to the operating system, they are simply files, like any other files that exist within the server. Open systems operating systems utilize a software layer, called a *file system*, to provide a human readable method of accessing files and managing space on disk storage. When the storage is used as a backup target for direct storage (network storage can be different, as you will see later), a single system must be responsible for the management of that storage. This is because data written to the storage must pass through the file system layer first before being written to the physical storage (see Figure 3–13).

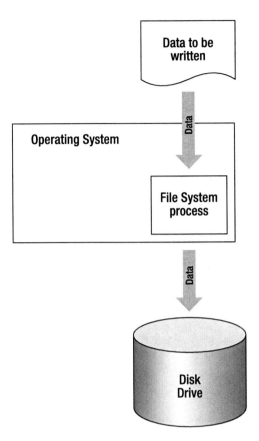

Figure 3–13. Data flow through file system process

The mechanism for this process is typically a program (called a *service*, or *daemon*, depending on your flavor of operating system) that intercepts the data I/O requests and manages the flow of data in order to keep track of the data being written. As a general rule, the process that manages the file system is only aware of the file systems that are locally present on the server on which the program is being written. This is based on the heritage of the open systems operating system: a stand-alone system with local storage that performs a fixed set of tasks.

Because the storage is defined as local, when a file representing a backup is written to the system receiving the backup, there is no way for the operating system to share the file with other discrete operating systems (particularly if they are of a different type from the originating operating system) because the process controlling the file system cannot directly present the file system to another system. Even though the backup software is aware of the file containing the backup (using the same paradigm as tape backups), it has no way to have the operating system share that file, even if the backup software could recognize the file once it moved to the other system (more on this later). In standard configurations, backups that are written to DAS cannot be shared between backup servers. Of more fundamental importance is that the storage cannot be *automatically* shared between backup servers to provide the ability of multiple servers to balance storage requirements across multiple sets of storage (although there are specialized file systems called *clustered file systems* that can span physical servers and be shared). Products such as Quantum StorNext FileSystem or Symantec CFS can be installed on related systems linking them together via the file system. However, they typically are not used as backup targets because they are very expensive to implement and do not perform well as backup solutions.

Note the word *automatically*. Although there is not a method to dynamically share direct attached storage between multiple servers to provide load balancing, there is a method to allow different servers to utilize the storage. When the process within the particular operating system manages the storage, it registers the storage as an object to direct data to and from. This registration process is called *mounting* (the term is borrowed from the early days when tapes had to be physically mounted onto the tape readers before the data could be read for a particular process). The inverse of this process is *unmounting*—removing the storage and deregistering it from the file system process. Once storage is unmounted, it can then be remounted at will by different physical servers if they can reach the physical storage on which the file system has been written. Also, the new server must be able to read the formatted file system, which means that the server must have its own copy of the process associated with that particular file system; typically, this limits the mounting ability to like operating systems. So, although HP-UX has a file system called jfs, and AIX also has a jfs, neither operating system can mount the other. The exception is Linux, which can mount many different types of file systems, ranging from ufs on Sun Solaris to Windows NTFS.

What does this have to do with sharing disks for backups? If the physical disk can be logically removed from one operating system and logically attached to another, the file system created under the first system can be read by the second; then the backup software can move disk storage between servers as done with tape. The process of this would look like Figure 3–14.

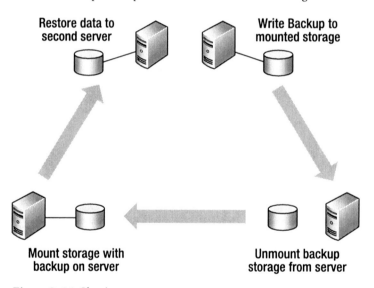

Figure 3–14. *Sharing storage process*

There are problems with this method and it is fraught with danger. In order to make it work, the physical connectivity must exist to allow direct parallel access to the disk drives that contain the file system. Using SCSI, this is a difficult (nearly impossible) task to accomplish reliably. However, this is a simple matter using FC. Because at its heart, FC uses a network paradigm to provide communication, it can (and frequently does) allow parallel access to a single disk device by multiple servers. Where the problem comes in is with the communication and control of this access. As stated before, FC only provides the communication pathway to the devices and makes no assumptions about the "correct" way to utilize a particular target device. As such, the operating system, being the ultimate party responsible for writing data to the device must manage that connectivity, including locking devices or files on shared file systems. Because this is a function that the operating system must handle, there is no way to automate this process other than by creating a separate process, external to the backup software, that would unmount and mount the file systems between the desired systems. At best, however, this would represent a manual process that would be very invasive in the overall backup flow as well as being difficult and unreliable to implement.

Network Attached Storage (NAS)

Again, fortunately there is an easier way. Disk-based backup targets can also be presented using the local area network protocols over TCP/IP. Such targets can be provided by stand-alone systems or through specialized appliances called *filers*. Storage that is provided over the LAN is commonly referred to as *network attached storage* (NAS). Protocols such as Common Internet File Service (CIFS) and Network File Service (NFS) are used to present NAS storage to clients and provide the ability to present a shared view of a single file system to multiple systems.

How does this work? Instead of building out the file system locally for the backup server to use directly, a file system is built on a remote server. The remote server can be in appliance format or simply be an operating system, loading on a general purpose server, with a file system that contains the required data. This file system is then "shared" or presented over the IP network by specialized software that allows access to the file system just as if the file system were locally mounted. This software must be running on both the source (to present the file system) and the target (to receive and interpret the data for the local server) in order for this to work. The software on the receiving end creates a device that can be mounted just like a physical device on to the local system—the exact same process as "Map Network Drive" on a desktop computer. But the more interesting component is on the remote side.

Because these methods are based on network protocols and not storage protocols, they have the same characteristics as other network-based applications, namely the ability to allow multiple connections to the same network resource. How this works is that the software on the remote side receives connection requests from the client. After these requests are authorized, the connection is made, and the client now has the ability to manipulate the files on the remote server just as if they were locally mounted. All servers requesting the same information receive the current state of the remote file system in parallel. On the remote side, because data is received from the clients to the file system, it is written to the local file system, which is being shared just as if local applications were writing the data (which, in essence, they are). Because multiple systems can write to the same devices, the problem of wasted file system capacity can potentially be reduced. Space that was previously isolated because it could not be utilized by a particular backup server can now be made available to multiple servers via a network share. However, it comes with some costs and caveats because all things do.

Before we address this, however, it is constructive to discuss the two protocols that are used to affect this architecture: CIFS and NFS. CIFS is the more commonly known of the two protocols because it forms the basis for all Windows File Shares. CIFS uses a technique known as the Server Message Block (SMB) to present file systems to clients for use, as well as other resources shared by Windows, such as printers and other devices. Because Microsoft developed CIFS to run by utilizing SMB, and no other file sharing mechanisms use SMB for file sharing, CIFS and SMB are used interchangeably. Because SMB is such a generic method of presenting devices, it must be able to handle and convey the current state of these devices as they are being accessed by the various clients. This ability to determine what is being done to devices remotely as changes are made and then incorporating the new information into a local view is known as being *stateful*. Because SMB is a stateful protocol, when implemented using CIFS it allows the local server to maintain knowledge about what is happening on the remote server with respect to the file system being accessed. If the state of the remote server changes unexpectedly, because CIFS is also stateful (by virtue of SMB being stateful) the connection is reset, invalidating all pending communication to the remote server (including reads and writes of data). This generally requires an explicit reconnection to the share provided by the server and starting the read or write operation from the beginning—no midstream restart is possible. The stateful nature of CIFS also can lead to a large amount of network overhead in simply determining the current state of the remote server, thus reducing the overall potential transfer rates of data from clients to servers. CIFS is almost exclusively used only in Windows environments; however, many UNIX and Linux implementations optionally provide the freely available software package, Samba, which allows these platforms to access file shares (and other services) based on SMB.

As a counterpoint, the NFS is almost the complete opposite of CIFS. NFS uses a natively developed protocol, in conjunction with standard remote procedure call (RPC) methodology, to facilitate the presentation of file systems to remote clients. NFS is almost exclusively the domain of UNIX and Linux operating systems; NFS clients are available commercially for Windows, but are very rarely seen in the field. As opposed to being stateful, NFS was historically a stateless protocol (this has changed in NFSv4— more later), meaning that the current state of the remote server is not maintained locally and can change without notification to the client. However, failed connection still cause issues on the client—different issues, but somewhat safer issues depending on how the NFS share is accessed.

As of NFSv4, this all-or-nothing approach of using hard or soft mounts has changed slightly. NFSv4, or version 4, of NFS implements a stateful approach to the client/server relationship, allowing for the determination of server state by the client dynamically. This stateful nature of NFS now allows for the (relatively) graceful notification of applications of the fact that communication to the file or set of files located on the NFS server was lost. As discussed, all file transactions were simply blocked in previous versions. Unfortunately, a side effect of this was that because there was no way to interrupt the attempts to access the file, there was also no good way to stop access other than through extreme methods— stopping the application and potentially rebooting the system to clear the application file connections to the now nonexistent files. However, NFSv4 does not go as far as CIFS in the maintenance of state. If a single-client connection failed on a CIFS server, the entire remote server stack typically is reset to reestablish state across all connecting clients. This means that even if one client could still access a share and another could not, both clients were reset, terminating all active I/O without prejudice. NFSv4, on the other hand, has the ability to reestablish state independently between clients, which only requires that clients that lost connection flush their previous state and reload the current state of the NFS share on reconnection.

By default, NFS shares are mounted *hard*: in a state where if the client cannot confirm the ability to communicate to the remote share, it will retry the write indefinitely, blocking all further access to the share from that client, and holding all pending transactions until communication can be returned. Unfortunately, this process will stop all upstream processes as well, such as the backup that is attempting to write to the NFS share via the client. The result is a backup that looks like it is stopped abnormally midstream (*hung*). On the positive side, once the communication is restored, assuming that the backup has not timed out due to inactivity, the backup continues to write data exactly where it left off as if nothing had happened. No restart or connection reset is required, and the only thing lost is time in the backup window.

Never use soft NFS mounts when using NFS shares as backup targets!

The *soft* mount option is an alternative to the hard mount. A soft mount states that if communication is lost, the client will wait for a specified period of time and then resume communication with whatever is available at that point in time. If the communication has not been restored, this typically means that the process reads from the local disk on which the NFS share had been mounted and then processes all transactions to that target versus the intended NFS share. Obviously, this can result in "bad things" when talking about backups; backups can easily be corrupted using soft NFS mounts. If a soft mount fails during a backup, then, to the backup application, the ability to write simply pauses for a period of time—the same period of time that NFS uses to timeout its connection to the remote server. Once the timeout completes, the application continues to write data to the local storage, right from the point it paused, creating a partial backup image on the local storage. If the connection is resumed, still midstream, the backup pauses again and resumes writing to the remote storage, creating a corrupt image on the remote side as well.

Given the different characteristics of these two protocols, there are differences in the advantages and limitations of implementing a disk backup strategy based on either of these protocols. There are, however, more commonalities, including determining how much data can be backed up to a single NAS device. In the direct attach storage model, the method for determining the amount of storage required was relatively straightforward. With NAS storage, there are additional variables that must be taken into consideration when sizing the storage. Instead of the data being transferred from the client to the backup server to the storage, the model is now the data being written from the clients to multiple backup servers, which are then consolidating all the data flow and targeting it to a single NAS device.

As a result, the total throughput to the storage on the NAS device is the cumulative transfer rate requirements of all servers that are utilizing the NAS storage. So if a single backup server has several clients, the total of which transfer data at 5 MB/sec, and this is replicated across 5 other clients, the cumulative required transfer rate to the NAS target is 25 MB/sec. This also means that on the NAS device, the back-end storage must be able to handle the number of IOPS that are associated with this throughput requirement. As the number of servers attaching to the NAS target increases, the backend IOPS requirements also proportionately increases as well.

Another factor to consider that is along the same lines is the network connectivity. There are two components to consider when looking at the network connectivity: available transfer bandwidth and the number of packets per second into the network interface. The first is relatively simple: if the interface on the NAS server is a 1 GB interface, and the interfaces on all clients pointing to them are 1 GB interfaces, there is a good chance that the NAS interface will be the bottleneck. This is because all of the clients are attempting to move data at the exact same speed as the NAS interface, resulting in too much data attempting to be transmitted in a given unit of time. Increasing the number of network interface card (NIC) interfaces on the remote NAS side will increase the number of targets that are available for a given speed. This will reduce the contention for a given interface, but will not increase the maximum line speed seen by the clients to the NAS. Here is why: say you have a NAS device with 4 x 1 GB interfaces. Assuming that all clients have 1 GB connectivity to the SAN, the fastest speed that the NAS can receive data from a single client is 1 GB/sec. It is not 4 GB/sec as some would have you believe. Although there is 4 GB of bandwidth available, it is broken down into individual 1 GB interfaces.

Think of it like cars on a freeway—there can be three cars on a three-lane freeway, but they can only travel a maximum speed of the posted speed limit (see Figure 3–15). The best solution to move data (or cars) faster is to raise the speed limit, but for both cars and network packets, it increased the impact of collisions (yes, there are collisions on networks; more on this later).

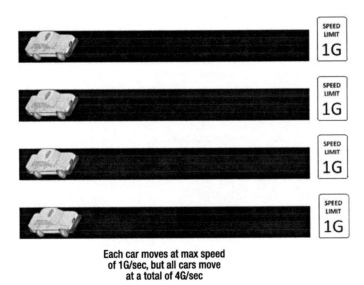

Each car moves at max speed
of 1G/sec, but all cars move
at a total of 4G/sec

Figure 3–15. Parallel "network packet" transmission speeds

The other aspect of network connectivity to NAS storage is that of the number of packets generated by a given client set. Let's take our previous example and have the clients have 100 Mb interfaces, all pointing to our 1 GB interface on the NAS. How many clients could you run in parallel and not create a bottleneck at the NAS interface? If you said 10, you would be correct, but why is that the case? It is not simply the case of dividing the speed at the target by the speed at the source. That simply provides a ratio of speeds, not the actual amount of traffic that can be handled by the NAS interface. To find that out, you need to calculate the number of Ethernet data chunks (packets) that can be handled by a particular interface per second. To find the theoretical maximum number of packets that can be received or transmitted for a given speed, use the following:

$$P_s = S_I /1532$$

Where:

P_s—Packets per second
S_I—Maximum speed of the interface in bytes per second
1532—Size of an individual Ethernet packet

So a 1 GB Ethernet interface works out to be approximately 87,000 packets per second, and 8,555 packets per second for a 100 Mb interface. To find the maximum number of connections, simply divide the NAS interface P_s by the P_s of the client. In general, this will match the ratio of the speeds, but it is important to understand why that is not accurate.

Additionally, each 1532-bit Ethernet packet actually sends only 1500 bits of information. This is due to the fact that the packet actually contains information in the header (the first 32 bits) that provide both source and destination information for the packet. Although for an individual packet it is not much of a difference, when applied to hundreds of thousands of packets, the quantity of data adds up. Ethernet is also limited by the protocol. Packets are not guaranteed for delivery, which leads to retransmission of packets, potentially causing a cascading degradation of overall performance.

To illustrate this, let's look at another example. Suppose that you have 9 clients all running 100 Mb interfaces to a single 1 GB interface. When you run a test of each individual client, you find that three of the clients can push data at full speed (not possible in reality, but bear with me for the purposes of the example), and only one seems to push data at 50 Mb per second. When you run all the clients to the NAS target, the throughput of the 8 good clients drops to around 90 Mb/sec, and the bad client stays at 50 Mb/sec. What is going on? When you look at this example, if you simply use the sum of the speeds, you would expect that the transmission rates of the individual clients would stay the same regardless of being separate or together. However, when you look at the number of packets generated, the story is actually told. Going back to the example, the network administrator comes to you and tells you that the bad client has to retransmit about 50 percent of its packets and that is why the performance is so slow. The effect of these retransmissions is to reduce the potential number of packets available for receipt, not only for the bad client but for all other clients to the same interface at well (see Figure 3–16).

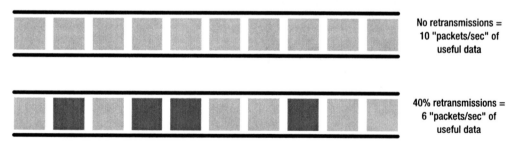

No retransmissions =
10 "packets/sec" of
useful data

40% retransmissions =
6 "packets/sec" of
useful data

Figure 3–16. Effect of retransmission on throughput

So although the bad client does not directly affect the other clients in a vacuum, when combined into a single target, the number of packets is cumulative, and any retransmissions or other deleterious packets will reduce the total number of packets that are available to the general population.

This is a good point at which to reintroduce our two NAS protocols: CIFS and NFS. Being a stateful protocol, CIFS has the side effect of generating a lot of network traffic that has nothing to do with data transfer *per se*. This traffic takes the form of state information that flows back and forth between all clients connected to the NAS server and represents protocol overhead that will reduce both the maximum throughput rate by reducing the number of packets available for actual data transfer. NFS, on the other hand, is a stateless (until v4) protocol. State information does not flow back and forth in the data path, so the overhead associated with NFS is less than that associated with CIFS. This results in a net increase in both the throughput available and the number of connections that can be accepted by a given Ethernet interface for a given speed. Given the choice between NAS protocols, strictly from an efficiency standpoint, NFS wins hands down. This might be changing, however. With the release of both Vista and Server 2008, Microsoft announced the implementation of SMB 2.0—a more efficient version of SMB that maintains state without the same level of network transmission required from the original SMB. As of this writing, the jury was still out on the increase in efficiency. On the NFS front, the impact of the "stateful" v4 implementation was also not determined, so when looking at NAS targets using these protocols, keep in mind the effects we have discussed here.

So, getting back to our backup NAS target, what is the effect of all this? It is important to understand that the throughput of backups to NAS targets is heavily dependent on the state of the LAN, as well as the number of connections and the data output speed and the overall network health of the clients attached to the NAS device for their backup. So although simply having a 1 GB or 10 GB connection is a great thing, it does not guarantee that your backups will move any faster because many other factors other than just the speed of the interface have an effect on NAS backup targets.

There is a third type of backup target that combines the properties of locally attached storage with the expanded connectivity offered by LANs, avoiding the need for the specialized skill set required for SAN design and administration, as well as the increased cost of equipment iSCSI. Simply put, iSCSI is putting LUNs (or tape drives, for that matter) created by a particular array controller on to the LAN and allowing clients to connect to them as if they were locally attached storage. This provides the ability to centrally manage storage and provide higher speed LUNs than would be available to local servers, but does not require the implementation of any specialty hardware other than a separate IP connection to allow hosts to connect to the storage. iSCSI does not offer the ability for multiple parallel connectivity in the same way as NAS storage. This is because the same paradigms used for local attached storage are reused for iSCSI storage, but just transmitted over a different medium—much as how FC was implemented. Sizing iSCSI storage targets is a hybrid of both the NAS and direct models: you need to assess the IOPS required for a particular connection, but also assess the number of packets per second that would be generated for the collection of servers attaching to the iSCSI storage to ensure that the particular Ethernet interfaces were not overloaded. In addition, because iSCSI is based on Ethernet, all the packet and other connectivity issues associated are also inherited. iSCSI is good for smaller environments that can tolerate variances in performance and are just getting into centralized management of storage, but do not want to implement a full SAN-based environment. Because both disk and tape can be emulated across iSCSI, inexpensive hybrid approaches to mixing both tape and disk solutions become available to the smaller environment. More detailed design requirements of hybrid solutions and target selection will be addressed later. However, before considering iSCSI as a backup target, assess the reliability of your network and the possibility of using other more reliable methods of creating backup targets. Issues such as having to rescan for devices not automatically detected at boot time and device performance degradation as a result of network utilization are items that need to be considered when looking at iSCSI as an option.

So when do you decide to use disk as a backup target? Disk backups are good backup targets because they represent a fast and easy-to-deploy method of creating a backup solution, using proven and well understood methods and techniques. Disk backup targets can be quickly brought up by any system administrator who has installed storage on a server and can be easily integrated into both NetWorker and NetBackup. In addition, NAS-based disk backups have the added advantage of providing connectivity via LAN connections and can also maximize the storage use by reducing islands of storage that have been fenced off by direct attachment. The disk resource is better utilized as a whole, without dedicating specific resources to meet specific needs. NAS-based backup targets also are easier to grow because entire NAS systems can be deployed without the need to stop systems in order to deploy additional storage. Simply issue a mount command (or Windows share mount) and away you go.

However, disk backups are not the cure-all. Disks are not portable. If you need offsite copies of your backups, having disk backup targets as your only type of backup is not workable. Also, when using regular disk backups (not the more advanced type as will be discussed in Chapter 5), there is not the benefits of compression or other storage techniques that can natively shrink data down to the smallest possible footprint. In addition, disk requires a large amount of environmental resources when compared with tape. It is easy to grow a tape environment: simply buy more tape cartridges—no additional hardware is required. However, to grow a disk environment, you have to deploy additional power/cooling/space for the disk drives, which introduces additional cost. Speaking of cost, the cost per MB of disk is much higher that than of tape. Table 3–3 shows disk advantages and disadvantages.

Table 3–3. Summary of Disk Advantages/Disadvantages

Disk Targets

Advantage	Disadvantage
Consistent speed	Expensive (when compared to tape)
Short-term retention	Does not scale well for long-term retention
Ease of implementation	Space management is highly interactive
Ability to share disk targets between servers	Not portable
Has many ways to connect, depending on the requirements of the solution	Connection types can require specialized knowledge to implement and maintain (e.g., SAN implementations)

Given the advantages and disadvantages, which are summarized in the table, disk is best suited in several areas. Disk is great as the primary backup target, with some type of replication of the backup to other media for long-term storage. This allows the administrator to get the speed and the reliability benefits of disk targets for the first backup. As the backup ages, it can be moved off to tape storage for longer-term retention, freeing up the storage for new backups.

Disk is also useful for quick backups that do not require any type of long-term retention, and where the growth of the backup size is relatively small. Backups of small offices, remote sites, or other areas that only require short-term backups of localized data and do not want to deal with the hassle of managing tape cartridges are also good candidates for disk.

Summary

In the beginning of this chapter, you looked at the original backup medium: tape. Tape provides a very mature, well-known, and superficially inexpensive method of storing backups. However, weaknesses, such as the sequential nature of tape, the mechanical complexities, and the highly variable nature of the throughput to tape devices are rapidly relegating tape to secondary or tertiary storage medium in many environments.

Disk storage overcomes some of these disadvantages. With the ability to receive data quickly, have multiple streams storing backups simultaneously, and having the ability to present the storage in a number of different ways, depending on the need, disk shines as a backup storage media. But disk also has its weaknesses: the cost of the media, lack of portability, and difficulty to ensure full utilization of the media make disk not as optimal as it seems on the surface.

The physical backup media discussed in this chapter represent the classic approaches to backup targets. These media types have been in use since the beginning of the computing era, and are well tested and mature technologies. However, mature and proven are often at dead ends technologically and cannot grow well to meet the needs of the 21st-century data center or of the highly distributed nature of computing today. The next several chapters will examine the state of the art in backup technologies and their implications for these classics.

CHAPTER 4

■ ■ ■

Virtual Backup Media

Physical media have been the basis for the backup since the first large-scale computer systems. However, physical media, as previously shown, have a number of limitations. The ability to allocate resources to the right areas, the details required in management of the backup media, and the general overhead required to simply maintain physical media can make physical media environments difficult to manage at scale.

Enter virtual media. *Virtual media* emulate the physical hardware with the goal of reducing or eliminating the management and hardware issues associated with physical media. By eliminating complex hardware and cartridge systems associated with physical media and replacing them with simpler, commodity disk drives, virtual media also has the advantage of increasing the overall reliability of the backup environment. Virtual media provide these advantages without changing operational procedures or requiring any modification of backup software to account for a new media type. Also, as will be shown later in the chapter, in some cases performance can be increased through better use of the bandwidth on the media used to connect the virtualized media to the backup servers.

Virtual backup media are traditionally associated exclusively with the *virtual tape library (VTL)*, but recently have newer incarnations using protocols that allow the virtualization of other types of backup targets to create new types of backup media. For now, let's review this most common of the virtual backup media: the VTL.

Virtual Tape Libraries

If you think about a physical tape library in more general terms, what is it, really? A *physical tape library* is simply a box that contains slots that stores tape cartridges, a connection to which tape drives can be attached, and containing a device (a robot) that can move the cartridges from the slots to the drives and back on command.

The function of a VTL is simply to take the concept of a physical tape library and implement it in software. The software presents connection points to the input/output (I/O) ports that look like their physical counterparts. So when a virtual library is created, to the operating system the library behaves *in every way* just as a physical library would. The virtual cartridges (the record within the library representing the data stored in a particular location) can be *inserted* into virtual drives, *ejected* from the virtual library (moved from the *library* table to the *nonlibrary* table within the software, and inserted back into the library (the reverse of the eject operation). Within a single physical VTL multiple libraries can be created (see Figure 4–2), thus allowing migration of virtual cartridges between libraries by ejecting and inserting virtual cartridges.

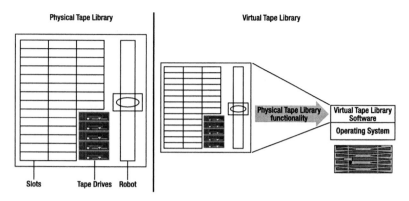

Figure 4–1. *Physical vs. virtual tape libraries*

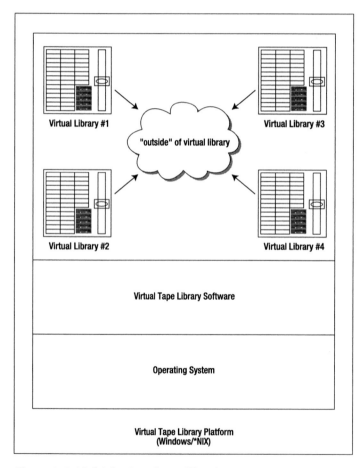

Figure 4–2. *Multiple virtual tape libraries*

This behavior of the VTL—providing a look and feel that is identical to a physical tape library—is simply a function of the identification strings that are sent as part of the protocol that is used to communicate back to the server. The same is true for virtual tape drives: they are just software-created connection points that respond to requests from the I/O port with the hardware identification strings that would be used if they were physical devices. This transmission of hardware identification strings by the software is known as *emulation*. When a VTL is said to emulate a particular library, the virtual tape library software is responding to the commands and requests that are issued by the backup server with the same hardware identification strings that the actual hardware would respond with. This makes the backup server think that a physical library is on the end of the connection, instead of a piece of software. The emulation takes every element of the library and translates this description into a software representation. The emulation covers both the capabilities and limitations of the particular library. So if a particular physical library that is emulated holds only a maximum of 100 physical tape cartridges, the emulated library is typically artificially limited to 100 cartridges as well. But this does not have to be the case. Because the emulation is simply a software response to a hardware request, and any slots and cartridges in the virtual library are simply pointers that are created by the software (a database of pointers), the size of the table containing the pointers can be arbitrarily large—extending beyond the limits of the physical tape library being spoofed. The VTL software can even allow the limits of the real hardware to be exceeded. An example is that the emulation of a 100-slot library can be made to have 1,000 slots in the virtual edition of the library, simply by changing the configuration in software of the library emulation.

Virtual tape drives are emulated in a similar fashion. When a virtual drive is created in a VTL, a responder is created as a connection point for requests coming in from the I/O port. The software emulator responds to requests for the various tape functions (load, eject, move forward, move backward, and so on), just as the physical tape drive would. Again, the emulation covers both the capabilities and limitations of the particular tape drive model being emulated, including the maximum size of the cartridge. The emulation can even insert delays into the processing to simulate tape operations—delays that might be necessary to ensure that the backup software running the tape drive does not get outrun by emulation. But as with the tape library, this is by convention and is not required. Because the cartridge is simply a series of pointers into the back-end storage media, the number of pointers can be arbitrarily large—thus creating virtual cartridges that are different sizes from their physical counterparts.

Given these two facts, why would you not simply create a virtual library with an extremely large number of slots, with virtual cartridges that emulate a particular drive type, but are custom sized to the needs of the particular backup? This will not work because of limitations built into both the operating systems of the servers and the backup software running on them. One of the advantages of VTLs is that because they look, act, and smell like physical tape libraries, *no change* to the backup software is required to implement them. Performance tuning items, such as multiplexing and other performance tuning factors, can have a much larger impact on the performance and storage capabilities of the backup on virtual media than the creation of customized tape cartridges.

This also can introduce limitations, particularly in NetBackup. When NetBackup (and CommVault, to some extent) identify a particular tape library, they know how many cartridges can fit within the particular library. As an example, if you connect a Sun L180 library to a NetBackup server, the NetBackup server will only recognize a *maximum* of 180 slots within the library. This is because the library specification within NetBackup for that particular library type is hard-coded to use only 180 slots. Originally, this hard code of the library specification had two purposes: to prevent malformed requests for slots by the software that either did not exist or could not be accessed (causing a library fault condition within NetBackup), and as a mechanism to license the particular capabilities of libraries based on the number of slots within the library. Until recently, these hard-coded limitations persisted within the software and limited the capabilities of VTL vendors in creating arbitrarily large libraries.

The situation is somewhat more complex for tape drive emulation. In order for tape drives to be accessed by either NetBackup or CommVault, the operating system on which they run must be able to recognize the virtual tape drives and manipulate them at a low level. Drivers, which are specialized software, are implemented to access the tape drives. One of the most important features of these drivers is the ability to figure out when the tape cartridge is full. But how does the operating system know how much data can fit on a tape? The answer is that it doesn't really know, but is relying on responses from the tape drive. The tape drive will attempt to put data on the tape up to the point where it is indicated that the cartridge is out of tape. The drive then sends a signal to the operating system, saying that it is out of tape. But the neither the operating system or the tape drive know how much data is on the tape—only the number of tape blocks that have been written and the number that are left. So if the operating system is not telling the backup software how much tape can fit on a cartridge, how does CommVault or NetBackup know how much tape is left? The answer is that they don't—there is no way that either product can determine the amount of space left on the tape cartridge. The only information that the software has is the fact that the end of the tape has not been reached and the amount of data that has been written to the tape.

However, with virtual drives this calculus changes—any amount of data can technically be put on to any cartridge of any particular emulation—technically, you could create a single cartridge that encompasses the entirety of the VTL. The backup software would be able to write to this cartridge and would indeed write as much data as possible to the cartridge. However, this might fail, either on the read or write, depending on how the driver accesses the tape drive. NetBackup provides specific drivers to use for particular classes of tape drives. These class drivers replace both the operating system (OS) native and device-specific drivers, thus providing NetBackup with particular control over how and where blocks of data are written to the media. In particular, NetBackup uses the concept of a pass-through driver, commonly known as the SCSI generic (sg) driver to allow for direct control of the tape device. This driver, combined with the specific class driver, allows NetBackup to bypass the regular operating system driver mechanism and control the transport mechanism, thus allowing NetBackup to precisely place data on the tape. While this has the advantage of using the media to the full potential, it also has a downfall. If the class driver does not understand the data being received from the device (physical or virtual) because *more* data has been written to a piece of media than would otherwise normally be possible, there is a potential for backup loss that which can only be detected during a restore operation (the driver might not understand the block pointer addresses being requested for a particular recover operation) or might exceed the addressing capabilities of the particular class of tape driver. If a virtual tape drive is created that does not meet the parameters expected by NetBackup, the backup might fail unexpectedly as suddenly the values passed back from the *tape device* (virtual tape drive/cartridge) do not match.

For CommVault, the issue is less pronounced. Because CommVault does not install CommVault-specific drivers for tape (again, virtual or physical), it relies on the functionality of either the OS native or manufacturer-specific drivers. CommVault can be easily fooled into thinking it has a particular drive type because it uses a custom tool, ScanScsiTool, to detect, read, and report on the drive type identification information embedded in the virtual tape drive. While this might make CommVault think that a particular tape drive is attached, it also makes assumptions regarding the function of the drive, particularly with respect to expected positioning and location addresses. CommVault might not correctly interpret positioning and location information returned by the virtual media during backup, causing unexpected backup failure. Worse, the backup might appear to succeed, but a restore from the virtual media might fail as the media locations required for portions of the restore might appear to be invalid to CommVault during the restore process—thus failing the restore from a successful backup.

However, possibly the best reason to match the size of the virtual tape emulation: avoiding confusion or capacity planning issues caused by creation of custom cartridge sizes. When creating duplicate or AUX copies of the backups from the virtual to physical tape with standard size cartridges, it is a simple matter to calculate the number of physical cartridges required for exporting the data—the virtual cartridges are either an exact match or a known standard multiple of the physical cartridge size. For instance, if an LTO-2 cartridge is used as the virtual backup media, and is intended to be exported to an LTO-4 cartridge, for every two LTO-2 virtual cartridges, a single LTO-4 cartridge would be required (at least for planning purposes).

When using custom size cartridges, this calculus is variable, particularly if a number of different size custom sizing methods are applied. In the previous example, in order to plan for the number of export cartridges required for the custom virtual cartridges, the operator would need to know both the size of the custom cartridge and the utilization of the cartridge. This calculation would vary depending on which individual cartridge happens to contain the backup images that need to be replicated out to physical cartridges—a process that can rapidly become complex and difficult to manage. In order to avoid this extensive management process, it is operationally simpler to create standard cartridges.

A word here about emulation and its importance: it really isn't important at all. That might sound surprising: doesn't the emulation determine the amount of data you can store on a cartridge? Yes, it does, but with a VTL you can create any number of cartridges up to (and in some cases beyond, as you will see shortly) the limits of the disk capacity. (See Figure 4–3.) What typically drives the concern around emulation is the ability to copy the cartridges out to physical tape once they are created. This actually has no bearing on the type of virtual cartridges that are created. Both NetBackup and CommVault, when copying backups between media, copy the backup image by default rather than the cartridge.

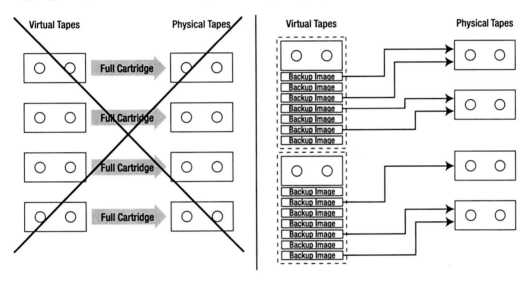

Figure 4–3. *Backup replication from virtual to physical*

This means that if you use CommVault to create a secondary copy of backups from one cartridge to another, NetBackup will look at each individual *image* versus each *cartridge* and copy the image and not the cartridge. CommVault works in a similar manner: when an AUX copy is created, the copy of the backup is moved, not the image of the entire cartridge. (See Figure 4–4.) This relegates the selection of a particular emulation type down to one of convenience and ease of management.

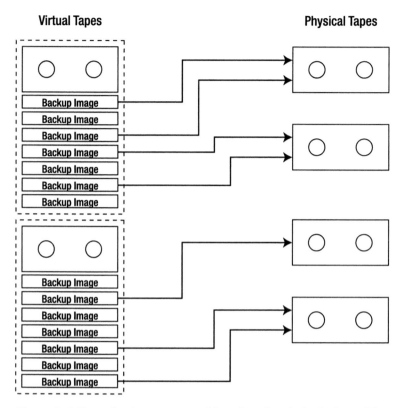

Figure 4–4. Exporting images to matching virtual and physical cartridges

It might be convenient to select an emulation that is either of the exact type of physical cartridge that is being exported to, thus allowing an exact analogue between the virtual and physical. This simplifies the management aspect of cartridge and space management down to counting the number of virtual cartridges consumed and acquiring the appropriate number of physical cartridges, depending on the size of the backups to be exported. This type of mechanism can also be used to direct backups to different tapes, depending on factors external to the size of the tape cartridge, such as retention times or physical storage locations. If is necessary to reimport the physical tapes back into the virtual library for some reason, the correct cartridge sizes and types are always available for the import process. This ensures that if the physical cartridge is full, the target virtual cartridge that would be used for the import would be able to hold the entire cartridge without any splitting of backup images from the physical cartridge. (See Figure 4–5.)

The risk of this type of strategy is that of loss or damage. If there are a relatively large number of cartridges in the export, it becomes increasingly likely that some or all of the data required for a restore is spread across a substantial portion of the cartridges. If one of the cartridges is lost or damaged, the restore might not be possible, or only partially successful if some of the data can be recovered from the remaining cartridges.

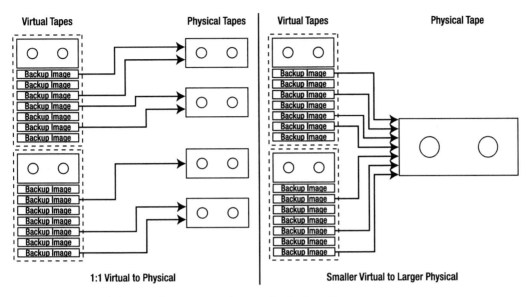

Figure 4–5. *Consolidation of images onto larger physical media*

An alternative is to use this image replication mechanism to consolidate many smaller emulated cartridges onto a fewer number of larger tape cartridges. This provides the ability to reduce the number of cartridges necessary to acquire and store to the minimum possible. During restore processes that require the physical tape, only a small number of tape cartridges are required to process the restore because all the required backup images have been consolidated. This also reduces the risk of any one cartridge being lost or damaged, resulting in the inability to restore due to missing image data.

However, this has a risk that is opposite of the many cartridges solution: the loss or damage of a single cartridge might cause the loss of entire backup image sets, including those not related to required restores. Additionally, reimporting the backups on the larger cartridge back into the VTL requires an image-by-image restore back to distinct cartridges, not just a bulk import. Finally, the large cartridge model also does not allow management of multiple backup retention requirements, on cartridges that are utilized to the maximum capacity possible.

So what to do? The decision to export from VTL to physical tape and select a virtual and physical cartridge size is largely dependent on the requirements for storage and will have to be selected based on the amount of data to be backed up, compared with the amount to be exported. These requirements are further balanced by the operations necessary to not manage large numbers of cartridges (whether virtual or physical), a process that introduces operational complexity and thus can inject human error into the backup process.

But, as you can see, the selection of cartridge type is a matter of reference and support; reference to the backup application to allow it to manage the amount of data that is put on a particular cartridge and support of operating systems for particular tape drive types.

Emulation is much more an environmental management discussion versus a discussion of technical capabilities. In older versions of operating systems, individual drivers were created for each individual tape type—allowing for specialization of the driver to meet the capabilities of the particular device being presented. However, this is generally no longer the case. The operating system vendors (or creators in the case of Linux) have built two layers that eliminate the need for specialized tape device drivers—the generic tape driver and the generic SCSI driver, or the pass-through driver. This is the same method that NetBackup introduced with the sg or pass-through driver. The generic tape driver is simply that—a generic driver that controls any type of serial tape device that is presented to it.

The caveat is that there is generally a configuration file that is related that allows the driver to identify devices and their capabilities when they are presented. So the same driver can attach to many different types of devices, simply by creating an entry describing the capabilities of the device within the configuration file. The classic example of this is the st.conf file within Solaris. The st.conf file describes the capabilities of a number of specialized tape drives, as well as provides general support for all other type of drives that issue a SCSI identifier that indicates that the device is a tape type device. However, even Sun/Oracle has recognized that native drivers are a much more efficient method of device management—their inclusion within Solaris has largely rendered the manual configuration of tape devices via the st.conf file irrelevant. It is included here more as an instructional example as opposed to an actual configuration issue to be resolve. The point is that all aspects of tape control, whether virtual or physical, are handled through the use of general driver types versus specific tape drive device drivers, simplifying the device configuration process and further driving emulation to the point of management convenience instead of a technical requirement discussion.

VTL Types

Under the covers, VTL systems are composed of one or more servers, called *engines*, which provide the emulation services. Most engines run variants of UNIX or Linux, depending on the vendor. There are three types of VTL configuration:

- *Gateway*: VTL configuration in which only the VTL software engine and platform is provided. Any required storage is provided and configured by the end user of the VTL solution.

- *Software*: The Software VTL is deployed just like any other type of software. A supported platform is selected; the end user installs the operating system to the software specifications, attaches appropriate storage, and installs the software.

- *Appliance*: The appliance VTL is a fully self-contained unit; no end user configuration of the storage or primary installation of software is required. Appliance VTL types typically use storage that is either proprietary to the VTL vendor, or at a minimum, specially configured to match the performance requirements of the VTL software. The VTL storage is not user configurable for any other purpose other than VTL utilization.

All three methods have their advantages and disadvantages (see Table 4–1). Both the Gateway and Software models allow the use of user resources, purchased as needed by the end user. This can result in a solution that is significantly less expensive than the Appliance model as hardware that is already owned can be used to provide VTL services. However, there is a large downside. While there are typically recommendations regarding the types of servers and storage to use, performance of these types of VTLs can vary widely. This is due to the fact that there is no way for a vendor to determine the performance characteristics of different combinations of servers (including operating system versions, drivers, other software, and so on) and storage systems, thereby your mileage might vary on how they actually perform.

Table 4–1. Comparison of VTL Types

Type	Advantages	Disadvantages
_Gateway	Allows use of existing end user storage resources.	Back end storage must be correctly configured to attain maximum performance.
	Provides standard platform on which VTL software runs—software runs consistently across deployments.	Storage capacity must be managed directly.
		VTL performance can be inconsistent.
	Medium cost—balances cost of VTL software and platform with the use of existing storage resources.	Storage cost to support VTL might be equal or exceed the cost to simply purchase an Appliance type solution.
_Software	Requires use of end user resources for all aspects of the hardware portion of the VTL solution.	Completely dependent on correct selection of platform for VTL stability and performance.
	Fully user-configurable to meet needs of environment.	Operating system on which VTL software is run must be maintained just as with other type of software. OS patches and changes can have indeterminate effects on the VTL.
	Generally lowest cost—simply a purchase of software.	Back end storage must be correctly configured to attain maximum performance.
	Can potentially run on a variety of hardware combinations.	Storage capacity and platform resource usage (CPU/RAM) must be managed directly.
		VTL performance can be inconsistent.
		Storage and platform cost to support VTL might be equal or exceed the cost to simply purchase an Appliance type solution.
_Appliance	Simple installation—no configuration required of OS/storage within VTL.	Cost can be high.
	Storage growth is straightforward—appliance manages deployment as storage is added.	Resources purchased as part of appliance solution cannot be reused for other purposes or repurposed after the VTL reaches it end of useful life.
	VTL performance and stability is consistent and measurable—no variability introduced by either storage configuration or operating system changes.	Specific drive types/sizes/speeds are locked in—cannot take advantage of any major jump in drive capacity/speeds. Often require a forklift upgrade.

Another downside is that of capacity management. In the Gateway and Software models, capacity must entirely be managed by the end user. Unless the user has purchased the maximum amount of storage for the VTL ahead of time or has a quantity of storage that is identical to the storage configured for the VTL, addition of unlike storage will have a profound effect on the performance of the VTL, with the likelihood of the effect being negative. Why? Because, depending on how the data for the VTL is placed on the disks, there will not be a continuum of storage performance that will provide for consistent performance.

Figure 4–6 illustrates the problems with adding different speed drives to VTL environments. X, Y, and Z represent different drive speeds relative to each other. Assume for the moment that the speed of the Y type drives are slower than those of the X drives. Backups that happen to hit the faster X type storage will perform at a different rate than those using the larger storage, and backups that span storage types will be completely indeterminate of their performance from one instant to the next. Add a second speed of storage, type Z, that is faster than the type X storage. Now portions of the backup that happen to hit the Z storage will be written and accessed faster than the rest of the backup, stored on the slower X type storage. Backups that span all the types of storage will suffer even more indeterminate performance—different pieces will perform at different rates at different times.

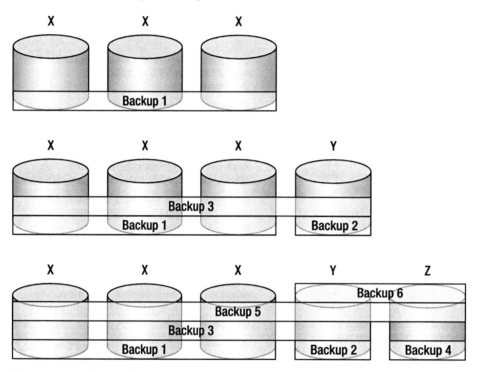

Figure 4–6. Backup performance variances

Appliance model VTLs help to eliminate these types of performance differences by enforcing standardization of storage upgrades to only matched drives or, at best, very similar drive types. This provides known, consistent, and standard methods of implementation, growth, and software.

This also has the side effect of not being able to add newer types of storage to increase capabilities of the VTL. For example, if you have a VTL that consists of 500G drives, and 2T drives with the same performance as the 500G drives become available, the only way to utilize the new drive type is to replace the VTL. Additionally, storage that is shipped with Appliance model VTLs are typically not available for general use and not even typically able to reuse once the VTL is retired without significant rework of the system. The disk storage on the back end of the engines typically use medium performance drives, such as SATA, configured into logical protected logical unit numbers (LUNs). The use of medium performance drives helps hold the acquisition cost of the VTL down, while providing a good balance of storage capacity and performance.

The storage is generally configured in some configuration sets of redundant array of inexpensive disks (RAID) devices, depending on the storage vendor, usually either RAID 5 or RAID 6. This allows for the maximum use of storage in a particular configuration, while providing protection of the backups in the event of a drive failure. Medium performance drives are sometimes used to artificially limit the performance of a VTL appliance; the software cannot necessarily take advantage of the performance provided by high-end drives, so there is no benefit to supplying them as part of the solution. However, as VTL software has matured, this is less and less the case and the reverse is becoming true. The software, combined with an appropriate platform selected by the VTL vendor, has the capability of outrunning existing storage.

Virtual Tape Allocation Models

When creating virtual tapes within a VTL, there are two different models by which the storage is allocated: preallocation and capacity on demand. *Preallocation* is the process where the space allocated to each cartridge is immediately allocated during the creation of the cartridge (see Figure 4–7). In this way, only the number of cartridges can be created on the VTL that there is space for. Preallocation also has a performance impact on the cartridges and the VTL in general. When this method is used, blocks are written to the VTL in sequence to the virtual cartridge. This allows for fast reads when restores are needed because related blocks are in physical proximity to each other. This also enables the implementation of drive spin-down: the ability to shut down or slow down disk drives within an array to save both power and cooling costs, but to reduce some of the normal wear and tear on the drives, potentially extending their life.

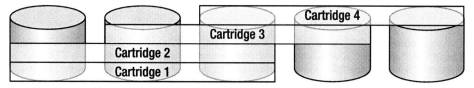

Figure 4–7. *Virtual cartridges distribution across LUNs—preallocation*

When using preallocation of cartridges, performance can be affected when read and write operations occur on different cartridges simultaneously. When the cartridges are created and storage is allocated, a number of cartridges can share the same set of LUNs. When a backup is written to a single cartridge, performance is as expected. However, when simultaneous backups are written, particular to cartridges that happen to share the same physical storage, performance of all cartridges can degrade. This impact is especially felt when performing read and write operations on co-located cartridges, as the LUNs are attempting to satisfy both operations simultaneously. This is typically seen during normal operations where backups are running during cloning/copying operations to physical tape.

Capacity on demand is the process where a header is created during the creation of the virtual cartridge, but the space for the cartridge is not allocated. As space is needed, the VTL attaches additional chunks of storage to the virtual cartridge, until the defined size of the cartridge is reached. This allows more cartridges to be created than actual physical space on the VTL, a process known as oversubscription. Oversubscription is useful to create a large number of cartridges to be allocated to multiple virtual drives. This creates the ability to more fully use the empty spaces that are created on preallocated cartridges when backups do not fully fill the cartridge. Creating cartridges in a capacity on demand model also has performance benefits that solve the issues that are created when using the preallocation model. Capacity on Demand does this by allocating blocks from various LUNs as they are requested when writing the virtual tape (see Figure 4–8). This has the effect of spreading blocks over all the LUNs of the VTL, effectively randomizing the read/write pattern of the VTL as a whole. This ensures that any simultaneous read/write operations that occur have a high probability of not hitting the exact same LUN, thus avoiding contention. However, the downside is the reverse problem. Because the blocks are now written randomly across all the LUNs of the VTL, reads of individual backup images can be slower than using the preallocation method. Typically this is not an issue as the performance differential is not usually significant, and they are outweighed by the benefits of using capacity on demand, which is why it is generally the recommended configuration for VTL cartridges.

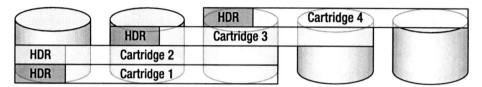

Figure 4–8. Virtual cartridges distribution across LUNs—capacity on demand

VTLs all require direct connectivity of some type: IP connectivity of VTLs is not an option natively (although iSCSI can be used, it is not recommended) because VTLs completely depend on the SCSI protocol to provide device services. Most VTLs offered as complete solutions utilize Fibre Channel (FC) connectivity, with smaller units still offering traditional cabled SCSI. Software VTLs typically offer greater connectivity options because they typically support the connection methods that the guest operating system supports. Appliance VTLs are the most limited in connection options, generally offering only FC support.

Why VTL?

So, if a VTL is simply a tape solution in a box, why do it at all? Why not just use tape or traditional backup to disk? There are a number of answers to this, some of which are controversial. Remember, a VTL is a hardware and software solution that provides an emulation of a tape environment, not an actual tape environment. The distinction is important. While a VTL can do many of the functions of a tape environment, it cannot do them all. VTLs eliminate many of the issues that are associated with tape drives, without sacrificing the functionality that tape provides.

In the previous chapter, it was mentioned that one of the largest issues with tape-based backups was the mechanical nature of the solution. Between the mechanics involved with the physical tape drive itself, to the complexities of the robot control, to even the mechanical nature of the tape cartridge itself, the fact that there are so many moving parts is a wonder to the ability of the solution to work for any time at all. However, with VTL, this mechanical complexity is reduced significantly. While the VTL has all the appearances of the mechanical components of the physical environment, none of it is actually implemented in the hardware.

But what about all those disks? There are a couple of ways to look at this. If you look at this solution from a disk perspective, there are methods of protecting data on disk that are not available on tape. RAID solutions, replication, and other methods protect against data loss by implementing automatic and transparent redundancy and error checking. If a single (or multiple disk in many situations) disk fails, data is not lost in most VTL implementations—the RAID and parity check implementations within the VTL protect the data from loss. In addition, disks, while complex and sometimes failure-prone, especially in large numbers, are much less mechanically complex than the simplest tape system. This allows disk drives to have a generally lower failure rate (as measured by the Mean Time Between Failure, or MTBF), which leads to higher availability rates and less data loss.

In addition to virtually eliminating the mechanical reliability issues of tape, VTL solutions also reduce many of the performance issues with tape. With tape, there had to be a minimum amount of data rate flowing to the tape drive in order to keep the tape transport running. If this data rate floor is breached, the transport had to stop and wait until enough data was available to start the streaming process over again. This start/stop/start cycle is known as *shoe-shining* and leads to a significant loss of performance and increased tape failure rates. However, with a VTL solution, the data move to the virtual drive without having to significantly adjust data rates (disks do adjust rates, but they are insignificant to this discussion). This is because the disks operate at a constant speed and take in data without having to worry about the mechanical movement of a piece of media over a fixed head. In a disk solution, the ingest rate has a *ceiling* limit of the number of IOPS (input/output operations per second) that the particular disk solution can handle. This is diametrically opposed to a tape solution which has a *floor* limit on the minimum data rate required to keep the tape drive moving.

Note Tape solutions ingest data at the rate of the slowest client, while VTL solutions ingest data at the speed of the fastest.

What this really means is that the VTL does not slow down for slow clients; it simply takes the data as fast as the client can supply it, while the tape solution must maintain a minimum ingest rate to keep data flowing. In this way, VTL solutions eliminate many of the performance issues seen by physical tape solutions.

As environments grow, additional resources are needed by the backup environment to expand both capacity and performance. When using physical media, this meant that the administrator would have to request the media, find physical space for the tape drives, ensure that all the infrastructure was available (and if not, request that too), shut down the entire library so that the tape drive could be added, and finally configure the tape drives into the backup solution. This process is both lengthy and expensive, requiring the interaction of a number of different groups as well as the purchase of additional hardware to support the solution. But what if you could simply click a button and add hardware without adding hardware? This is precisely the problem that a VTL solves over a physical tape solution. The VTL provides the ability to minimize the disruption involved when adding capacity to the solution. Because the VTL is simply a piece of software, it is a simple matter to add capacity—simply edit the existing tape library, add the required virtual devices or cartridges, present the new devices to the appropriate systems, and configure them into the environment. Expansion of capacity does not require the huge process that a physical tape requires because the administrator is simply making a software change and not having to add physical hardware to support that change. Remember, virtual drives are simply software sockets to which the operating system hardware drivers attach. These attachments are effectively software-to-software and are not limited in the number of attachments that can be made.

However, there are limits to this model. Let's look at two different cases to illustrate the limitations of this model. First is the bandwidth case. As the typical environment grows, one of the main limiting factors in getting backups completed is the number of data streams that can be run in parallel. In the physical tape environment, this is simply solved by adding more and more tape drives, up to the limit of the infrastructure. Tape bandwidth can theoretically grow without bound—or at least grow to meet any reasonably sized bandwidth requirement with linear scalability. However, the VTL does not grow in the same way. There are two reasons for this. First are the design and limitations of the disks themselves. Disks perform based on the number of IOPS that can be pushed to a disk or set of disks. Within the VTL, there are a limited number of disks, and therefore a limited number of IOPS available for use *globally* within a given system. The creation of more and more virtual drives simply provides more connections to the same maximum number of IOPS, and not more connections to a fixed ingest bandwidth, as a physical environment has to offer. One of the most common mistakes in designing a VTL solution is to create huge numbers of virtual cartridges to meet a backup need. What generally happens in these situations is that the overall performance of the VTL decreases below the maximum rated performance by a significant factor because the large number of virtual cartridges a creating a significantly greater number of IOPS than the disk system can handle. The solution is to look at the number of parallel streams and ensure that these streams are not generating IOPS that are greater than the maximum number of IOPS rated by the VTL system.

The second case is the connection case. When physical tape devices are added to the environment, they bring along a new set of connections to the system. The more drives added, the more the total amount of bandwidth to the devices is available. However, in VTL systems, there are a fixed number of connections to the infrastructure, generally four to eight connections total for a VTL as a whole. As virtual tape drives are added to the VTL environment, they will compete for the available ingest bandwidth of the VTL system as a whole. So even if the preceding warning was heeded and the number of IOPS is not exceeded by the backup streams, if there is not enough connectivity available to get the data to the disks in the first place, any number of virtual drives will not add any increases in performance. The other common mistake in transitioning from physical to VTL devices is the assumption that increasing the number of virtual drives will magically increase the number of connections and therefore allow the designer the ability to get a large amount of data backed up simply by adding more virtual tape drives (and by corollary, more connections). This simply is not the case as we saw above.

While these are considerations to be cognizant of when putting together a solution, they typically only raise their head in large environments. In general, a single VTL connection can replace a significant number of physical tape drives at a fraction of the space/power/cooling required, and still have better throughput when put against real world data. It is tempting when implementing a VTL to simply assign all servers a large number of virtual drives and allow them to use as many as possible. However, this will typically lead to one or both of the previous situations, and decrease the VTL performance overall, rather than increase the overall performance of the environment by replacing a nondeterminant device (tape) with a more determinant one (disk). However, a related advantage along the lines of creating larger numbers of devices is the ability for VTLs to facilitate the creation and installation of larger numbers of backup servers that write to media: MediaAgents or Media Servers.

In order to understand how VTLs allow for the creation of more media writing servers, we will introduce the concepts of tape time (TT) and available tape transfer rate (ATTR). *Tape time* is the total amount of time available for use by the sum total of the number of tape devices in a particular environment, measured in seconds. The time available for use is effectively the measure of the backup window—the tape drive is no longer available for the first window if the second window has started. *Available Tape Transfer Rate* is a measure of the transfer rates of each individual tape drive, multiplied by the TT, with the result summed over the total number of drives available.

In a physical tape drive environment, there are two use cases for the distribution of physical drives across media writing servers: nonshared and shared tape environments. Before we move on, this would be a good time to review the concept of drive sharing, using either NetBackup Shared Storage Option (SSO) or CommVault Dynamic Drive Sharing (DDS) and its implications on tape drive utilization. In the previous chapter, we discussed the ability of both NetBackup and CommVault to take advantage of idle physical drive time by providing a resource scheduler that allocates idle tape drives to designated systems for use. The drives were used by the Media Server/MediaAgent until they were completed with the task at hand and then handed back to the Master Server/CommServe for reallocation to new servers.

In the nonshared case, the total amount of TT and ATTR available to any particular media writing server is directly related to the number of devices attached to a particular server. In this case, it is easy to give one media writer more available TT and ATTR than another simply by physically attaching an additional physical device, up to the limit of the connecting bus and the performance of the particular server. However, there is no guarantee that the additional devices will be used effectively. Clients might not necessarily always be assigned to the media writer that has free resources, potentially leaving physical tape drives, and therefore available TT and ATTR stranded. An attempt to normalize this by assigning additional media writers will work, but leave throughput available at some point as there can be at most a 1:1 correlation between a media writer and tape device in the nonshared case.

The shared use case attempts to reconcile this by having multiple media writers attached to multiple physical devices, in an attempt to balance both the performance characteristics of the media writers and the TT and ATTR potential of the devices. However, as the media writer performance begins to degrade, simply adding additional media writers to boost performance reduces the amount of TT and ATTR to any particular media writer, without a corresponding increase in the number of physical devices to balance the additional media writer potential performance. This balancing act can quickly get out of control, creating an unmanageable mesh of media writer and tape devices in a vain attempt to achieve a total tape time and available tape transfer rate number that is suitable for the environment.

As shown in Figure 4–9, the number of connections to manage for a particular device grows quickly and the math to calculate potential performance of this type of environment can get complex fast—quickly to the point of not being able to determine potential performance of a particular MS/MA due to the complexities in determining how much actual ATTR would be available for any particular connection because of the number of other connections vying for the same device.

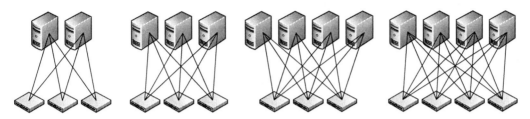

Figure 4–9. Illustration of connection difficulties

So how does VTL solve this problem? Simple—by reverting back to the direct connect model, but eliminating the penalty for being unbalanced in terms of TT and ATTR. How does this work? In a VTL environment neither SSO nor DDS are necessary or actually desired. Why? The simple reason is that if an additional drive is required, simply add a new virtual drive to the existing virtual library and assign it to the system where the resource is required. It is not necessary to share drives as they are not physical resources, which was the primary driver in creating drive sharing in the first place. Because any number of virtual devices can be created to meet a particular need, there is not any need to share devices. In fact VTL resources are wasted when doing drive sharing.

To illustrate, let's look at an example. Assume you have two systems that are backing up to a single VTL. The VTL is lightly loaded and has plenty of resources available. If you implement drive sharing between the two systems requiring backup, this requires that the backups be operated in series—one backup after another. This is because although the back-end devices are parallel access devices, they are still being presented as serial devices. This means that they can only be accessed one at a time.

If the same systems use two virtual devices, they can run in parallel. Each system will move data independently of each other and be able to complete the backups in half the time that the shared system would be able to. In fact, if the VTL has not reached the maximum number of IOPS on the back-end storage, both backups will run at full speed and will not have any effect on the other. Contrast this with the shared option described previously: because the backups have to run serially, the total amount of time to complete both backups is more than double the amount required for completing the backups in parallel. Additionally, because the VTL has plenty of capacity (measured in terms of both inbound bandwidth and backend IOPS), the capacity not used in the shared model is wasted—the single system cannot use all of the available capacity, which is then left idle.

Because drives are not shared in the VTL model, the amount of time that drives are shared is not relevant. In addition, the number of drives available is also not necessary to calculate. Because virtual drives are simply software connections, any number of them can be created on a given connection, and not have an effect on performance. As long as the total number of IOPS at peak utilization is not exceeded, any number of devices can be created. As a corollary, any number of servers can be attached to these connection points as well. The implication of these two statements is this: as long as the amount maximum number of IOPS is not exceeded and the connection bandwidth is not exceeded at peak usage. The bottom line is that when looking at the potential number of Media Servers/MediaAgents that can be connected to a particular VTL, the only relevant measures are the ability of the MediaAgents to move data, the total bandwidth available for transport to the VTL, and the available ingest rate of the VTL (implying the number of available IOPS on the back-end storage).

Compare this with the media writer–based physical devices. The number of potential media writer servers in the physical case is limited by a number of different factors, all of which reduce the maximum TT and ATTR available for use by a given media writer. However, because the ingest rate of a VTL is fixed, regardless of the number of virtual devices assigned, each device receives an equal percentage of the potential ATTR based on the number of simultaneous backups and the speed at which the data is transmitted by the media writer. TT is no longer relevant—it can simply be increased by adding additional virtual devices. Thus, more work (backups) can get done in the same unit of time because the number of devices that can be brought to bear against a backup load is simply a function of total performance of the media writer and the ingest rate of the VTL.

VTLs also have advantages other than the ability to provide simple scalability of environments. Remember the discussion disk targets and how backup software was designed for use for serial-based tape devices, making implementation of disk devices difficult. VTLs overcome this limitation by providing a front-end view to the backup software that looks to the backup software like a traditional serial tape device. However, as we have discussed, the back end utilizes disk as the storage platform. This means that there is not a requirement to rewrite or redesign existing backup software to be able to implement a VTL back end. This also means that designs that currently use physical tape as the backup target can simply substitute VTLs for physical tape. While this type of direct substitution will not yield an optimized design, it can provide a good starting point for implementation of a VTL-based solution.

There is another advantage of VTLs when they are used to complement tape as well. Many organizations have a requirement to ensure that copies of backups are retained in an offsite location, in order to provide a modicum of protection against physical destruction of the source data center. Many times the easiest way to implement this is to make a copy of the backup from the VTL to a physical tape and then send that tape offsite. This has several advantages over simply creating a physical tape directly.

The primary advantage is an effect known as *tape stacking* (see Figure 4–10). We saw this effect previously in the discussion of the consolidation of backups from VTL onto physical media. Tape stacking optimizes offsite copies of backups by creating a contiguous, nonmultiplexed copy of the image, while putting as many backups on the media as possible. How does this process work?

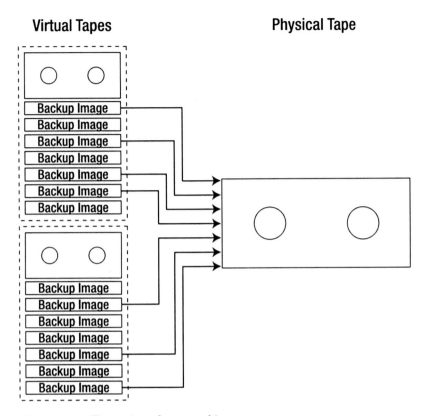

Figure 4–10. Illustration of tape stacking

In order to explain this, let's review how backups are typically written to tape media. Many backup environments, in order to balance client throughput against cartridge utilization, virtual or physical, opt to multiplex their clients. From the discussion on backup software, multiplexing is the ability of backup software to take the backup streams from multiple clients and coalesce the streams onto a single device or set of devices, interleaving the blocks from the various clients onto the backup media. While this optimizes the backup stream, when used for offsite backups, clients that require offsite retention are lumped in with ones that do not. This means that more tapes than are necessary are generated and sent offsite as effectively all backups are sent offsite. In addition, while these backups are optimally configured for backup, recovery of individual client files from multiplexed backups can be slower. The reasons for this were discussed in previous chapters, but to recap, this is due to the fact the backup software must reassemble the backup by skipping over the chunks that are not needed for the restore and retrieve the ones that are needed.

What tape stacking does is make a nonmultiplexed copy of the image by reading the image from the source media and writing it back to a second piece of media in a sequential format. But if you are making a copy back in to sequential format, aren't the performance advantages of using multiplexing negated? No, assuming, that the MA/MS can process data streams to media (both read and write) well above the shoeshine thresholds of physical tape. The reason why multiplexing is used for client backups is to normalize the overall data stream performance by smoothing the low performers with the high performers. This results in a data stream that is as full as possible, with the benefit of keeping media spinning as quickly as possible. However, the MA/MS has a constant, known, high-speed rate of data export to media, so multiplexing when making copies of backup images is not necessary. So the fragmented images that are stored on the primary media are transformed during the copy process to nonfragmented images in a fraction of the time required that would be required to create the primary images in the first place. This allows the secondary piece of media, which typically is physical, to stream data in restore operations as quickly as possible for any particular backup image by not having to skip over data blocks that are not related to the restore in question.

Because tape stacking represents a copy of the image, by definition, the image is specifically selected for copy, thus eliminating all other unrelated backups from the target media. This might seem like a trivial statement, but it is an important concept to grasp. Remember that a multiplexed backup contains backups from many different sources. When the demultiplexed copy of an image is made, only the blocks from the desired backup copy are copied to the target media. This creates a contiguous image on the target media of the desired backup media. In addition, because each successive image is also contiguous, the media is used to its full potential because there is as little wasted space as possible.

Replication

Of course, the whole point of making copies of tapes is to get copies of the backups to another location in case of a failure of the primary, or to ensure that the primary copy has a redundant one in case of corruption. However, it is exceedingly difficult (nigh impossible) to ship VTLs offsite to support such events. For this reason, physical tape copies, with all their faults, are still the standard for making offsite secondary copies. But what if you could simply make an electronic copy of the cartridge at a remote location? Remember, the backup image is simply a collection of blocks on a set of disks—a file if you will. Files can be copied, even VTL files. That is effectively what replication is—the ability of a VTL to make a replica of the set of blocks located locally on a remote VTL, thus creating an offsite cartridge without using a single piece of physical tape.

However, there are several caveats to the VTL replication. The target of VTL replication will create an exact copy of both the data and metadata of the cartridge on the remote target. This might be a trivial statement, but it has an important impact on the usability of the replica. Most VTLs, when making a replicated copy, also replicates the cartridge information along with the data. This means that there are effectively two cartridges having the same identification information with the same information. If this situation occurs within the same CommCell or datazone, the backup software will, at best, ignore the second copy, or at worst be able to access either copy. In order to use the secondary copy, the backup software must logically eject the virtual cartridge and then reimport the replicated cartridge on the remote side. Both the source and remote VTLs are treated as individual libraries as far as the backup software is concerned. Because VTLs operate in the same way as real libraries, including the ejection of cartridges, this does not require any special processes. Think of it in terms of physical libraries—if a tape is needed to be moved to an offsite location and put in to another library, you would take the cartridge physical out of the first library, transport the cartridge to the remote location, and insert the cartridge back into the library for reuse. The cartridges replicated through VTL replication need to be treated in the same way, with the same result.

Second, in order to create the replica on the remote site, all the data must be copied between the source and target VTLs prior to having the remote copy available for use. This caveat can create distance limitations as the quantity of data that can be replicated can exceed what can be effectively replicated. In order to evaluate this, it is necessary to be able to calculate the amount of data that can be transmitted on a give link, during a given period of time. This figure can be calculated using the following formula:

$$\frac{\left(D_t = \left(\frac{(S)_{Mb}}{8} \right) * (W_h * 3600) \right)}{1024}$$

Where
D_t = Data transferred in GB
S_{Mb} = Link speed in Mbits
W_h = Available transmission window

Let's look at an example to illustrate this. During a given cycle, 1 TB of data is backed up to 4 cartridges within a VTL. There is a requirement to replicate the VTL to a remote site within 12 hours of completion, which is connected to the primary by a DS-3 link, approximately 45 Mb/sec. Assuming that the link can be fully utilized by the replication process, the most that can be transmitted during the period is approximately 237 GB of data. This is shown following:

S_{Mb} = 45 Mbits/sec
W_h = 12 hours

$$\frac{\left(D_t = \left(\frac{(S)_{Mb}}{8}\right) * (W_h * 3600)\right)}{1024}$$

$$D_t = \frac{(45/8) * (12 * 3600)}{1024}$$

$$D_t = \frac{5.625 * 43200}{1024}$$

$$D_t = 237.3$$

Clearly, not all the data backed up to the VTL can be replicated given the link speed. Even if the VTL compresses the data at 2:1, only half of the data can be replicated in the given time. The purpose of the example is to simply show that there must be a great deal of consideration given to the network bandwidth needed to transmit the cartridges, and that replication might not replace traditional copies of virtual cartridges to physical in all cases.

VTLs represent a significant improvement over tape—eliminating the mechanical and serialized issues with tape, while retaining compatibility with both legacy backup software and operating systems. While VTL does not replace physical tape, it greatly reduces the need for tape to the absolute minimum when applied appropriately.

Other Virtualized Media and a Look Ahead

VTL was the only type of virtualized media for a number of years. Then, in 2006 Symantec developed and released a method of providing virtualization of storage, optimized for backup: the OpenStorage API (OST). OST provides a method of taking vendor-provided storage, providing a standard interface to NetBackup using an API instead of software that forces a particular type of emulation. Because OST generalizes backup storage, the storage can be optimized for any type of backup and tuned to meet the needs of the environment.

The API consists of two parts: one provided embedded in the target storage appliance, and a part supplied by the storage vendor and installed as part of NetBackup. The second piece is the integration point between NetBackup and the storage, and it should be installed on all Master Servers and Media Servers that will use the storage. The API's function is to simply instruct the storage to take backups of certain types, but does not specify how to write the image, or how to format the storage. In addition, the API also allows for NetBackup to tell the storage to perform optimized replication of select images, avoiding the need for demultiplexing the backups prior to replication. Additionally, these replicated images are both ready for use once the replication is completed—the API takes care of tracking the images separately. However, while the name of the API implies it is universal, it is far from it. There are only a few vendors that make use of the API—one of which is a major deduplication vendor, which will be discussed in the next chapter.

CHAPTER 5

New Media Technologies

For a number of years, backup was boring: move data to tape and then make copies of the tape. Then the virtual tape library (VTL) was introduced, making backup slightly less boring, but basically a variation on the same theme of moving data to tape. Recently, a number of new technologies and techniques have been introduced that have sparked a revolution of sorts within the backup world. In addition, new types of platforms, specifically the advent and widespread adoption of server virtualization technologies, have provided new methods of providing backups that do not fit the traditional notion of backup. In this chapter, the technologies of deduplication, continuous data protection and remote replication, VMWare Recovery API, and cloud targets will be examined.

Deduplication

One of the most talked about new technologies is *deduplication*, which is the process of analyzing data at the subfile level and storing only those elements that have not already been stored on the media. Some definitions of deduplication only have this comparison done at the file level, such as a single Word document that has been individually stored in multiple locations—all of which are being backed up. However, this is not deduplication, but is actually a process known as *single instance storage*, or SIS. When true deduplication is utilized, new data is read, broken down into blocks, compared with the blocks that are already stored, and only the new blocks are stored. Blocks that already exist are created as pointers to the data already stored. This reduces data by only storing the blocks once for every subsequent pass of data. This data reduction is measured, not in terms of the amount of data stored, but as a ratio of the data processed to the data stored (referred to as a *deduplication ratio*). Typically, good deduplication will achieve ratios of 10:1 and will in many cases regularly reach over 15:1.

A word here about deduplication ratios (or *data reduction ratios*, as they are also known): from a mathematics standpoint, the dedup ratio is simply the inverse of the percentage of data reduction, as shown here:

$$DD\ ratio = \frac{1}{1 - Data\ reduction\ \%}$$

For example, if a backup is reduced in size by 85 percent through the use of deduplication, the resulting deduplication ratio would be the following:

$$DD\ ratio = \frac{1}{1 - .85}$$

$$DD\ ratio = \frac{1}{.15}$$

$$DD\ ratio = 6.66\ or\ 6:1$$

Conversely, if the deduplication ratio is known, the amount by which the original backup is reduced can be calculated. This number is useful for understanding just how much data a particular backup is, or would potentially take to store on a particular system. In order to estimate this reduction percentage, the following calculation can be performed:

$$Data\ reduction\ \% = \left(1 - \left(\frac{1}{DD}\right)\right) * 100$$

As an example, if a vendor advertises that a product has a 12:1 deduplication ratio, how much would the backup be reduced by? Applying the previous formula results in the following:

$$Data\ reduction\ \% = \left(1 - \left(\frac{1}{12}\right)\right) * 100$$

$$Data\ reduction\ \% = (1 - 0.083) * 100$$

$$Data\ reduction\ \% = 0.916 * 100$$

$$Data\ reduction\ \% = 91.6\%$$

But how do you calculate the deduplication ratio in the first place? The deduplication ratio is measured by taking a specific data set, storing it in a deduplicated format, and measuring the amount of new data that is actually stored. The deduplication ratio is the ratio of the bytes backed up, divided by the bytes stored, as shown here:

$$DD\ Ratio\ (actual) = \frac{Bytes\ backed\ up}{Backup\ bytes\ stored}$$

The deduplication ratio, like many statistics, can be misunderstood or used to misrepresent the actual usefulness of deduplication. Many deduplication products advertise the ability to achieve deduplication ratios of 10:1, 15:1, 20:1, or higher. The ever increasing values of the deduplication ratio seem to imply that the difference between a 10:1 deduplication ratio and a 20:1 ratio would represent a very large decrease in the amount of data actually stored on a particular device. On the surface, this looks like a big difference, but consider Figure 5–1, which represents deduplication ratios that are applied against a 1 TB backup.

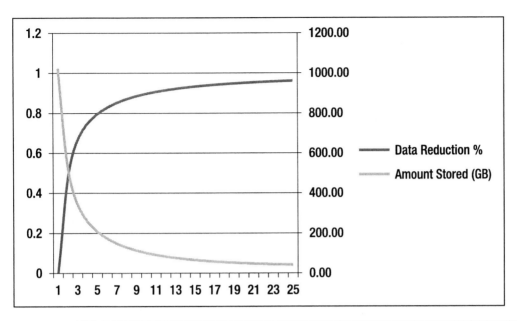

De-dup ratio	Data Reduction %	Amount Stored (GB)	De-dup ratio	Data Reduction %	Amount Stored (GB)
1:1	0.00%	1024.00	13:1	92.31%	78.77
2:1	50.00%	512.00	14:1	92.86%	73.14
3:1	66.67%	341.33	15:1	93.33%	68.27
4:1	75.00%	256.00	16:1	93.75%	64.00
5:1	80.00%	204.80	17:1	94.12%	60.24
6:1	83.33%	170.67	18:1	94.44%	56.89
7:1	85.71%	146.29	19:1	94.74%	53.89
8:1	87.50%	128.00	20:1	95.00%	51.20
9:1	88.89%	113.78	21:1	95.24%	48.76
10:1	90.00%	102.40	22:1	95.45%	46.55
11:1	90.91%	93.09	23:1	95.65%	44.52
12:1	91.67%	85.33	24:1	95.83%	42.67
			25:1	96.00%	40.96

Figure 5–1. Deduplication ratios versus amount stored

The graph and associated table in Figure 5–1 show the relationship between the deduplication ratio, the amount of data actually stored (versus the 1TB example backup), and the percent by which the backup is reduced in size. As the deduplication ratio increases, the amount of data stored decreases, but the difference between the deduplication ratios, as compared with the difference between the amount of data stored, is the interesting data point to review. While the dedup ratio climbs, the difference in the amount of data stored decreases—this is what is expected. What is interesting is that the difference between the amount of data stored between two adjacent ratios gets ever smaller as the ratios increase. This is what is shown in the graph and table in Figure 5–2.

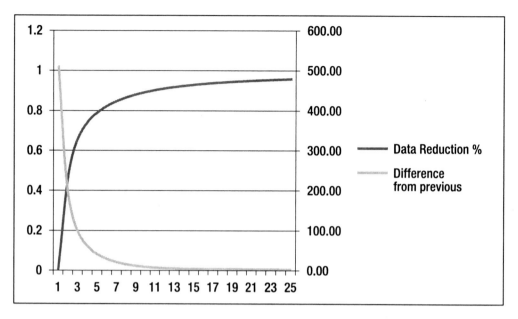

De-dup ratio	Amount Stored (GB)	Difference	De-dup ratio	Amount Stored (GB)	Difference
1:1	1024.00	0.00	13:1	78.77	6.56
2:1	512.00	512.00	14:1	73.14	5.63
3:1	341.33	170.67	15:1	68.27	4.88
4:1	256.00	85.33	16:1	64.00	4.27
5:1	204.80	51.20	17:1	60.24	3.76
6:1	170.67	34.13	18:1	56.89	3.35
7:1	146.29	24.38	19:1	53.89	2.99
8:1	128.00	18.29	20:1	51.20	2.69
9:1	113.78	14.22	21:1	48.76	2.44
10:1	102.40	11.38	22:1	46.55	2.22
11:1	93.09	9.31	23:1	44.52	2.02
12:1	85.33	7.76	24:1	42.67	1.86
			25:1	40.96	1.71

Figure 5–2. Deduplication ratios with differences against a 1 TB backup

As the deduplication ratios increase, the amount of data that is saved from being stored, represented by the Difference column, shrinks dramatically, especially when compared with the original size of the backup. The message: when comparing products based on deduplication ratios, larger ratios do not necessarily make a significant difference in the actual value provided. And a comparison of deduplication ratios is not a strong method of comparing products. For instance, if Product A advertises a 20:1 deduplication ratio, and Product B advertises a 25:1 ratio, for a 1 TB backup, the difference in the amount of data actually stored is only 10 G of storage—*a difference of less than 1 percent of the original 1 TB backup.*

Great—the deduplication has reduced the data, but what does that really mean and how does it work? Let's take a slightly odd example to illustrate how deduplication does its work: if you had to back up a colony of bees, what would be the most effective way to do it?

The first thing that would be done would be to identify the basic components of a single bee— wings, legs, black stripes, yellow stripes, and head. Then you would make a copy of each component of the first bee—the first backup in the deduplication storage. Each component is a *block*, in deduplication parlance. However, bees, like anything else, are not uniform—there are different numbers of stripes, different widths, bigger wings, and so on. So as new bees are looked at to be backed up, any variations are stored, and the pieces that are the same as the ones previously stored are "discarded."

Now add different types of bees—say honeybees to bumblebees. From a structural standpoint, the bees are the same, but there are now wider variations in the bees. There are also similarities—namely the black and yellow stripes. A deduplication methodology would back up only the differences between the different types of bees, but only one yellow and one black stripe backup—common to both bee types—are actually stored.

In order to build the bees back from the components, you would take the unique components that make up the particular bee you are restoring, add in the right number of yellow and black stripes (the commonly stored components), and instant bee!

Notice something interesting about the preceding example? As different file types that are put into the deduplication storage are actually stored, only the unique blocks are stored. Also, while the deduplication ratio drops, it only drops due to the proportion of the new blocks to the already stored, not because the deduplication becomes less efficient. In the backup environment, this effect becomes very pronounced.

Note As more data is written to a deduplication device, less is stored as the probability of an individual block already having been stored increases.

The mechanisms of deduplication also actually do not look directly at the data blocks. Doing an analysis of individual bits of data would be extremely time- and resource-consuming. Instead, the various systems that provide deduplication use a signature mechanism to identify patterns of data. This signature is typically in the form of a mathematical summation of the bit values, known as a *hash calculation.* A hash calculation will typically generate a unique identifier for a given piece of data. This is particularly useful as the process can also work backward—for a given hash, a data structure can be regenerated from the hash value, assuming the mathematical mechanism for the original hash is known. Since hash values can be quickly calculated, easily compared, and quickly stored, they are used as the basis for the identification of blocks within deduplication mechanisms.

A hash, however, is simply a number—a large, relatively unique number, but a number just the same. Since this number is calculated using a standard method, using the value of the data at points within the file, it is theoretically possible to take two different sequences of values from two different files, and, using the same method for both, return the same value out of the method. This calculation of the same value from two distinct sequences of values within two different files is known as a *hash collision.* When a hash collision occurs, there is no way to determine which sequence is the sequence to use, given the two patterns.

If a hash collision occurs in a deduplication solution, the file that contains the block involved in the hash collision will not be able to be reliably restored. Why? The blocks that are part of the collision each contain vastly different data sequences—one that is valid; one that is not. If the invalid one is utilized, the resulting file will necessarily be corrupt and potentially unusable.

While it is theoretically possible to have a hash collision, the probability of one occurring is extremely small. Hash values that are typically returned from the calculation mechanisms are anywhere from 53 to 160 bits in size (ranging from 0-10^{48} as a hash value). Even on the low end, at 53 bits, using commonly available hashing mechanisms, the probability of a collision is on the order of 1 in 10^{-20}. As a basis of comparison, there have been (depending on estimates) fewer than 10^{17} seconds in the current age of the universe. If you were to generate a series of hashes sequentially, and each hash generation takes less than a second, it will still take longer than the known age of the universe to pass through all possibilities to determine whether there is a duplicate hash.

Fixed-Block Deduplication

In the bee analogy, the different components of the bee, or the bee *blocks*, were fixed in size—the bees were always chunked in the exactly the same way. When deduplication is applied to real files, there must be some way to determine a block size in the file in order to apply the deduplication mechanism. There are two different ways to do this: pick a fixed size for the deduplication analysis or determine a block size based on some indicator within the data stream.

Many products rely upon a *fixed-block* mechanism. It is relatively easy to implement as the data stream is simply broken into blocks of a fixed size, identified, and compared with existing blocks. If the block already exists, discard it and create the pointer to the existing block. The downside of this mechanism has to do with what happens when data changes within a particular data stream. This is illustrated in Figure 5–3.

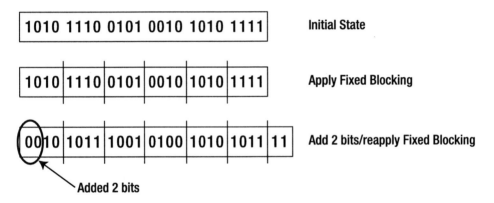

Figure 5–3. Fixed-block deduplication

The first line represents the initial state of the data as it has been written, simply as sequence of bits. Next, fixed blocking is applied; in this case, a blocking factor of 4 bits is applied. This represents the initial state of the deduplication; in this case, there are 2 blocks that are common in the data stream that would be deduplicated. Then, in the course of normal operations, 2 bits are added to the front of the data sequence, which shifts the blocking. Note what happens to the deduplication. While there are still two blocks that have a common structure, all the other blocks are now different than they were previously, with respect to the blocking factor applied. Even more, not only are the common blocks different from the common blocks in the first state, almost all the other blocks are now different from the first state as well. This type of "new" data from a deduplication perspective has a highly detrimental effect on the reduction in data stored, thus reducing the overall deduplication rate by storing more data than is necessary. The amount of "new" data that results from the de-duplication window shift becomes more pronounced with larger block sizes. The larger block sizes result in a larger number of bit-level combinations. The larger number of possible combinations increases the probability that a single combination has not already been seen.

Variable-Block Deduplication

There is an alternative to fixed-block deduplication that solves many of these issues that make it less efficient in some cases: *variable-block deduplication*. It performs an analysis of the data and finds data "markers" that determine the points at which to place the block points. Let's take our original diagram showing deduplication and apply a "variable" deduplication scenario (see Figure 5–4).

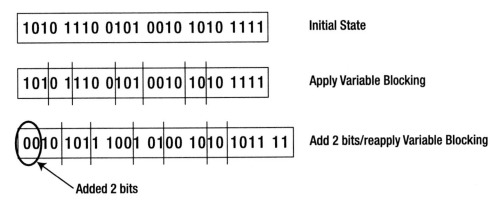

1010 1110 0101 0010 1010 1111   **Initial State**

101|0 1|110 0|101|0010|10|10 1111   **Apply Variable Blocking**

00|10|101|1 100|1 01|00 10|10|1011 11   **Add 2 bits/reapply Variable Blocking**

Added 2 bits

Figure 5–4. Deduplication ratios versus amount stored

Again, we start with the initial state of and apply a variable blocking factor, based on a marker. The *marker* is a measure of probability—how probable is it that the sequence of blocks will reoccur within the set of data represented by the block size. In this case, the blocks vary in size from 2 bits to 6 bits. Now we add the same data to the original data that that was added in the fixed block and reapply the variable blocking. With this particular marker mechanism, almost all the blocks have already been seen in the previous blocking set, thus providing a very good deduplication ratio, as the amount of data actually stored is significantly reduced. This is a very simplified example, but it demonstrates the basic principles of the concept. The actual math behind this is extremely complex and is actually covered by several patents.

Data Type Limitations: Media, Mystery, and Mother Nature

Deduplication is not good at backing up all types of data or all data profiles, however. Bad deduplication candidate data types can be summed up as the 3 Ms: media, Mother Nature, and mystery.

Media files, such as .mp3, .jpg, and other formats, represent compressed data types or data types that typically do not exhibit many repeatable patterns. Prior to backup, compression of data effectively removes any repeatable data patterns that may have previously existed, as the compression is designed to take any repetitive data and replace it with specialized pointers and markers. Most media files, in order to save space but retain the majority of the resolution (either visual or audio) of the original source, employ various means of compression to shrink the overall file size. Even those media data types that are lossless and not compressed do not deduplicate well. In order to illustrate this, think about what a digital picture is: a set of encoded pixels that represents various shades of color or a collection of red/green/blue pixels in various shades that represent a single dot of color. When you take a picture, it is a unique point in time, never to be exactly duplicated. While there may be some common point, the overall composition of the picture will effectively be completely different, even if you take many pictures in quick succession. This will produce, from a binary standpoint, entirely new patterns of binary data that were probably not seen by a deduplication method previously, thus low deduplication rates.

Mother Nature is related to data gathered in relation to scientific studies, typically imaging data or large quantities of statistical data such as hydrological or seismological studies. On the surface, this data is seemingly random. So from the deduplication perspective, the data is also random—and random data does not deduplicate well.

Finally, *mystery*, or *encrypted*, data also does not deduplicate well. When data is encrypted, the point of the encryption is to hide the essence of the data behind a wall of seemingly random data. Again, random data is anathema to deduplication, so encrypted data should be unencrypted prior to deduplication, or else the deduplication rate will be quite low, probably near 1:1, or no compression.

■ **Note** A quick note about security and deduplication—when data is stored in a deduplication format, it is effectively encrypted because any type of deduplication only stores unique blocks of data from the backups. These blocks can come from binary files, text files, documents, and so on, and are not unique to any particular type of file. As such, the block in and of itself does not contain data that could be identified specifically as a part of any file or set of files without the method to reconstruct the complete file from the series of unique blocks. Because these blocks are stored based on an index, independently of how they originally existed in the file, the data has been completely randomized and therefore completely encrypted. Re-encrypting blocks once they land is an unnecessary process that simply encrypts data that is effectively already encrypted. When confronted with a security challenge on a deduplicated backup, offer the challenge to reconstruct any particular file, given only the set of unique blocks to work with—a task that is virtually impossible without a map with which to place the blocks in the correct order.

Deduplication Types and Terms

Now that deduplication as a concept has been explained, how is it implemented? Deduplication is simply software, either preinstalled on hardware to provide an appliance type solution, or integrated as part of a backup solution. The deduplication software can be implemented in two different ways:

- *Source-based*: Performs the deduplication function on the backup client and then sends the resulting data stream to the backup target.

- *Target-based*: Performs the deduplication function after the backup client has sent the backup stream to the server writing the backup media.

Both types of deduplication have advantages and limitations, depending on the data types being protected.

In the target-based model, deduplication is performed in two different processing models:

- *Inline*: The deduplication is performed as the data is being received and is stored immediately in a deduplicated format.

- *Post-process*: The data stream to be deduplicated is stored in an intermediate storage area, or landing zone, and is then deduplicated as a scheduled process after the data has been fully stored. (See Figure 5–5.)

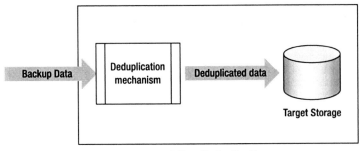

Inline Deduplication

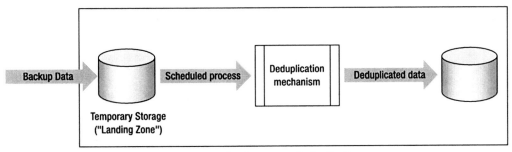

Post-process Deduplication

Figure 5–5. Inline vs. post-process deduplication

The *inline deduplication* process has the advantage of only requiring the storage necessary to actually store the data that has already been deduplicated. This represents the absolute minimum amount of storage required for the solution. However, inline deduplication solutions may have slower ingest rates than post-process solutions as the deduplication must happen on the data stream prior to actually storing the data on disk. This will necessarily slow down the storage or recovery of data (depending on the inline device architecture) as time is required to analyze the data stream for the common blocks and either store or reassemble the blocks—all within the confines of memory. Inline deduplication is most often found in appliance-based solutions, such as EMC DataDomain devices, but is also used in both the NetBackup PureDisk and CommVault deduplication solutions.

Post-process deduplication, on the other hand, uses a portion of disk as a temporary landing area for the data stream. This has the advantage of ingesting the backup stream as the fastest rate possible, but also can require substantial amounts of disk space, over that required for the deduplicated storage, as the landing area needs to be large enough to hold all the inbound data long enough to be processed and moved to the deduplicated target storage. Post-process deduplication is found in both appliance solutions, such as the Quantum DXi series, or simply as a secondary copy process from a traditional backup to secondary media, such as a Vault process in NetBackup, or an AUX copy process for CommVault.

Source-Based Deduplication

The first type of deduplication type is source-based. In a *source-based* setup, data is deduplicated *prior* to being sent across the Internet Protocol (IP) network to the storage target. The execution of the deduplication on the client can provide a significant reduction in the amount of data transmitted across the IP network, as only unique blocks are sent to the storage media, eliminating all the common blocks as part of the deduplication process. There are two major products that offer this type of deduplication: NetBackup and EMC Avamar. While this book primarily deals with CommVault and NetBackup, the CommVault solution, as of Simpana 8, is a target-based solution and processes deduplication after the client data has reached the MediaAgent. As a basis of comparison, it is instructive to see how Avamar works as a comparison with NetBackup in performing source-based deduplication. In a source-based environment, the backup client uses some type of mechanism to determine which blocks are unique prior to storage on the media.

In order to perform source-based deduplication, the regular NetBackup client is supplemented by the installation of the PureDisk deduplication plug-in to the standard client. This client performs local deduplication of the data prior to transmission on the Transmission Control Protocol/Internet Protocol (TCP/IP) network. The end target of the deduplication can be a standard NetBackup disk storage unit or a deduplication disk storage unit on a standard Media Server. The NetBackup client only sends the blocks that are unique within the particular client, and relies upon the target system to provide further deduplication. (See Figure 5–6.)

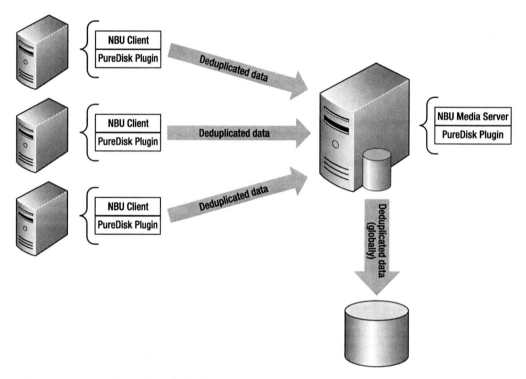

Figure 5–6. NetBackup client deduplication to deduplicated Media Server

While this provides a level of deduplication within the client and provides a good level of reduction in the amount of data transmitted, because the deduplication does not occur across clients, there is a potential for sending the same block twice. However, if the data deduplicates well, and the block size is relatively small, this should not have a large impact on network traffic.

Since the NetBackup deduplication client can use a standard Media Server, a standard NetBack disk media type can be used to hold the deduplicated backups. As such, the basic architecture of a standard NetBackup data zone does not change, although the back-end implementation of the actual Media Server infrastructure to support deduplication can be significantly more complex. (See Figure 5–7.) This will be explored more in the target deduplication section to follow.

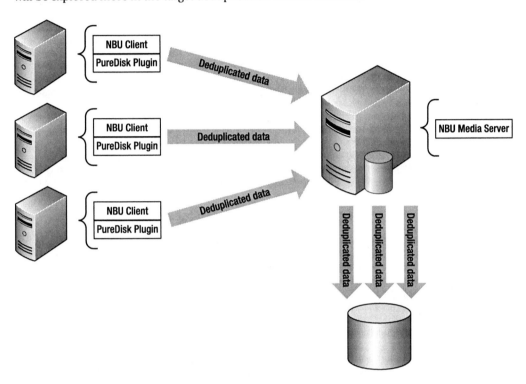

Figure 5–7. NetBackup deduplication to standard Media Server

As a contrast, EMC Avamar utilizes a different model. While it utilizes a client-based deduplication model, it allows for the ability to deduplication enterprise-wide. This is done by a complex process that generates hash signatures within clients and then compares the hash signatures with the central storage processor prior to data transmission. This method provides several advantages. First, the overall amount of data transmitted is reduced as only data chunks that are unique are sent to the storage unit. Second, when new clients are added to the backup, only those chunks that are not already stored on the central storage unit are sent. However, the storage mechanism for this is a dedicated appliance. The appliance is based on a node technology, which grows in capacity by adding nodes to the appliance. Since the addition of nodes consumes a significant amount of physical space, it is important that only data that deduplicates well be stored on EMC Avamar in order to minimize the number of nodes that are required to house the solution.

Target-Based Deduplication

In contrast with source-based deduplication, *target-based deduplication* performs the deduplication process after the data has reached the server or appliance that is storing the data. NetBackup has several different methods by which to implement a target-based solution: NetBackup Media Server with Deduplication, PureDisk, and NetBackup PureDisk Option. CommVault Simpana, on the other hand, provides only a single target-based solution located on the MediaAgent, which provides deduplication solutions for the CommCell. In addition to these solutions, there are appliance-based, target solutions that are fully supported by both NetBackup and CommVault that can provide a solution that offloads the deduplication process from the MS/MA.

So if source-based deduplication can achieve large-scale data reduction prior to even leaving the client, why do target-based deduplication at all? There are actually several reasons why. First of all, source-based is not an end all solution. There are practical limitations to the amount of data that can be processed in a given time, even with efficient hashing mechanisms, due to the limits of the local CPU, the efficiency of the storage and, in the case of EMC Avamar, the necessity to communicate with the storage servers to determine whether the block already exists prior to sending. High change rate systems also produce more data to churn through, as well as typically more unique data blocks, all of which require more processing on the local machine prior to sending to the target. Source-based deduplication is best suited for low change rate data sources and a file system that has a large number of small files, known as a high density file system (HDFS).

For other types of data sets, particularly large databases, the amount of processing and disk performance that can be brought to bear against a deduplication problem can only be performed by a purpose-built system—hence the need for a target-based solution.

NetBackup

To that end, NetBackup provides two basic solutions and two variations. The most basic solution is to implement deduplication on a NetBackup Media Server and use a *Disk Storage Unit (DSU)* to store the resulting deduplicated data. The overall architecture of this solution does not look much different from a regular NetBackup deployment, but there are some differences. The Media Server deployment model groups the clients participating in the deduplication, the Media (storage) Server that will hold the data, and any additional ancillary servers into a group called a node. The deduplication *node* is a logical encapsulation that defines the boundary of where the deduplication service ends—clients who participate in another node, or data that is deduplicated in another node is not deduplicated or stored relative to the original node.

Multisystem deduplication, such as that provided by the Media Server deployment model, is limited in providing deduplication only to those clients that are localized to the particular Media Server. (See Figure 5–8.)

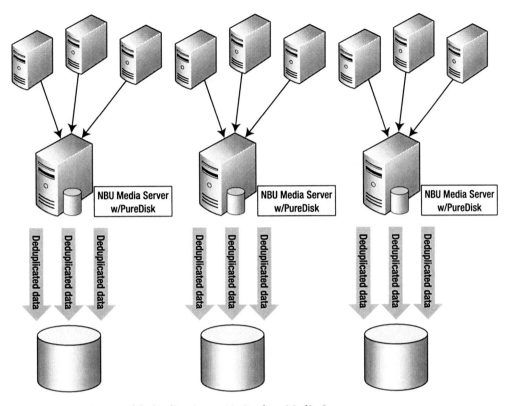

Figure 5–8. Isolation of deduplication to NetBackup Media Servers

In a standard design, the Media Server provides all data processing, including the calculation of the data block signatures, or *fingerprints*, as they are called; the management of storage attached to the Media Server that holds the unique data blocks; and the transmission of the metadata to the Master Server for tracking. In addition, a deduplication node can implement a secondary support server called a *Load Balancing Server (LBS)*. This LBS provides a method by which the calculation of the data block signatures, or fingerprints, can be further offloaded from the primary deduplication Media Server, thus reducing the overall load on the server and providing a modicum of performance increase. (See Figure 5–9.)

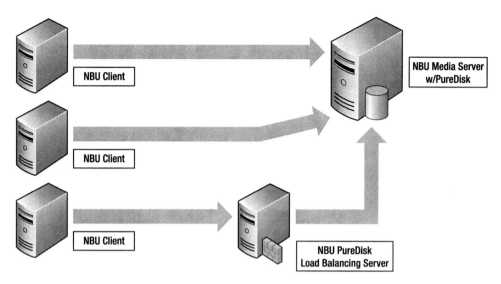

Figure 5–9. NetBackup Load Balancing Servers

However, this is not recommended until the CPU resources on the primary Media Server within the node is fully saturated and cannot process any more data during regular backup windows. This is because the LBS introduces latency into the backup process and only provides a calculation service, not a storage service.

An advantage of this method is that the clients that participate within the deduplication node can be a mix of client-based deduplication clients and non-deduplication clients. This has the advantage of applying client-based deduplication on clients where it is appropriate to use, provide a target-based solution for the remaining clients. The backups from both deduplicated and non-deduplicated clients can be combined on and jointly deduplicated on the Media Server, providing a means of combining both source- and target-based deduplication methods into one storage mechanism. (See Figure 5–10.)

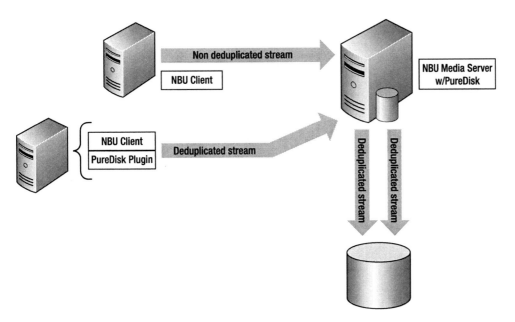

Figure 5–10. *Combined client/target NetBackup Media Server*

The second basic solution is the traditional PureDisk solution. While PureDisk provides the basis of the deduplication node described previously, PureDisk stands alone and is designed to be a stand-alone product (somewhat, as will be described later), and providing deduplicated backup services to sets of clients. The PureDisk solution has a unique architecture that is wholly separate from that described by a Media Server–based deduplication node. A PureDisk Storage Pool is a collection of servers and clients that provide a scalable method of performing deduplication using dedicated hardware that is purpose built, but not an appliance. PureDisk is purpose built using the PureDisk Operating System (PDOS), which runs on standard Intel x64 hardware. In this way, you can get many of the advantages of an appliance, without the expense.

There are a number of services that need to be installed as part of PureDisk to build a storage pool for use:

- *Storage Pool Authority*: Manager of all Storage Pool polices and storage

- *Metabase Engine*: A database of selected metadata regarding the data and clients backed up

- *Metabase Server*: Manages queries to the Metabase Engines

- *Content Router*: Deduplicated client data storage area

These services can go on as few as two physical servers or as many as needed in order to gain the storage and file count needed within the storage pool. The two services/servers that are added to the storage pool in order to grow the services are the Metabase Engine and Content Router. (See Figure 5–11.)

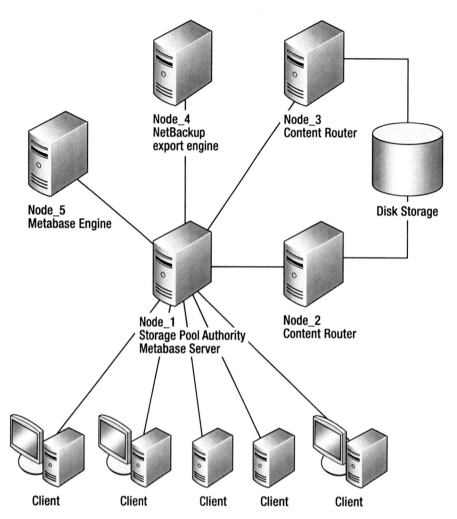

Figure 5–11. *PureDisk solution*[1]

Each of these services is generally added on separate physical servers in order to provide the required input/output (I/O) and processing services to the Storage Pool, as the collection of servers/services is called. Once the Storage Pool is built, the PureDisk software is installed on the clients. The standard NetBackup client software is augmented with a PureDisk plug-in if the client is going to participate in both a standard NetBackup environment as well as a PureDisk environment. The client is then associated with the storage pool and policies are built for the particular client.

While these two services can, and frequently do, stand apart, NetBackup provides other options that allow the combination of the two target deduplication methods into a different solutions that allow for variations in the available architectures. One of the more interesting combinations is the ability to

---

[1] From *PureDisk: Getting Started Guide*—Symantec Corp., p. 18.

connect a standard NetBackup Media Server to a PureDisk Storage Pool via the NetBackup PureDisk Option. This allows regular NetBackup clients to perform backups to a standard Media Server, but be able to gain the advantages of target-based deduplication. (See Figure 5–12.)

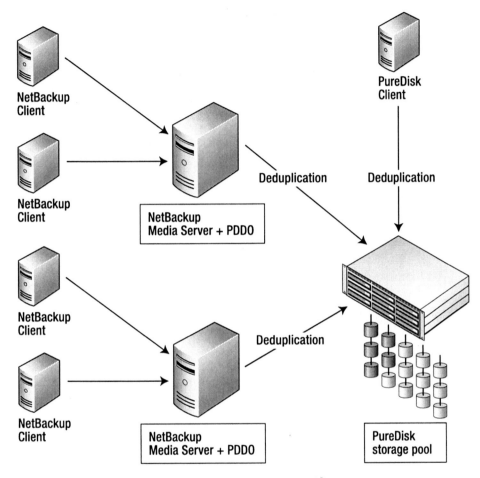

Figure 5–12. Using standard Media Servers with PureDisk[2]

The second configuration allows the opposite. The NetBackup PureDisk connector allows standard PureDisk clients the ability to get their backups into a standard NetBackup environment. This is accomplished through the installation of a NetBackup export engine into the PureDisk Storage Pool. The export engine allows the files to be reconstituted and placed onto traditional NetBackup media types, including tape, and managed as a traditional NetBackup Master server. This provides the ability to perform directed recoveries, or recoveries to client systems other than the client from which the backup was taken, from PureDisk clients to NetBackup clients.

───────────────────

[2] *PureDisk Option Guide*, Symantec Corp., pg 14.

CommVault

Although NetBackup has four different methods to provide a target-based solution—Media Server with deduplication Storage Pool, NetBackup PureDisk, NetBackup PureDisk Option for standard Media Servers, and NetBackup PureDisk Connector. CommVault only has a single method. CommVault provides the ability to perform target-based deduplication on a MediaAgent. When configured for deduplication, the MediaAgent creates a specialized area called a deduplication store. The deduplication store is effectively a database of block signatures and their locations within the MagLib configured to hold the deduplicated data.

Deduplication is configured at the subclient level and can be selectively implemented for all or part of a single complete client. The block signatures for the subclient to be backed up can be generated either on the client or at the MediaAgent. This allows for flexibility in placing this activity on either platform, depending on client/MediaAgent load. Also, no additional client needs be installed to implement deduplication to the MediaAgent. The architecture of the overall CommCell also does not change as well, making deduplication simply a choice of backup type, not a major architectural change to the environment. (See Figure 5–13.)

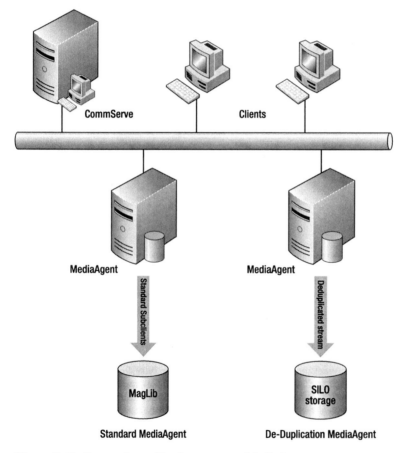

Figure 5–13. *Comparison of backup types on MediaAgents*

However, there are some limitations. In order to control the space utilization of the MagLib, it is necessary to purge, or "seal," the deduplication store and migrate the data to tape, or "silo," storage (as it is known in CommVault terms). While this moves the data on the MagLib to alternate storage, it effectively resets the deduplication, forcing blocks previously stored to be re-placed within the MagLib and the deduplication store. However, CommVault deduplication also allows for deduplication of secondary copies of subclients already backed up to other media types.

Continuous Data Protection/Remote Replication

Instead of backing up data on a regular basis, only taking a snapshot of a particular data set in time, it would be nice to have a backup of the data at any point in time, recover to any point during the retention cycle within minutes, replicate the backup as it is happening, and perform the same operations at the remote site. This describes the basic features of a backup method called continuous data protection (CDP) and continuous data replication (CRR). CDP is used for local data protection (within the same locale as the data being protected). CRR is utilized for replication of these types of backups to remote locations.

So how does this work? CDP works by taking each I/O operation at the disk level and splitting it into two parallel operations. This split of operations can be accomplished through the use of a specialized piece of software known as a *splitter driver*, or simply a *splitter*. Using the splitter, the first operation is written to the disk as normal, and the second operation is written to a storage location, along with the sequence number of the I/O.

The disk location in which the disk blocks are tracked is called a *journal*. There is a journal associated with each logical unit number (LUN) that is managed by the CDP software. As such, a storage area network (SAN) must provide the storage to the servers participating in the CDP software system. In addition to a sequence number, the software also maintains a timestamp with each block, with granularity down to the millisecond. Additionally, the software can be integrated with several different applications, mainly database applications. This allows the CDP software to associate the journal blocks to the application state. (See Figure 5–14.)

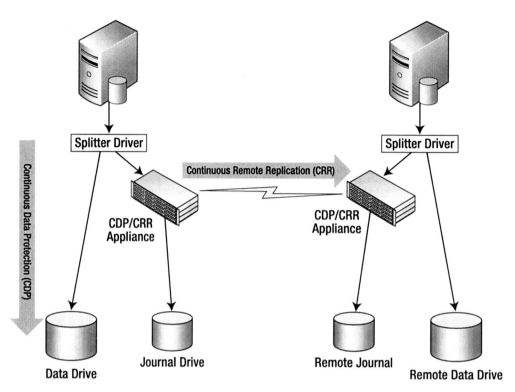

Figure 5–14. CDP and CRR

This effectively creates stateful backup of the application at any point in time. How? Since CDP maintains a sequential listing of all the blocks associated with the LUNs being protected, those blocks can be reapplied in reverse order, thus replaying any transaction back to any selected point. By associating the application, the effect is to have a backup of the application state to any point stored within the CDP software, down to the individual millisecond, or to a particular quiese or checkpoint that is generated by the application. By replaying the transactions, the effect is to restore data to any point, so CDP acts as a backup. (See Figure 5–15.)

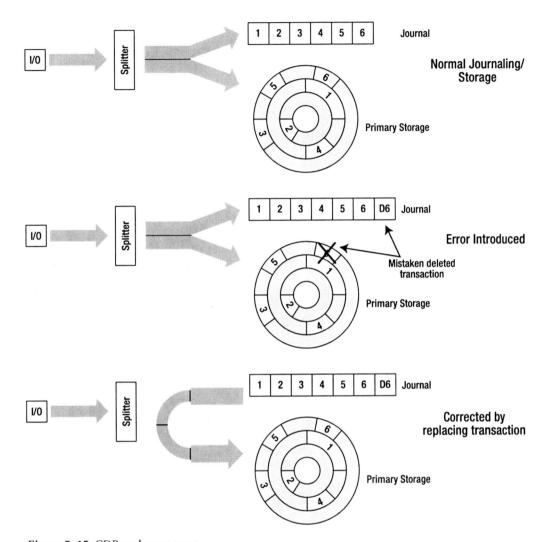

Figure 5–15. CDP replay on error

In addition, most CDP solutions give the ability to present the journal (at a previous point in time), plus the original storage as a "virtual" LUN that represents data at a particular point in time, without having to replay the journal on the master data LUN. Typically, this virtual LUN is a read/write copy, with the option to replay the changes on the virtual LUN back to the original, overwriting the original, or to discard any changes after the virtual LUN is released.

CDP can be implemented in several methods within the I/O path. The most common points of implementation are at the host, within the switch infrastructure of the SAN, and even within certain disk arrays. Within the host, the I/Os are typically split, utilizing a driver loaded onto the server that intercepts the blocks and sends duplicates to the journal as well as to the target disks. Switch infrastructure implementation is typically performed through appliances attached to the switch fabric, or to embedded devices within the fabric itself. When using this type of CDP, I/Os are sent from the host in the normal fashion down the Fiber Channel (FC) path. The CDP appliance is placed logically between the storage and the host, and intercepts the I/O as they are sent to the storage. The appliance then creates the journal entry and sends the original to the storage. The last typical point of split is within the array. The LUNs are assigned through the array controller and are designated as LUNs to have CDP applied. (See Figure 5–16.)

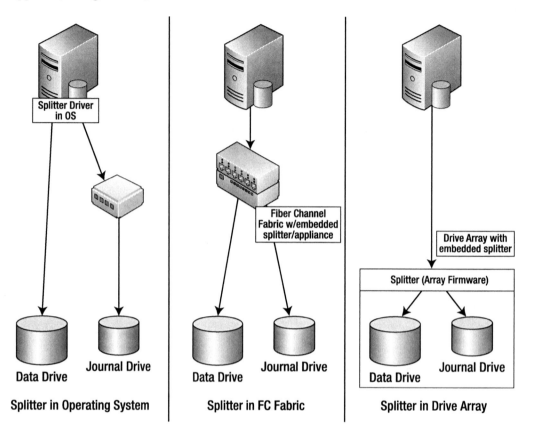

Figure 5–16. Comparison of CDP types

Continuous remote replication (CRR) is simply an extension of CDP. Instead of the journal being local, CRR establishes both a remote journal and remote copy of the data. The data is sent to the remote journal and committed, and then replayed to the remote copy to establish a ready-to-use remote copy. If there is a logical error, and the application needs to roll back remotely, the journal is simply replayed and applied to the remote copy. The data is then available for use in the desired state, although in a remote location. This is typically used in disaster recovery (DR) situations to provide short Recovery Point Objective (RPO)/low Recovery Time Objective (RTO) recoveries of critical data.

NetBackup provides a CDP-only solution through the use of RealTime—a software, host splitter-based solution. RealTime integrates with NetBackup, allowing the use of NetBackup to control the creation of point-in-time snapshots using the CDP solution. This designates the CDP snapshot as a primary backup and can be further stored on standard storage units (tape or disk). Conversely, this also allows the use of NetBackup to treat the CDP points of recovery as primary backup sources for recovery back to the original servers (or to alternate servers if the backup had been moved to alternate storage).

CommVault does not offer a true CDP solution, although it is badged as CDP. The CommVault CDP is actually a schedule replication process that allows the replication of file system data to alternate servers on a scheduled basis.

Cloud Storage

Another high profile technology that has appeared over the last several years is that of the cloud. When the term *cloud* is discussed, it is important to understand from what perspective the term is being used. *Cloud technologies* can refer to several different things: storage, application, or host clouds.

First, here is a quick discussion of the general characteristics of cloud environments. A *cloud environment* is typically an environment or resource that, to the end user, has no distinct physical resources associated with it, such as physical servers, or storage; utilizes IP connectivity (typically over the Internet); and is available in an on-demand model. This is similar to virtual server environments presented by products such as VMWare or Microsoft Hyper-V; the physical hardware used is abstracted from the guest operating systems by the virtualization product—the cloud abstracts the entire operating system or other types of resources from the end user. Cloud environments can offer specific applications for use, such as on-demand web servers, CRM environments, or databases; entire virtual server environments, in which users can upload complete virtual servers for execution remotely or simply offer an IP-based storage environment. Cloud storage differs from other IP storage such as Network File Systems (NFSs) and Common Internet File Systems (CIFSs) in several ways:

- Cloud storage does not provide a file system or directory structure view like NFS or CIFS. Instead, the storage requires a programmatic approach to storing data, and stores data in generic "blobs" rather than specific file types.

- The protocol used to communicate with the cloud, and move and manage data is a very lightweight (not resource-intensive) protocol. The protocol that is most widely used is known as REST—a protocol based on HTTP. This allows for applications to be able to transfer data without large impacts on network traffic that both NFS and CIFS enforce to ensure data integrity.

- Cloud storage also requires relatively strong authentication mechanisms to access the storage. This ensures that only authorized users should be able to access the data stored on the cloud.

- However, cloud storage does not provide for encrypted transmission or storage of data to and in the cloud environment. Encryption must be provided prior to transmission.

- There is not a fixed amount of storage in the cloud; however, users of cloud storage are charged for the amount of storage consumed by the cloud provider.

- Cloud storage is designed around "write few/read many" types of operations.

So where does cloud storage fit into backup? The cloud can be used for several operations. First as long-term storage: backups can be moved into the cloud from traditional backup solutions for long-term storage, particularly if those backups are truly archival backups (backups that are most likely not to be read except under exceptional conditions). Cloud storage is typically cheaper than the physical storage of cartridges in a vault, and infinitely more reliable.

A second use of cloud storage is for backups destined for business continuance (BC) and DR use. Since cloud storage is typically IP- and Internet-based, it is effectively accessible from anywhere. If a BC/DR event occurs, restoration from cloud-based backups can be to any server, anywhere in the world—even to virtual cloud servers. However, some cloud vendors are supported only within North America, so when considering cloud targets, it is important to understand the access limitations that are imposed. This can affect the last advantage of cloud storage: cloud storage can be used for transportable backups. Similar to the BC/DR events, backups sent to the cloud can be used anywhere. As a new technology, cloud storage capabilities are still developing—new uses and capabilities will be added as the cloud offerings mature.

CommVault offers extensive cloud support for targets. A cloud target is simply another media target within a storage policy, just like a MagLib or a tape target. NetBackup, while not having direct cloud support, can access cloud storage though gateway systems that emulate CIFS or NFS but utilize cloud storage as the backend to those protocols.

Summary

Backup storage technologies have come a long way since tape and even virtual tape libraries. Technologies such as deduplication, CDP, and cloud storage have revolutionized the backup industry and provided new options and opportunities for protecting large and differing types and quantities of data, storing it in ways and efficiencies that were not even possible using traditional technologies.

Deduplication has revolutionized the use of disk storage, making the cost basis of disk storage approach that of tape. It is also made replication of backups electronically, economically, and technically viable, as opposed to the transport of physical cartridges to remote locations. It can be implemented in many different ways. It can be applied either at the source of the backup or at the end point, can use different ways of analyzing the data to be deduplicated, and use different ways to write the data to the media. It is a very flexible method of efficiently storing data on disk media. However, it is not without its limitations and is not effective on all types of data. In short, deduplication is a powerful technology that has revolutionized (and will continue to revolutionize) backups as well as storage as a whole.

The introduction of CDP and CRR as backup methods provides ways to reduce windows and narrow recovery points to very small amounts of time by tracking transactions as backups. CDP and CRR also provide additional electronic replication methods for backups that can help to eliminate the need for tape copies—once a transaction is replicated, the backup is complete.

Finally, cloud storage abstracts the media target to the ultimate level. There is not any associated physical entity on which the backups are stored—it is simply a network target that exists "somewhere" on the network (the physical locality is largely irrelevant). This abstraction of locality, once fully developed into a mature technology, will again revolutionize the backup world by potentially eliminating local storage entirely in favor of a generic target that has no physical construct.

CHAPTER 6

Software Architectures— CommVault

The previous chapters have dealt with the various components of backup architectures. From this point forward, we will start to put the pieces together into specific designs that can be expanded upon various size environments. So let's look at some specific configuration mechanisms around CommVault and how they will apply to various environments. If you are not using CommVault, this chapter can safely be skipped—however, it may be instructive to compare different mechanisms of utilization in order to better understand how NetBackup functions in the same situations and general configurations.

General Configuration

In Chapter 2, we reviewed some of the components that make up a CommVault CommCell. Before we start putting them together, let's look at some of the more important configuration elements in detail. The elements that will be discussed here are as follows:

- Disk and MagLib types
- Disk writers
- Multiplexing
- Fill/Spill versus Spill/Fill
- Storage policies
- Multiplexing
- Data interface pairs

Disk and MagLib types

As review, a *magnetic library (MagLib)* is a disk-based storage unit that allows backups to be stored or staged for further migration to different types of media. When creating a MagLib, there are different types of MagLibs that can be created, depending on the disk type utilized. The three types of storage that are available for MagLib storage are the following:

- *Static*: Static storage is simply traditional disk storage directly attached to a MediaAgent, either through direct attached storage (DAS) or through a storage area network (SAN).

- *Shared static*: Shared static storage is typically provided via Transmission Control Protocol/Internet Protocol (TCP/IP) protocols such as Common Internet File System (CIFS) or Network File System (NFS).

- *Shared dynamic*: Shared dynamic storage is provided via two different methods— via a clustered file system (CFS) such as *Polyserve* or the Quantum StorNext file system, or via a SCSI-3 reserve/release mechanism implemented at the operating-system level for shared storage. The SCSI-3 reserve/release mechanism is typically very complicated to implement, can be unreliable as a method of enforcing shared locking, and is not recommended for implementation in shared storage environments.

From the various disk storage types, the MagLibs are created. Just as with the disk types, there are two different types of MagLibs:

- *Dedicated MagLibs* are created on a single MediaAgent and can be created on any type of supported disk storage.

- *Dynamic MagLibs* are created between MediaAgents and utilize either shared static or shared dynamic drives to create the linkages between MediaAgents.

In addition to better utilization of storage when using shared storage, MediaAgent can also share backup images as well as use shared index cache areas. This allows one MediaAgent to have a client backup, and another to be able to restore the backup that was created. This provides a simple method of scaling MediaAgent capabilities without isolating storage resources or having only a single point of restore for any particular backup.

Disk Writers

Disk writers are processes that are created to write inbound backup data to MagLib storage. The creation of multiple writers allows the ability to write data in parallel, thus increasing the efficiency with which data is written. Writers are assigned per drive (or *mount path*, as it is known in CommVault).

A mount path can be a physical device or a network share—basically, any type of valid target media can be defined as a mount path. The number of writers is typically set at 2 for initial configurations of mount paths. This is adequate for a simple RAID 1, or mirrored, disk that is used as a mount path. However, for more involved RAID types, such as RAID 5, the number of writers should be increased.

CommVault generally recommends that no more than six writers be applied to a particular mount point, however, as the performance of individual systems varies, more than six writers may be able to be applied on systems with high-speed CPU and storage, with multipath storage as these types and combinations of elements can absorb more parallel processing. This applies regardless of whether this is physical storage or network attached storage (NAS)–based storage. The best method of tuning this is to start with the recommended six writers and increase them over time until overall performance tapers off. Then reduce the number of writers until performance picks back up.

Writer maximums are also assigned by a library as well. When a MagLib mount path is created on a MediaAgent, it is assigned to a *library*, hence the name MagLib magnetic library. The library then acts as a collection of MagLib mount paths that can be managed as a single entity. But consider what happens when a number of mount paths are collected and operated as a single unit. Each mount path may have been independently tuned for maximum performance. However, when operated in parallel, if all assigned writers are executed at the same time, the overall performance of the MediaAgent will suffer as the writers in aggregate will overload the MediaAgent. The writer maximums for the library prevent this situation by limiting the number of writers in aggregate that can be executed at once, regardless of the setting of the individual mount paths.

Multiplexing

Multiplexing is the ability to interleave different streams backup into a single writer, as shown in Figure 6–1.

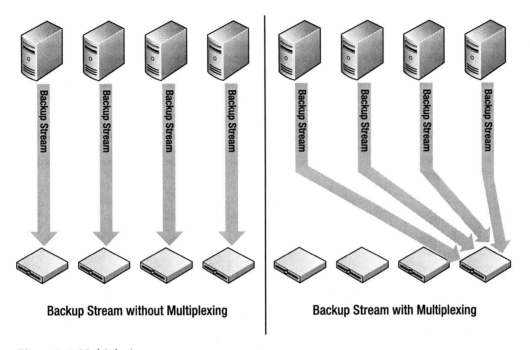

Backup Stream without Multiplexing   **Backup Stream with Multiplexing**

Figure 6–1. Multiplexing

Multiplexing allows backup clients of varying performance to intermix their backups and allow a writer to reach maximum performance. Here's an example. Imagine that you have 12 clients, each of which can generate 5 MB/sec of performance during a backup. The MediaAgent has 2 mount paths, each with 6 writers, can ingest 60 MB/sec of backup per mount path, and Spill/Fill is enabled for the 2 mount paths. Without multiplexing, each mount path will get three clients, each client using one writer. This has the effect of only generating 30 MB/sec of throughput to each mount path, half of what it is capable of, as well as leaving six of the clients waiting for resources. However, if a multiplex factor of 2 is set, each writer will get 2 streams, 1 from two different clients. This has the effect of boosting the effective ingest rate to the maximum performance, as well as removing the queued clients waiting for resources. Multiplexing is useful for filling pipelines of data efficiently and is particularly useful when writing directly to tape resources. This is a mechanism that can be used to ensure that the tape resources do not have the "shoeshine" effect, as was discussed in Chapter 3 by ensuring that the minimum throughput is always maintained by virtue of combining slower streams into single writers for an aggregated throughput that is greater than any one client can produce.

Fill/Spill versus Spill/Fill

So if you have a number of mount paths, how do you ensure that the performance is balanced in a way that makes sense within your environment? CommVault provides two mechanisms to balance the number of writers against the workload presented: Fill/Spill or Spill/Fill. The Fill/Spill mechanism states that a single mount path will reach its maximum number of writers before starting writers for the next mount path in the MagLib. This has the effect of concentrating writers on a single device, to the exclusion of others. While this may have useful effects when dealing with dissimilar performing mount paths within a MagLib, by providing a mechanism to fill the higher performing mount point before moving to the lower one, typically this is not the desired mechanism as it tends to overload and overfill one mount path over all others.

The recommended mechanism is Spill/Fill. This mechanism distributes the load to writers in a round robin fashion between all mount paths within the MagLib. (See Figure 6–2.) It provides an even distribution of writers, load, and storage capacity among all mount paths, leading to a balanced distribution. This works well if the mount paths are relatively equal in performance and capacity, which is a recommended configuration.

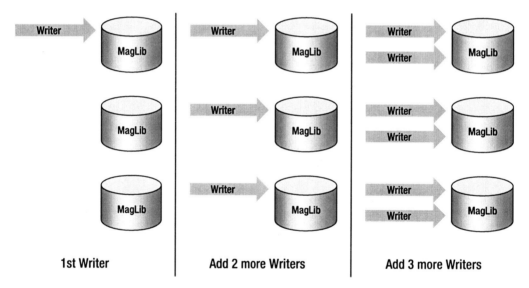

Figure 6–2. Spill/Fill

Storage Policies

Storage Policies (SPs) take many of the common elements that make up a backup and combine them into a single entity that can be managed. Storage Policies consist of the following items:

- Clients

- Target MediaAgents

- Number and type of copies (via a reference Copy Policy)

- Data path

- Retention

- Library and drive pools

The Storage Policy has the effect of defining exactly how the client is to be backed up, where and how long the backup is stored, and how the data gets from the client to the MediaAgent. There are two types of Storage Policies:

- *Standard*: Standard Storage Policies can define both a full and incremental/differential backups types.

- *Incremental*: Incremental Storage Policies are actually policies that can provide a separate set of policies for incremental/differential backups than the Standard SP. This can be useful if you want to have a different combination of elements for your incremental backups, say a different MediaAgent, from your full backups.

Storage Policies actually reference several different types of secondary policies to allow the adjustment of the parameters of the Storage Policy quickly and easily. Schedule Policies provide the mechanism by which both the full/incremental/differential relationships are defined, as well as the time period in which they are performed. By having the Schedule Policy separate from the Storage Policy, it provides a means to change the backup schedule of entire sets of clients simply by changing a single entity.

Storage Policy Copy Policies define the type and number of copies of backups or media that are made. There are two types of copies:

- *Primary*: Primary copies are simply the initial copy of the backup. Secondary copies are those copies that are made of the Primary and stored on different media.

- *Secondary*: Secondary copies are created by AUX copy jobs that execute the policies within the Copy Policy. There are two types of Secondary copies:

  - *Synchronous*: Synchronous copy is a complete copy of the *source* of the Primary copy. This effectively clones the source media to a separate media target, say for long-term storage. Synchronous copies can be made from full or incremental backups on the Primary.

  - *Selective*: Selective copies, on the other hand, are full copies of backups that have occurred on the Primary media. Selective copies are only made from full backups and can be time-consuming due to the size of the backups that need to be copied.

Both types of copies have the advantage of implementing a mechanism that is similar to tape stacking (described in Chapter 4). The backup copy can be configured to demultiplex the original backup, creating copies that contain contiguous, compacted copies of the original backup and are faster to restore from, given that the interleaving of different backup streams has been removed.

Data Interface Pairs

When configuring clients, CommVault expects to be able to resolve only one network interface on the client. However, with the Data Interface Pairs setting, it is possible to associate more than one interface between systems. This allows the ability to have traffic spread across multiple network interfaces, or to have an alternate interface associated with the system in question—allowing an alternate path to the same system. While Data Interface Pairs can be used in the event that a path fails, it is not an automatic process and will require manual intervention.

CommCell with Single Target

The most basic configuration is that of an environment with a single target for media and a single CommCell. This single CommCell would consist of only a single CommServe, which could act as both a MediaAgent and CommServe simultaneously. This configuration provides a very basic environment in which to implement a CommCell and is a microcosm of all the elements of a CommCell. However, this type of implementation is typically only found in very small environments as the ability of the MediaAgent to ingest data can be rapidly overshadowed by the performance requirements of the CommServe portion of the unified platform. For most implementations, the additional cost of a separate MediaAgent server will save costs of expansion as the backup need grows.

CommCell with Single MediaAgent

This is the most common environment in most CommVault configurations. This configuration consists of CommServe and a single MediaAgent that provides backup services to the CommCell. This configuration also forms the basis for all other environments to follow.

The configuration provides the basis for *horizontal scalability*. Horizontal scalability is the core of any good architecture, regardless of product. This is the ability to provide increases in capacity without the necessity to add additional control mechanisms, such as a CommServe—effectively creating a new CommCell. This is particularly important in CommVault as clients backed up in one CommCell cannot be restored in another CommCell without an extensive client migration process that involves migration of licenses, media, and other elements.

In this configuration, the CommCell should have two types of media present: disk and tape. The tape configuration can be either physical tape or virtual tape library (VTL), but it must be a type of media that is intended to provide a low-cost, alternate copy of the media, freeing up the more expensive disk-based storage for use in other backups. This also provides secondary protection against failure of the MediaAgent, particularly the disk storage associated with the MagLib used as spool storage. Simply having a single MagLib storage may seem effective and can be useful, but it provides a risk of having all backups be completely associated with the MediaAgent. This is because the MediaAgent maintains the metadata regarding the location of backups that are created on that particular server—this data is not maintained on the CommServe. If the environment grows or the MediaAgent fails, it is easier to integrate a new MediaAgent and rescan the data than it is to transfer disks (physically) to a new replacement MediaAgent (in the case of MediaAgent failure) to re-create backups on the replacement.

The requirement of having secondary copies external to the MediaAgent can be mitigated without requiring the use of tape. If shared storage is used, such as CIFS- or NFS-based storage, the risk of losing primary backups when a particular MediaAgent fails is reduced. This is shown in Figure 6–3.

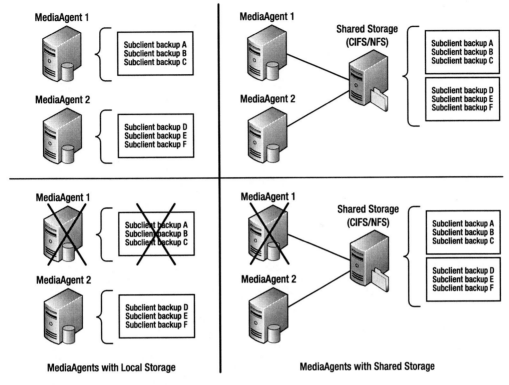

Figure 6–3. *Use of local storage versus shared storage for MagLibs*

Additionally, if storage is required for a MagLib attached to shared storage, the storage can be simply added to the provider of the CIFS or NFS share and it is available to any MediaAgent attached to the storage server. In this case, a secondary copy would *not* need to be created, and the Storage Policy Copy Policy would not use the MagLib as spool storage. However, it still may be prudent to create a secondary copy for use as an offsite copy or for further protection.

Storage Policies are created for every client that points toward the MediaAgent within the CommCell, leaving only the disaster recovery (DR) backups to occur on the CommServe itself. This offloads all major I/O operations to the MediaAgent—at least with respect to backups—and frees the CommServe to deal with the maintenance and standard operations that are outside of the backup cycle. Where possible, multiple network interfaces should be used to provide additional bandwidth to the MediaAgent in order to stream data to the target media.

From an overall construction perspective, the MediaAgent should utilize MagLib storage as a temporary, or "spool," copy of the backup. When used in this manner, the Storage Policy Copy Policy automatically executes an AUX copy job at the completion of the backup to create a Synchronous or Selective copy, based on the type of backup and the desired collection. Once the copy is complete, the MagLib is purged of the original Primary backup, and the AUX copy is promoted to the Primary. (See Figure 6–4.)

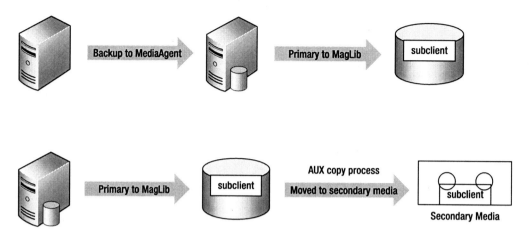

Figure 6–4. *Spooling backups via AUX copy*

When looking at the growth scenario, simply having all the backups stored within a single set of internal disks does not provide a mechanism to easily move clients and their backups between MediaAgents without extensive copying of data between the "new" and "old" MediaAgent. When looking at this type of configuration, it is important to identify how to grow such an environment. If this type of configuration represents a small environment, without the potential to grow out of the single MediaAgent, simply providing internal protected (RAID) storage for the MagLib, tuning the disk writers appropriately to the storage type, and directly connecting the external storage are the appropriate solutions. Figure 6–5 shows the difference between local storage and shared storage and how they relate to growth scenarios.

Although more difficult, the direct connection of external storage, in particular disk storage, does provide a mechanism for growth. Regardless of connection type, any external types of storage—disk, VTL, or physical tape—can be connected to other servers via various connection mechanisms, primarily the sharing of connections to the storage types via Y cables, SCSI-3 reserve/release protocols, or combinations thereof. (These mechanisms were discussed at length in Chapters 2, 3, and 4, and should be reviewed when considering this type of method.) The method also limits the number of servers that can share the resource for growth, typically to no more than two, so if growth is slow, this type of connection may last the lifetime of the backup solution; otherwise the use of shared physical connectivity between devices will not work.

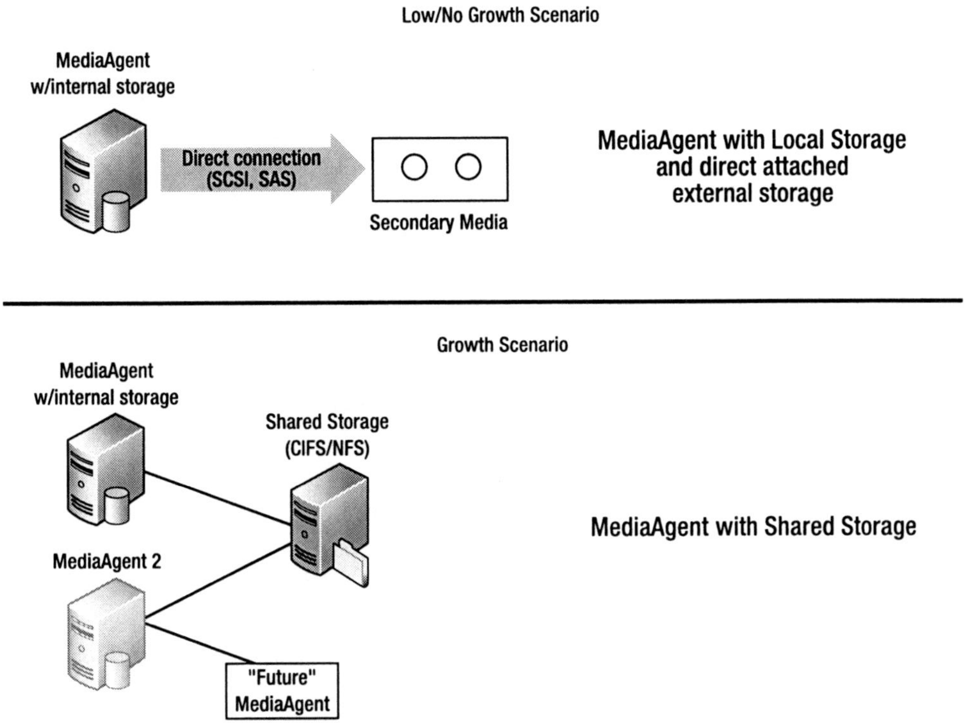

Low/No Growth Scenario

MediaAgent
w/internal storage

Direct connection
(SCSI, SAS)

Secondary Media

**MediaAgent with Local Storage
and direct attached
external storage**

Growth Scenario

MediaAgent
w/internal storage

Shared Storage
(CIFS/NFS)

MediaAgent 2

"Future"
MediaAgent

MediaAgent with Shared Storage

Figure 6–5. Storage connection scenarios

However, in the case of physical tape libraries or standalone tape drives, it is much simpler to add an additional connection directly to a new tape drive, thus avoiding the pitfalls of sharing physical connectivity. In the case of a tape library, this is a simple reconfiguration of the library within the CommServe. The new tape drive will be detected by the CommServe, and the library should be reconfigured to rescan itself (from within CommVault—the library already knows about the new drive internally), and CommServe places the drive within the library. The new drive is then available for use, either on the existing MediaAgent or on one newly added to the environment. (See Figure 6–6.) Stand-alone drives are simply attached as needed and associated with the MediaAgent on which they reside.

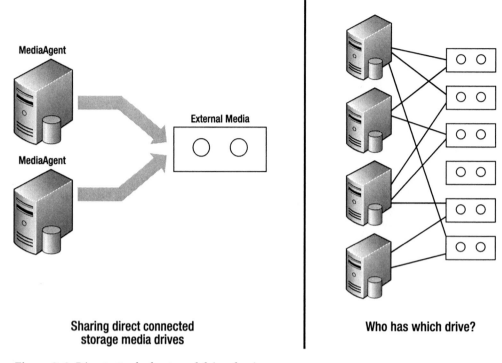

MediaAgent

External Media

MediaAgent

**Sharing direct connected
storage media drives**

Who has which drive?

Figure 6–6. *Direct attached external drive sharing*

The more important point to take away from this is that the only physical device that is relevant in the configuration is the physical library, not the MediaAgent. In a configuration in which the MediaAgent is logically detached from the storage, whether disk or tape, the data that is important is stored in the external component. The MediaAgent can be changed out, renamed, or shut down, and the backup data remains intact. This abstraction of the actual backup data from the physical server that performs the work should be the basis for any design that uses media writing servers, such as MediaAgents, in their design.

While the focus of external storage is on the use of either disk or tape libraries, CommVault does provide a drive pooling mechanism to group stand-alone drives into logical groups to be managed in a similar fashion as would be completed for a tape library. However, this will still require manual intervention for insert/eject operations on each of the physical drives attached. Unless the environment is completely static, represents a remote office location with extremely limited space, or has other constraints that severely limit the hardware that can be installed, *it is strongly recommended that small tape libraries be deployed instead of multiple tape drives, even in the case of a single tape drive being required for the backup*. The deployment of small libraries avoids the necessity to remember to physically insert/remove tapes from drives and provides a small cache of tapes that can be used in the case of a backup overrunning a single tape and an operator not being present to switch tapes.

In addition, the small tape library also provides the ability to grow easily, effectively doubling throughput simply by adding connections, but not doubling the management overhead of now inserting tapes (correctly) into different drives. The small library also aids in media management by providing the ability to insert/remove tapes on a bulk basis (for weekly offsite storage or tape rotation, for example) versus managing individual tapes that can be more easily lost. Costs of small libraries, as well as other small form factor devices such as VTLs and autochangers, are typically not significantly higher than the cost of two drives, plus the costs of losing that first organizationally critical backup and provide a much better level of protection than the single tape drive. Overall, the cost of the loss of the backup will more than pay for the cost of the hardware in the long run.

Advanced Storage Connectivity

For environments that have a potential for faster growth, it is desirable to implement more dynamic types of storage connectivity: iSCSI, CIFS/NFS, or Fibre Channel–based storage. iSCSI implementations, while providing connectivity to external storage, is a good choice for the MagLib-only implementation, is not the best choice for potential growth scenarios. This is because the iSCSI protocol does not allow for shared access to a common disk area or file system because the native iSCSI protocol is not set up for shared access to common logical unit numbers (LUNs), as is the Common Internet File System (CIFS) or Network File System (NFS).

This limitation does not preclude its use in a growth environment, however. A shared storage environment, such as a low-cost drive array that acts as an iSCSI target, makes an excellent, low-cost option to provide storage to a single MediaAgent, with the option of adding additional MediaAgents to account for future growth. The only limitation of such a setup is the inability to access a common index cache—thus isolating each MediaAgent to its own disk storage. However, utilizing iSCSI provides the ability to have a common platform, with a relatively efficient protocol, that can provide storage services to CommCell needs as well as other application needs, with a minimum of cost and a high utilization of storage resources. If you are considering iSCSI as a storage platform, there are excellent resources available that can cover the advantages and disadvantages of this protocol for general use. They should be consulted prior to making any decisions regarding the implementation of this storage model.

A CIFS/NFS implementation, as discussed previously, also provides an inexpensive method of implementing MagLib storage that can easily be expanded for use from a single MediaAgent. MagLib storage utilized in this way should be targets for both the data store and the index cache. The placement of the index cache on the shared storage allows any current or new MediaAgent to access a common cache—effectively giving any MediaAgent access to the metadata, and therefore the backups, generated by any other MediaAgent.

Storage utilization is high as the CIFS/NFS share utilizes common storage and manages the storage platform as a single entity, not as discrete LUNs in the iSCSI solution. CIFS and NFS are also mature protocols with well-known limitations regarding their implementation (refer to Chapter 3). The major limitation that should be considered when planning for a growth model is the protocol overhead. CIFS in particular typically has a very high overhead requirement that can impact the amount of performance that can be provided. Many manufacturers rate their NAS storage throughput using NFS statistics, which are significantly faster than CIFS, so when comparing storage solutions for their suitability for backup targets, ensure that a minimum of a 15 percent difference in performance is accounted for if CIFS will be used as the NAS protocol. While this overhead may not be visible in a single MediaAgent model, it can become visible after more MediaAgents are added to the share.

Another factor to consider is the management of the storage on the CIFS/NFS provider and its impact on the overall performance of the storage being provided for use by the MediaAgent. A simple storage layout (for instance, a single RAID 5 group shared as one "lump" of storage accessible by all shares) may be sufficient for a very small number of MediaAgents; such a layout will quickly lose performance as more demand is placed on it. The configuration of the back-end storage on a NAS solution is important, even when starting out.

While RAID 5 and RAID 6 storage configurations look attractive from a storage capacity standpoint, especially when starting with NAS storage targets, the growth of the environment must be considered. Once a RAID configuration is selected for a particular set of storage, it is almost impossible to change without significant effort, including outages for the environment. Parity RAID configurations such as these will perform acceptably when used by one or two MediaAgents, but as the demand on this type of storage configuration grows, the performance will rapidly decline. So, when considering a NAS storage model for MediaAgent storage, plan for the fastest possible storage configuration on the back end of the NAS provider in order to account for growth in the environment.

For those environments that are starting small, but anticipate very fast growth and high performance requirements, Fibre Channel is the way to go. However, as the most expensive and management-intensive option for MediaAgent storage, it is not to be considered lightly, and there must be preparations made in terms of training and expectations prior to implementation. Fibre Channel provides the highest speed storage, up to 8 Gb/sec in current implementations, and can be shared between servers at the LUN level. Since Fibre Channel uses a dedicated SAN to provide storage services, it is typically not subject to the same type of issues that iSCSI and CIFS/NFS implementations suffer from. Figure 6–7 shows a generic SAN topology.

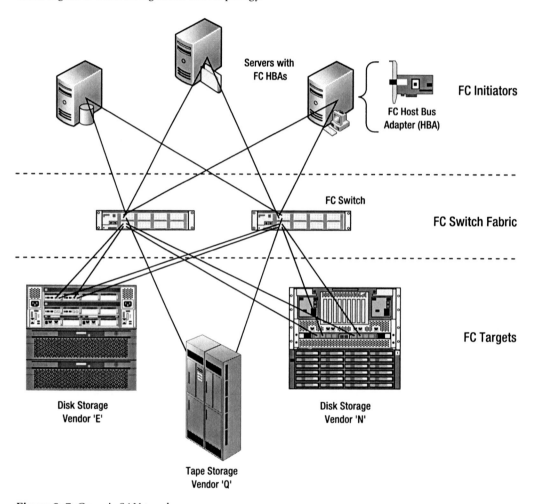

Figure 6–7. Generic SAN topology

Fibre Channel implementations do require a number of specialized components that make them a choice for single MediaAgent implementations only in situations where growth will be accelerated and performance is at a premium. MediaAgents participating in a SAN environment require specialized interfaces, HBAs, in order to connect and access the storage offered on the network. Storage arrays also must be attached to this network, which may remove the array from other types of connectivity, depending on the array vendor and model. The SAN requires connectivity management that is completely separate from that provided by standard TCP/IP networks, which in turn require specialized knowledge to design and maintain.

This is changing: a new technology, call *Fibre Channel over Ethernet (FCoE)* is emerging that promises to allow both Fibre Channel and TCP/IP network protocols to run on the same physical connection, with no degradation of either from a performance or reliability perspective. In its current form, FCoE is very limited where and how it can be deployed, however, as the standards and resulting protocols mature, the knowledge base required to manage storage networks will slowly converge into a single group.

MediaAgent implementations with SAN-based storage typically utilize dedicated LUNs for MagLib implementations in order to provide high-density, high-speed storage for use as storage targets. (See Figure 6–8.)

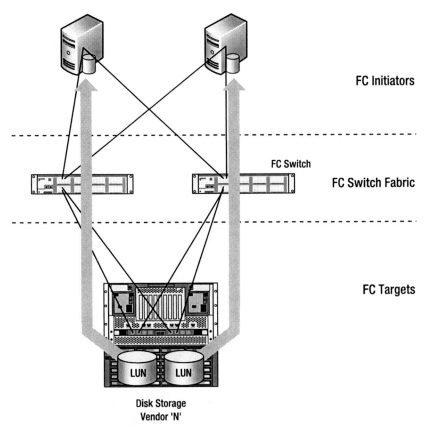

Figure 6–8. Dedicated FC LUNs for MediaAgents

This storage is located on a common set of arrays that provides the ability to manage the storage from a single location, thus allowing storage to be effectively allocated, both from a capacity and performance perspective. This type of storage allows both the MediaAgent to be easily replaced in case of a failure or upgraded while maintaining the storage contents because they are externally located. A SAN-based disk also allows for the utilization of physically smaller MediaAgents. Since the server that contains the MediaAgent does not have to also hold all the storage associated with the particular MediaAgent as the critical storage resides externally, there only needs to be enough storage to hold the operating system, plus the CommVault software. Servers implemented this way still do not share storage from a CommVault perspective or share storage from an operating or LUN perspective, but do share storage array locations.

While Fibre Channel implementations can provide shared storage from the LUN level, it does not guarantee that these shared LUNs will be able to be utilized at the MediaAgent for a shared environment. Just as with iSCSI, Fibre Channel LUNs cannot violate any of the constraints that the operating system that is using the LUNs place on the use of shared storage. In contrast with iSCSI, however, Fibre Channel provides the ability to share each LUN between servers. Fibre Channel does not arbitrate the use of the LUN, however; there is no inherent control mechanism in Fibre Channel that prevents access to a common LUN from one server while another server is using the LUN in question. Fibre Channel relies on upper-level mechanisms, provided at the operating system level, to arbitrate between server requests. For a shared storage environment, the mechanism that provides this level of arbitration is a CFS. The CFS provides communication between servers that participate in a shared LUN environment to ensure that writes between all servers are coherently placed on the LUN, the writes by other servers are known by all other servers using the shared LUN, and simultaneous requests for the same area of disk are arbitrated according to a common set of rules. Examples of a CFS file system are the PolyServe FS and StorNext FS.

The CFS provides the mechanism by which multiple MediaAgents can access a common set of LUNs and provides a shared area in which both index caches and data volumes can be created for use by all participating systems. This allows the use of non-IP–based storage mechanisms such as Fibre Channel to create a common index cache and subclient storage area. As was explored earlier, this provides the ability for any MediaAgent to use the subclient backups created by any other MediaAgent that both share the index cache and are within the same CommCell. However, the CFS must be installed *prior* to use by the MediaAgent, and must be installed on all systems that are or will use the common area in a shared infrastructure. Conversion of an existing file system is typically not possible; it would require manual migration of data from standard file systems to the CFS. In terms of CommVault, this would be the equivalent of executing a combination of Selective and Synchronous copy jobs, followed by expiration and cleanup of the originating standard file system to move the data. In the single MediaAgent discussion, this means that either the need for additional MediaAgents be accounted for during the planning phase of the design and a CFS is installed; or that the overhead of either keeping existing MagLib storage on standard file systems, followed by alteration of the appropriate Storage Policies to point to the new MagLib created from the CFS is accepted.

CommCell with Multiple MediaAgents

Once the single MediaAgent environment has grown beyond its bounds, the next logical expansion point, as defined by a horizontal capacity model, is to add additional MediaAgents to provide potential capacity from both a storage and throughput perspective. Secondary MediaAgents may be deployed to support general-purpose uses such as growth in the number of clients that need backup at a particular time. Alternatively, a combined client/MediaAgent deployment may be made to allow a particular backup client the ability to move data directly to media instead of through a general-purpose MediaAgent. One or both of these will usually be deployed as part of the expansion into multiple MediaAgents.

In either case, secondary or tertiary MediaAgents are deployed to solve shortages or address projected capacity issues with both throughput and storage ability. These two resource areas are not necessarily dependent on each other, and a shortage on one does not imply a shortage on another. Frequently one of the resources is consumed far quicker than the other, which forces a decision to move to the expansion via an addition.

Network Resources

Network resources are consumed with every backup, but are relinquished with the conclusion of every backup. When a backup starts, it sends network traffic in the form of backup data to the MediaAgent; when it completes, that traffic ends and any bandwidth consumed is freed for use by other clients performing backups. As more clients utilize the existing connections on a single MediaAgent in parallel, less and less bandwidth becomes freed per unit time. At some point, the network interface becomes used at its maximum capacity (it is *saturated*). At saturation, no additional traffic can be added to the interface at a particular time without impacting the performance of all other users of the same interface.

Notice a couple of items:

- Discussions of network performance initially centered on point-in-time measurements.

- Network saturation can occur periodically, but can be recovered from by removing traffic.

The moral of the story: before adding additional MediaAgents or network interfaces to solve network performance problems, look the overall traffic pattern and compare it to the backup schedule. *Most of the time, network performance issues can be solved simply by moving the time when backups start to times when other backups are finishing. This sounds simple—and is. However, it is the most overlooked solution to performance problems, particularly those around network utilization.*

The reason it is overlooked has largely to do with the two previous bullet points. While network utilization is measured as point-in-time snapshots, the tendency is to think that because a network interface has reached saturation during one snapshot or window, the entire interface is therefore saturated at all times.

How do many administrators schedule backups? The backup window starts at a particular time, and all backups start at the very beginning of the window or may be staggered within a few hours of the backup window. This generates a traffic utilization pattern that looks like Figure 6–9.

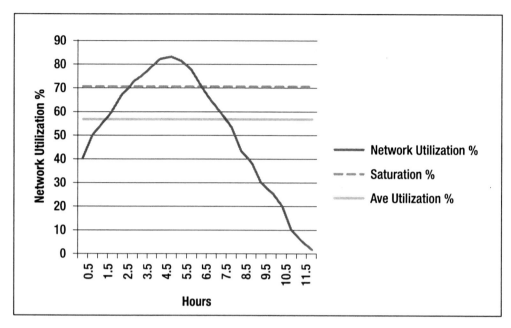

Figure 6–9. Network overutilization

Note that all the work comes during the beginning of the backup window and rapidly tapers off after the first half of the window. In this particular case, the maximum (saturation) utilization is at 70 percent of the theoretical maximum—any activity that happens above this saturation value will degrade in performance globally over all connections. Said another way, there is a traffic jam—too much traffic on too few lanes. After the middle of the window the traffic rapidly declines because the short running backup jobs have completed, leaving the longer-running jobs to have the remaining bandwidth. But notice what the average utilization is for the entire window—it is well below the saturation value. But most administrators design for the first half of the window and create an ever-increasing requirement for network bandwidth that does not necessarily need to be satisfied. Plenty of bandwidth is available, but it is being inefficiently utilized throughout the backup window.

If a client starts at the beginning of the windows and finishes within a couple of hours, why not move the client start time to occur after longer running backups complete, but still allow it to finish within the allotted window? It effectively removes network traffic from the interface and allots it to jobs that need to run for longer periods of time. When this type of approach is utilized, the network utilization curve should look like Figure 6–10.

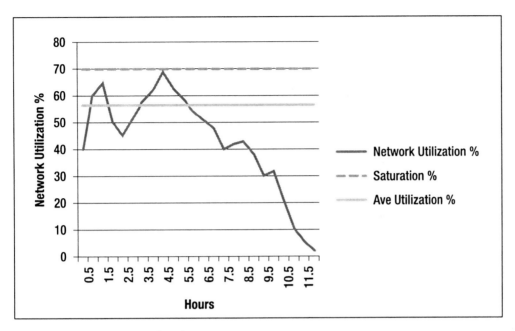

Figure 6–10. Proper network utilization

While the average and saturation points are roughly the same, the load when distributed across the window never reaches saturation at any point during the window. Longer-running jobs are still started at the beginning of the window, and there are peaks and valleys depending on other factors, including starting new batches of jobs. But overall the exact same workload will actually complete *faster* with the same around of resources because all jobs are not competing for the same network bandwidth, thus allowing all jobs to get as much bandwidth as they can consume and be able to transfer data faster. This is referred to as an increase in work per unit time—the individual jobs may or may not run any faster, but overall the backups complete faster because the bandwidth bottleneck has been removed.

The best way to apply this approach to solving network saturation issues is to first characterize jobs in terms of *window required* not *performance*, *size*, or *type*. Once this characterization is complete, assign like *performing* jobs in terms of the window size, to the same start time, taking into account the length of time each set of jobs takes to complete. This should produce a performance that resembles the previous one.

As jobs grow longer, more clients utilize the MediaAgent; the average utilization begins to reach saturation, and/or the peaks cross saturation and stay above the line for longer periods of time. At this point, additional resources should be considered, although they do not imply a second MediaAgent…yet. Adding an additional network interface to the same physical MediaAgent may extend the life for some period of time, without the addition of a physical server. The network interface provides additional bandwidth for use by the collection of clients by doubling the amount of potential bandwidth available.

The addition of more interfaces can be accomplished by three different methods:

- *Software* Configure CommVault to use discrete network connection points, configured as Data Interface Pairs

- *Extension of existing network* Create network interface bonds or teams.

- *New network hardware* Replace slower interfaces with newer, faster ones, such as replacing 1 GB interfaces for 10 GB ones.

As discussed earlier in this chapter, the Data Interface Pair solution involves the addition of a secondary network interface, assigned its own IP address different from the primary address, to which clients connect. The Data Interface Pair feature allows the definition of paths to MediaAgents that have IP address/hostname combinations that do not match the primary IP address/hostname, but refer to the same physical machine. This allows the ability to define specific paths, through a combination of Storage Policies and Data Interface Pairs, over which specific clients should communicate. In this way, the administrator can definitively define and balance traffic across discrete paths, all managed from within software.

While the use of Data Interface Pairs provides a definite and managed way to route traffic, it can rapidly become unmanageable with a larger number of servers or in situations where the amount of bandwidth that a single network interface can provide is not sufficient for a single client or set of clients. In this case, a hardware/operating system–based solution, interface bonding/teaming, would be appropriate. This method uses drivers within the operating system to take like network interfaces, combine them together, and present them as a single network interface with X times the amount of bandwidth, where X is the number of discrete interfaces that have been combined together.

As Figure 6–11 shows, while teaming is not exactly a linear increase in performance, teaming does provide a significant amount increase in available bandwidth available for use. To the MediaAgent software, the teamed interface appears to be a normal network device, and the client simply sees a IP connection point and does not have any knowledge of the device types, at least from an TCP/IP perspective.

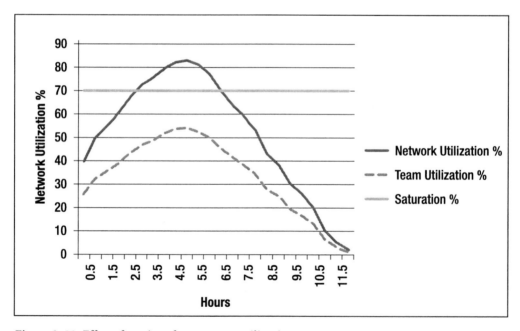

Figure 6–11. *Effect of two interface team on utilization*

There are several different methods of implementing teaming. The available methods will vary from operating system to operating system, but can be categorized into the following three types:

- *Active/passive* This method of teaming provides protection only against link failure, and actually does not increase bandwidth in any way. If the operating system or drive only supports this method, implement Data Interface Pairing instead.

- *Link aggregation (802.3ad)* This is the formal IEEE method of implementing teaming. The implementation involves the creation of the combined interface at the operating system layer, which then communicates with the switched network to establish the optimal routing of traffic between the server interfaces. This requires that the switch that the team is connected to supports 802.3ad, and be configured to use the protocol for the ports to which the server is connected. While this is the best possible load balancing available, *it is typically not implemented due to the management overhead from both the server and network teams, and requires costly switches and management software licenses.*

- *Load balancing*—This is an operating system/driver–implemented method of implementing a teamed approach that does not involve the use of an 802.3ad switch. The driver determines the interface that is the least lightly loaded and utilizes that interface. There are generally two types of load balancing implementations:

  - *Transmit Load Balancing (TLB)*—This is a transmit-only load balancing mechanism. Receive is handled by a single interface. While this may have some uses for MediaAgents using TCP/IP-based storage, such as CIFS/NFS, it will have no effect on inbound client traffic. Implement Data Interface Pairing if this is the only type available

  - *Adaptive Load Balancing (ALB)*—This is a full transmit/receive load balancing mechanism implemented at the operating system level. ALB rewrites the MAC address of one of the interfaces for all outbound packets and allows any of the participating interfaces to accept the same MAC address. While this is the best method of host-based load balancing, it does introduce overhead in the network stack, thus reducing overall potential performance. However, this performance reduction, in most cases, will be negligible. Implement this method if available on the operating system.

The caveats to the addition of additional network interfaces are centered on the other components of the MediaAgent: CPU, memory, bus type, and disk I/O capacity. If any one of these components is near maximum utilization (or even hovering around 60 percent) when using a single interface, the addition of additional network resources will not have the desired effect—and may actually decrease performance overall. This is because the new interface will add additional load to these other elements and may reduce performance overall because now one or more of these elements is now overloaded and slowing down overall performance. At this point, additional physical MediaAgents should be considered.

The last method of increasing network performance is to replace older and slower interfaces with newer and faster ones. The most common network interface in use, and the one that is included in almost all newer servers, is the 1 Gigabit Ethernet interface. This interface uses a standard RJ-45 copper connector that has been the basis for Ethernet networking since the mid-1980s. Gigabit Ethernet, however, is beginning to be replaced with 10 Gigabit Ethernet interfaces. This new interface represents an almost 10x increase in performance over traditional Gigabit, but it has some limitations. In the current releases of 10G, there are only two types of NIC interfaces supported: LC optical and twinax (neither of which is compatible with existing wiring infrastructures). Standard RJ45 NIC interfaces, known as 10GBase-T, are just now becoming available, but are not in wide use due to the strict cabling requirements needed for the copper interfaces. If this route is selected, it represents a complete augmentation of existing network infrastructure with new 10G infrastructure, either copper or twinax, which will represent a significant cost. This route would only be recommended if 10G infrastructure has already been deployed as part of the organization's overall network plan.

The addition of a MediaAgent is a judgment call as much as a technical call. This is because although the MediaAgent is not fully utilized at this point, an additional load cannot be placed on it without reducing overall performance—effectively stranding resources in an unused state. The judgment call is from an organizational point of view. Can the organization tolerate the extension of windows judged against the cost of adding new hardware and licensing, and the adjustment of Storage Policies to rebalance the load across the new resource? This question unfortunately cannot be answered definitively from any formulaic or technical point of view, and must be judged almost completely from a cost perspective. However, as the backup administrator you can take the current performance and supportability, extrapolate out the growth effect on both, and present the case based on a datacentric approach.

Storage Resources

Determining the inflection point at which an additional MediaAgent must be added from a network perspective can be difficult; however, the view on the storage side is more complex. Storage performance is driven from a number of different variables, all of which are interrelated and make a determination of performance issues a complex process. Whole books have been written on this subject, but a few general recommendations and configurations will be addressed here:

- Assess storage last

- Ensure proper storage configuration

- Split MagLib storage into multiple chunks

- Use multiple paths to storage

- Tune disk writers to recommendations

Assessing storage performance should only be undertaken once all other components on the MediaAgent have been addressed—network, CPU, memory, and bus configuration all need to be assessed for utilization issues prior to looking at storage performance. This is because these elements are higher in the data flow "stack" than storage; storage is at the bottom of the stack. Backup data flows into the network interface (the "top" of the stack), is buffered and processed on the physical server (CPU and memory are at the middle of the stack), passed on through the bus to either the controller or HBA (depending on storage type), and then passed to the physical storage itself. Any elements above the storage innately affect (limit) the amount of data that can be sent to the storage and thus the overall performance of the storage. However, incorrectly configured, laid out, or utilized storage still has a significant effect on the overall performance of the system. While storage is the bottom of the stack and is affected by the upper layers, storage is also the slowest component of the stack and has the most incremental effect on overall performance. *Once storage is configured properly, the amount of incremental gain in overall system performance will be negligible, but improperly configured storage can impose a significant impact on system performance.* CommVault in particular requires optimal disk layout as it is heavily dependent on disk for many aspects of operation.

When configuring disk storage for use as a MagLib on a MediaAgent, the tendency is to lump all the available storage into a single mount point or LUN and simply have the largest single MagLib available for use. While this may provide a simple way to manage the disk storage space, it is not particularly efficient nor does it provide the best possible performance. When looking at the design of storage layouts for MediaAgents, it is better to split the storage into multiple drive letters, or mount points, create multiple mount paths to the storage on the MediaAgent, assign a number of disk writers to each mount point, and configure Spill/Fill to spread the disk task among the writers.

The exception to this rule is when a single internal controller is used with a small number of drives. Since the number of drives is limited on internal storage, it is best to create RAID groups that span the drives, giving the best possible performance for the LUN. In the internal controller model, the limiting factor becomes the performance of the individual drives, and the constraints on the maximum number of drives that can ever be available for use. In this case, each drive presented as an individual LUN will be slower than the drives grouped together, all combining their available performance into a coordinated whole. (See Figure 6–12.)

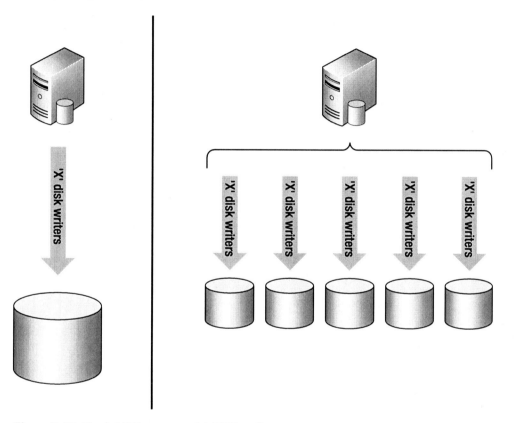

Figure 6–12. Single LUN versus multi-LUN performance

From the CommVault perspective, more mount paths equal more potential disk writers. According to best practice, six disk writers is the standard starting point for RAID 1/0 configurations, and the maximum number for RAID 5 configurations. This number can be increased, depending on the number of drives participating in the RAID configuration; however, the overall number of writers per mount path is limited. So by having a small number of mount paths, or even one mount path, the total number of writers will be completely gated by the number of writers to that single file system.

But by increasing the number of mount paths, the numbers of disk writers increases in proportion to the number of mount paths. So adding a mount path doubles the number of writers, a third path triples the number, and so on. This pattern can be continued up to the limit of the capabilities of the

MediaAgent system to handle parallel processes and to process I/O to the drives. As writers are added, the maximum number of writers of the MagLib as a whole gates the ability of the system to assign writers, so while each individual mount path may be able to have x writers, if the sum of all x over the number of drives exceeds the maximum number of writers for the MagLib as a whole, the number of writers actually running will be reduced. This allows MediaAgents to continue taking on storage capacity, while not exceeding their performance thresholds for overall optimal throughput. However, this global optimization will necessarily be at the expense of the performance of the individual mount paths.

For instance, if the maximum number of writers is set to 18, and there are 3 mount paths, each with 6 writers each, the addition of a fourth mount path with 6 writers will effectively reduce the number of disk writers to 4 (4 mount paths * 4 disk writers = 16 < 18 maximum). The addition of a fifth mount path would reduce it to three—half the maximum of six writers. This has the net effect of cutting the available performance of the individual mount paths in half and thus wasting potential throughput performance. (See Figure 6–13.) This must be caveated by looking at the net ingest rate, however. If the ingest rate does not exceed the total ingest rate possible by the disk writers, the storage has really only been added for capacity—no real performance impact is felt, and the MediaAgent can continue as is.

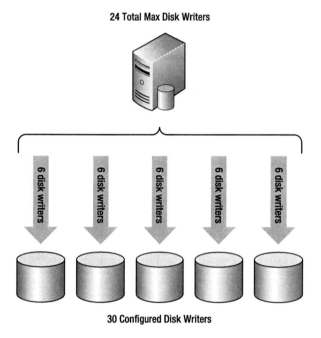

24 Total Max Disk Writers

6 disk writers   6 disk writers   6 disk writers   6 disk writers   6 disk writers

30 Configured Disk Writers

6 configured disk writers will never get used!

Figure 6–13. *Maximum vs. configured disk writers*

When working with multiple controllers or external drive arrays, the smaller multiple mount path method is preferred. Configuring disks into multiple LUNs works better for a number of reasons, even given the same number of disks. When creating a single large LUN, there is a tradeoff between optimizing the performance within the storage array and creating larger LUNs. (See Figure 6–14.)

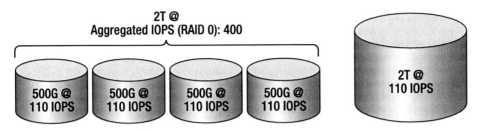

Figure 6–14. Performance trade-offs between size and IOPS

As was discussed in Chapter 2, drive performance of RAID-based storage is far better than that of single disks because the potential IOPS available for any particular drive operation is greater when combining a set of disks that any single disk can provide.

There is a limitation to this, however. When the RAID striping utilizes two disks on the same controller, or "wraps" the RAID set, the controller has to deal with twice the read/write activity for any particular operation to the single LUN, which decreases performance. (See Figure 6–15.) So to avoid this performance penalty, the size of any particular RAID LUN is limited, depending on the configuration of the storage enclosure that houses the physical drives. RAID LUNs, however, can also be put into their own RAID groups, thus increasing performance, as all drives are now participating in the LUN, and no wrapping is occurring to decrease performance.

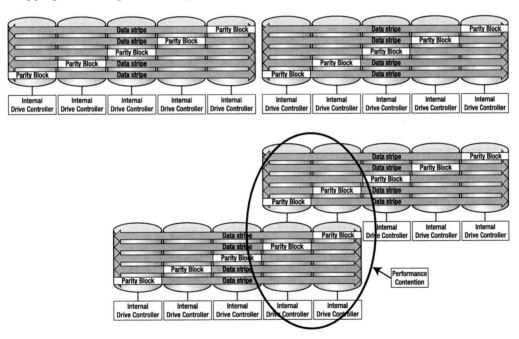

Figure 6–15. Optimal (top) versus suboptimal (bottom) RAID configuration

Great! The problem of having a single large LUN seems to be solved, but what happens if you have to grow that LUN? Since the RAID group is bound two ways—once across the individual RAID groups, and once across the physical disks to create the RAID groups, you cannot simply add drives to the configuration as it will provide an unbalanced configuration that will not perform predictably or consistently. In order to grow the group, the RAID configuration across the LUNs has to be torn down either new RAID groups created using the new and old disks, or a completely new RAID group created and then the RAID configuration replaced on the new combinations of the disks. *This works great, except for the fact that deconstructing RAID groups destroys the data on the group—effectively erasing any backups that were on the LUN.*

The solution to the problem is not to use RAID LUN configurations of RAID groups, but to create smaller ones that end up presenting multiple LUNs to the MediaAgent, rather than a single large LUN. When additional storage needs to be added, simply create a new RAID group configuration and present it as a new mount point to the MediaAgent, and set the configuration appropriately. Setting up the storage in this way also provides optimal performance both from the operating system and CommVault perspective.

By providing multiple paths via the different file systems that have been created for the operating system to use, the I/O load is more evenly distributed between internal processes within the kernel, and both CPU and memory are more efficiently used as a result. With more efficient use comes better performance overall. If a particular file system happens to have more load than the others, it is easy to detect at the OS level and manage from the application level. If there is one, or very few, large individual file systems that are created, there is effectively only one or few paths that can be taken to read/write data from any area. This can create a bottleneck at the operating system level and decrease performance. This is a much simplified view of the operations of the file systems at the kernel layer, but the concept is sound—more file systems can equal better performance, given enough backup streams.

The optimization of this is dependent on the number of backup streams as compared with the number of file systems. If there are fewer backup streams than file systems, this optimization does not add value to the overall performance. However, if the number of backup streams exceeds the number of file systems, and they are balanced via backup software mechanisms across those file systems, the load on any particular process or CPU thread will be balanced with all others doing the same work, thus making efficient use of the available CPU and memory.

As with everything, there are limitations. As some point, if the number of file systems becomes too great, there are too many operations that need to be completed in parallel—thus slowing down the overall performance of the system. This works in a similar way as the network bottlenecks, and finding a balance is the best. In practice, the reasonable administrator would never be able to configure enough file system mount points to completely overwhelm a system, but it is important to understand the basic concept and be able to look at the effect on CPU and memory when adding file systems to the MediaAgent.

So the storage has been addressed, and the operating system and CommVault software has been addressed, but what about the piece that connects them: the controller/HBA? As a whole, there is not much to tune at this level, but there is the issue of paths. When using external storage, frequently there is the ability to provide multiple paths to the same piece of physical storage or LUN presented. To the operating system, in a default configuration, this would look like two different pieces of storage, not the same storage—a particularly confusing problem. The issue is similar to that described when discussing shared storage—the SCSI or FC protocols do not describe specific mechanisms to access or control access to shared storage, but simply provide the means to do so.

Enter the *multipath I/O (MPIO)* drivers. MPIO drivers are specialized drivers, typically provided by the storage provider, that interrogate the external storage about the LUNs being presented to the particular system. If the MPIO driver determines that the same LUN is being presented down the multiple paths, it will present the multiple paths as a single path to higher layers within the operating system. In addition, most MPIO drivers provide the ability to schedule I/O operations to the external storage that has multiple paths, so the overall I/O bandwidth is increased and more I/Os can be sent than would be possible using a single path. Again, the more paths, the more bandwidth—with the limitation being the bandwidth ingestion rate of the array and the ability of the LUNs to absorb the I/Os being sent to them via the multiple paths.

A side effect of the MPIO drivers is that if one path that participates in the load balancing is taken offline, the remaining paths automatically pick the load up. However, the amount of available bandwidth on the surviving paths is reduced by the amount that was previously on the failed path. So if the backup is dependent on the full or nearly full utilization of all available paths, if a single path fails, the throughput should be expected to be reduced by a significant amount, with the net effect of slowing backups.

So, given all these factors in storage (RAID configuration, multiple mount points, disk writer counts, and MPIO drivers) how is the inflection point determined to add additional MediaAgents based on storage? When any one of the areas described previously exceeds 70 percent of available capacity or bandwidth, it is time to consider adding an additional MediaAgent to absorb the load. Note that this is *not* based on the capacity of the storage or the performance of the array. If the capacity of a particular mount path is becoming full (80–85 percent or greater), it is time to add an additional mount path. If the overall ability of the array to absorb additional IOPS is being reached, it is time to look at the addition of an additional array or to upgrade the existing array to be able to process more I/O. Neither of these conditions necessarily warrants a new MediaAgent.

However, when the addition of the mount path causes any one of these issues, it is time to consider a new MediaAgent:

- *CPU* Increase in CPU or memory load that would exceed 70–80 percent of utilization overall or cause a noticeable decrease in the overall performance of the physical server providing the MediaAgent services. This could be due to the number of processes or (much less likely) the number of file systems to manage pushing kernel performance limits.

- *Throughput measurement* No increase in throughput or a decrease in throughput at the disk layer when an additional mount path is added. This can indicate that the controller is becoming saturated with work. If there is only one path to storage, and a second path can be added to the same storage, this may help alleviate the issue. However, if this occurs in a multipath system, while the addition of yet more paths may help, it may be simpler to acquire an additional MediaAgent. This becomes more of a cost/risk decision than a technical one. For instance, if a MediaAgent has two paths to storage, with multiple mount paths, the controller may be simply overloaded. In this case, the addition of another set of paths (controllers/HBAs should always be added in pairs to maintain symmetry of operation) may offload enough of the traffic to rebalance the load and allow the MediaAgent to keep functioning. The downside is that the addition of the addition I/O path may expose CPU or memory weakness that was not detected because due to masking by the throughput issue—thus requiring an additional MediaAgent to solve.

- *Active disk writer count* The average number of writers per mount path drops to equal or below half the individual path configured maximum in a RAID 5 or RAID 1/0 configuration. Once the maximum number of writers per MagLib has been determined, the addition of additional mount paths will reduce the number of writers per mount path in proportion to the overall maximum disk writers.

The combination of network and storage factors, as reflected in overall system performance and server utilization, provides indicators as to how and when to deploy additional MediaAgents in the general case. However, what if a server is so large, or transfers data over the network at such a slow rate, that it is not practical to back up to a MediaAgent? In this case, a combined client/MediaAgent may be the solution. In most installations, the client sends backup data to the MediaAgent for storage on the appropriate media. In the case of the client/MediaAgent combination, the client self-references the

MediaAgent target and sends data directly to backup media that are locally attached, not to an external MediaAgent. Since the throughput to the storage can easily exceed that available to the network, especially given the shared nature of the network interfaces, the overall performance of the backup is increased, the network and storage load of a long-term backup is removed from the general MediaAgent with the potential net effect of all backups increasing in performance.

Some situations where a client/MediaAgent may be implemented are the following:

- *Total data size* Data to be transferred is too large to be transferred using the network speed available, within the backup-defined backup window.

- *Network transfer speed* The client is behind a firewall, located on a slow network link, or at the end of a wide area network (WAN). These three situations represent slow or impeded networks that can prevent backup data from being transferred.

- *Current MediaAgent load* The general MediaAgent is becoming overloaded due to the particular client load. For instance, if the general-purpose MediaAgent is backing up 100 clients, but a single client consistently and continuously consumes 40 percent of the network bandwidth and 60 percent of the storage, making that single client a MediaAgent will free those resources for use by the remaining 99 clients. This would prevent the purchase of a completely new piece of hardware, as when the client causing the issue is converted to a client/MediaAgent, the backup load is offloaded back to the client and freeing resources for the general MediaAgent.

The flexible deployment option of both general-purpose and/or client/MediaAgents allows the administrator to balance the needs of both large and small clients, crafting a solution that meets the needs of the enterprise as a whole, but is tailored to meet the needs of individual clients. By adding both types of MediaAgents, a CommCell can grow horizontally to very large scales, but what happens with the limits of an individual CommCell are reached, and when are new CommCells required? That is the subject of the next section.

Multiple CommCells

There are limits to single CommCells. The conditions that trigger consideration of the creation of additional CommCells are the following:

- Unreliable network links

- Locations separated by long network distances

- Legal or organizational needs

- Multiple large data centers

- Performance degradation on the primary CommCell

When placing MediaAgents at remote locations, it is important to be able to have reliable communications back to the CommServe in order to ensure that clients are properly scheduled and contacted, as well as to ensure that the metadata regarding the client backups is properly stored. If the network separating the CommServe and the clients is unreliable or has noise that causes a number of network packet losses or retransmissions, the communication necessary to make sure that clients are properly started and tracked either may not happen or happen in a way that slows the backup process down. An example is the placement of a MediaAgent in Fiji that is part of a CommCell based in San Francisco. The theoretical latency between the sites is on the order of 300 ms, and given the remote nature and the number of hops required to make the link, there would most likely be significant packet loss as well. If network issues such as these cannot be resolved, then by placing a secondary CommServe at the remote site, the communication becomes local and bypasses the issue.

Related to unreliable network conditions are the conditions associated with long-distance networks that can induce the same type of problems. As distances between points on networks increase, the round trip time of packets to travel between the sites also increases. This is known as the "time-distance" problem that encapsulates the issue of measured latency on long-distance network links.

In long-distance types of environments, although there may be plenty of network bandwidth available, if the distances that the network packets have to travel are more than 1,000 statute miles (approximately 1,600 km), the net throughput of the network may begin to drop. The drop in performance will slow the transmission of metadata from the remote site, thus reducing the overall backup performance. While this may not be noticeable for small data backups, for larger backups, particularly those consisting of large numbers of files, this increase in metadata transfer time becomes apparent quickly. Again, the addition of a CommCell at the remote site avoids the distance problems, localizing backups.

Many organizations have divisions that handle information that is sensitive, such as personal identifiable information (PII), information around financial transactions executed by broker/dealers, and other information of a sensitive nature. Organizations also may have subsidiary organizations that must remain separate for legal or regulatory reasons, including infrastructure pertaining to the business. Depending on the nature and requirements of the sensitive information, it may be necessary to create completely separate infrastructures, including backup infrastructure, in order to completely isolate the sensitive information from the general population of the organization or to support isolated physical environments created for the information. An example of a type of organization that requires this type of isolation is the Broker/Dealer division found within many U.S. banks. These divisions handle highly sensitive information that if released would have significant financial impact on not only the bank but also potentially the account holders, the companies that do business with the bank, and even companies that are traded through the Broker/Dealer division.

In order to support these types of environments, it is necessary to create a separate CommCell that fully contains the information regarding backups of this type of information. A common CommCell could not be used, as even the metainformation regarding the backups can be construed as sensitive information because it can convey the nature of the content or provide information regarding particular files or file types that would contain the sensitive information that is to be protected.

The last two situations involve numbers of *client density*. As the number of clients grows, the amount of metadata the CommServe has to manage grows exponentially. This is because although the number of files and backups can remain constant, because each file has to be tracked over time, the number of entries in the metadata database grows. As the number of clients grows, this process becomes more resource-intensive and eventually reaches the limits of the CommServe physical capability. This can happen within a single data center, particularly within large centers as the number of clients grows over the life cycle of the center.

The other effect of client density occurs when attempting to manage multiple large centers in a single CommCell. In addition to the number of servers in each large center, there is also a consideration of the network connectivity between the sites. The amount of metadata that is transmitted by the clients over a WAN link that connects the central to the remote site, can consume large portions (sometimes over 50 percent) of the link. If enough of the link is consumed, the overall performance of the WAN link decreases, thus decreasing the transmission rate of the metadata. The ultimate effect of the reduction in the rate at which metadata is transmitted is a corresponding decrease in the throughput rates of the client backup that rely on having fast, reliable metadata transfer rates.

In either case, the number of clients will dictate the need to install a secondary CommCell to manage the remote site as a separate entity. There are not a theoretical number of clients that will drive such a decision in this case. The inflection point that helps determine the point at which a secondary CommCell could be created is the overall performance of the backup environment, as compared with the performance of the CommServe with regard to CPU and I/O capabilities. Once either of these details approaches 80 percent of utilization on a regular basis, it is time to consider the addition of a secondary CommServe.

■ **Note** CommVault is unique because there is a standard process by which CommCells can be split in controlled fashion, creating entirely separate environments. This process involves creating a CommCell and then migrating the metadata from the original CommCell to the newly created one. However, this process can take time and requires detailed planning and execution, with CommVault Professional Services *strongly recommended*. Once a CommCell is split, however, it cannot be put back together, so the decision to split a CommCell must not be taken lightly. Once the CommCell is split, each CommCell is managed separately, which can make coordination and management of the enterprise difficult. CommVault provides a product called CommNet that provides basic unified reporting against multiple CommCells, but does not provide a method of unified management—that must still be accomplished by the discrete management of each CommCell.

These basic configurations and decision points form the basis of all designs using CommVault components. The combination of clients, MediaAgents, client/MediaAgents, and multiple CommServes provide the ability to start small and scale to as large as necessary to fit the particular environment in which CommVault has been deployed.

Summary

CommVault provides a flexible solution that allows the backup administrator to tailor the configuration to the needs of the organization. However, as was shown, the backup software is not the only element that needs to be considered when deploying or upgrading a CommCell. Items such as the configuration and performance of the LAN and WAN, storage configuration and layout, and the CPU and RAM consumption within the individual backup servers all go into thinking about how to deploy a CommVault solution. CommVault shares many similarities with the other product addressed in the book—NetBackup also provides some unique capabilities, such as the ability to have a controlled, repeatable split of CommCells into smaller units as operational necessities dictate.

CHAPTER 7

■■■■

Software Architectures—NetBackup

Where the previous chapter dealt with the specifics of CommVault, this chapter will look in depth at Symantec NetBackup. NetBackup shares many high-level architectural similarities with CommVault:

- *Central control server* Both use a central point of control for the backup operations within a zone of control, called a *Storage Domain* in NetBackup parlance. The central server is a Master Server in NetBackup, as compared with the CommServe in CommVault CommCells.

- *Distributed backup data writing* NetBackup uses Media Servers in a similar fashion as CommVault uses MediaAgents—to offload the I/O load associated with writing backups to the target media. However, NetBackup takes a different approach to the storage of the metadata than does CommVault, as will be demonstrated later.

As in the previous chapter, if you are an exclusive user of CommVault, this chapter may be extraneous; however, the comparison of functionality between CommVault and NetBackup may provide insight into issues that may arise in both environments.

General Configuration

In Chapter 2, we reviewed some of the components that make up a NetBackup Storage Domain. However, before we start putting pieces together, it is important to understand some of the more important tuning and configuration parameters that NetBackup uses. This is one area where NetBackup differs from CommVault—many of the tuning parameters used by NetBackup are set either in configuration files or in environment variables. This difference in configuration methods results from where each of the products was originally developed: CommVault was developed primarily as a Microsoft Windows–based application, whereas NetBackup evolved from the early UNIX environments—an almost exclusively command-line driven environment.

While there are many different tuning and configuration parameters, and there exist many debates regarding any list of the most important ones to review, most users and groups agree that the following are within the top 10 of any list to look at within a NetBackup configuration:

- Multiplexing/multistreaming

- Inline deduplication (twinning)

- Buffer tuning

- Secondary copy creation

Multiplexing/Multistreaming

These two terms are frequently confused, and will be relied upon heavily in the following discussions. So it is important to understand that they are distinct from one another and relate to completely different areas of backup performance.

Multistreaming is the ability to generate multiple backup jobs, or streams, from a single client as a result of the execution of a backup policy. This is useful for clients to back up different file systems, databases, or application elements at the same time, thus creating more work completed per unit time. Multistreaming happens at the client, prior to the backup stream leaving the client for the Media Server and is configured at the policy level. All clients that are contained with a policy that sets multistreaming are affected by the setting. It is important to understand this as if clients are included into policies with multistreaming that do not have the needed resources may have their backup stream slow down, or worse, slow the applications that are running on the backup server during the backup process.

Where multistreaming is executed on the client, multiplexing happens on the Media Server and is applied after the backup stream has left the client. *Multiplexing* is the ability to interleave different backup streams to optimize backup data transfer to the target media. Since multiplexing happens once the backup image reaches the Media Server, its application has no effect on the client configuration, *per se*. Multiplexing allows slow jobs to be augmented with fast ones in an attempt to prevent tape device shoeshining. As disk does not suffer from this effect, multiplexing backups to Disk Storage Units (DSUs) has no effect. Multiplexing is also applied at the policy level. Although both are applied at the policy level, multiplexing and multistreaming are completely independent of each other—one, both, or neither can be applied to any policy as necessary.

Inline Deduplication (Twinning)

Inline deduplication, also known as *twinning*, is a NetBackup feature that allows the creation of multiple copies from a single backup image, all running in parallel. This provides a mechanism to create a secondary copy without having to have a separate backup image duplication job to process an already executed backup. Inline deduplication is executed based on what NetBackup calls a *schedule*—a section within the backup policy that defines when a backup is executed. The Attributes tab of the schedule, as shown in Figure 7–1, has a check box for multiple copies—this is where inline deduplication is set.

This feature is implemented through job management—instead of creating a single backup job that represents the client/policy/schedule combination, NetBackup creates a new job for each copy created—a master job and a backup job for each copy. This *master job* is simply a special type of backup job that acts as the primary backup job for the client and a controlling job for each copy that is made. The master job is the only job that is receiving data directly from the client, with the remaining child jobs simply there to transfer the result of the master job to the media in a parallel operation. The subordinate jobs are autonomous from each other and semi-autonomous from the master job.

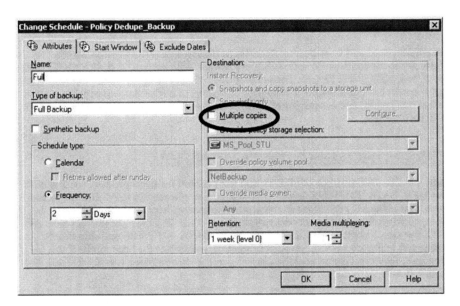

Figure 7–1. Multiple copies check box on the Attributes tab

This can be a very powerful feature and should be implemented with the following considerations in mind:

- *Performance*–To achieve the most consistent performance, all targets participating in the inline deduplication should be the same type with the same connectivity. This is not a requirement—there may be instances where different media types are needed, depending on items such as location, size of media, and so on. However, when tape or connectivity types are mixed, it can produce an indeterminate effect on the speed and reliability of the backup because the completion of the backup from the NetBackup perspective is dependent on the slowest device and on the completion status of the subordinate job streams.

- *Device resource requirements*–When implemented, the operation does not take away from existing backup streams. Said another way, it is necessary to effectively double the number of target devices that are currently in use.

- *Targeted implementation*—Target only those clients that require immediate secondary copies. All other clients should utilize normal duplication techniques (as detailed later).

- *Check Media Server resources*–Ensure that Media Server memory and CPU resources are available when implementing inline deduplication. Each device uses a set of buffers that resides in RAM on the Media Server. The RAM resources will double when inline is implemented. In addition, the number of processes that are executed to support inline also doubles, so ensure that enough CPU time is available to support double the number of bptm processes that normally run.

Buffer Tuning Parameters

NetBackup has multiple variables that can be tuned to alter the performance of the Master, Media Server, and Client, but there are three main parameters that are always adjusted: SIZE_DATA_BUFFERS, NUMBER_DATA_BUFFERS, and NET_BUFFER_SZ. These three variable control the basic data flow from client to targets through the control of the amount of memory allocated to buffer data streams in a an attempt to either shield slow devices from a onslaught of data, or gather data from slow devices in order to maximize throughput to faster ones.

SIZE_DATA_BUFFERS/NUMBER_DATA_BUFFERS

These two variables govern the size and number of buffers that are created for each process writing data to a particular device. The SIZE_DATA_BUFFERS defines the size of a single area in RAM that is reserved for use by the bptm process that processes the backup stream to the master bptm, which generates its own buffers to buffer the input from the child bptm processes. The NUMBER_DATA_BUFFERS defines the number of buffers, with the size, in bytes, specified by the SIZE _DATA_BUFFERS variable that is created. These two exist to provide the maximum amount of tuning to account for both sides of the performance equation: the data flow coming in, and the capacity of the device going out. By default, the value for each variable is as follows:

    NUMBER_DATA_BUFFERS = 16
    SIZE_DATA_BUFFERS = 65536

These are tuned by observing the output in the bptm logs and watching for either unused buffers or queued requests for buffers. If these conditions are observed, then increasing the number of buffers may help the situation. However, if the number of buffer queues continues to increase, then the throughput of the Media Server needs to be addressed. The size of the data buffers can be tuned to match the optimum throughput of the attached devices and/or host bus adapter (HBA). This allows blocks of data to be transferred and placed on the media without fragmentation.

The DATA_BUFFER tunables consume system memory, thus taking away from memory that can be used for applications and other system requirements. Since each bptm process consumes the number of buffers specified in NUMBER at the size specified in SIZE, the total amount of memory consumed is specified by the following:

$$M = N_S * N_D * \text{SIZE\_DATA\_BUFFERS} * \text{NUMBER\_DATA\_BUFFERS}$$

Where:

M = RAM required

N_S = Number of backup streams

N_D = Number of backup devices

Take the following example:

Media Server device count (N_D): 5

Number of backups per device (N_S): 5

SIZE_DATA_BUFFERS: 65536 (Default)

NUMBER_DATA_BUFFERS: 16 (Default)

When you apply this configuration to the formula above, the result is:

$M = N_s * N_D *$ SIZE_DATA_BUFFERS $*$ NUMBER_DATA_BUFFERS

$M = 5 * 5 * 65536 * 16$

$M = 26214000 \; bytes$

$M = \sim 25MB$

So, with a simple configuration in which 25 different streams are coming to a single Media Server, 25 MB of RAM is consumed. This is a relatively small number of devices and simultaneous streams to a single Media Server. If these variables are tuned, say by adding more buffers, increasing the size of each buffer, or both, the amount of memory consumed can increase quickly.

NET_BUFFER_SZ

This variable works in a similar manner to the NUMBER_DATA_BUFFERS and SIZE_DATA_BUFFERS, except instead of working on the media targets and data pathways, it works on the network pathway. The variable adjusts the TCP/IP socket buffer size in an attempt to provide a mechanism to ensure that the network has data to send, especially from slow clients. NET_BUFFER_SZ is set both on the client and the Media Server. The size of this value can be as large as 256 kB, with a default size of 32 kB. While the sizes of the NET_BUFFER between clients and the Media Servers are not required to match, for optimal performance, and to ensure that the NET_BUFFERs are filling the DATA_BUFFERS as quickly as possible, the two values should match.

NET_BUFFER_SZ is the value that is set on UNIX clients and on all types of Media Servers; however, on Windows clients, this value is set in the registry or within NetBackup as the Communication Buffer value.

Creating Secondary Copies (Vault/bpduplicate)

As discussed earlier, NetBackup offers inline deduplication to create copies of backups as the backup is happening by using parallel devices to create the copy. However, if this method is not used, secondary copies can be created after the fact using either the bpduplicate command or through the use of NetBackup Vault. Bpduplicate is a command-line-interface (CLI) command that takes an image name, list of images (via a script or time range), or media ID, and makes a copy on to new media. The retention of the new copy of the image can be changed during this process, creating two copies of the same image, each with different expiration times.

On the other hand, Vault is a licensed feature of NetBackup that not only creates copies of backup images but also manages the life cycle of the copies as well. As copies expire, are scheduled to move between locations, and are required to be recalled back into the environment, Vault tracks and generates reports that allow administrators to manage media that contain these images. Vault can manage media, containing duplicate images that are created after the backups are created or image copies that are created during inline deduplication. An interesting side note is that Vault actually leverages bpduplicate under the covers to create any needed secondary backup image copies.

Generic Configurations

There are several ways to configure NetBackup Master Servers. You might want to use a single target (where the Master Server is also the Media Server, or use a separate single Media Server, or, if you need additional capacity, you can set up a Master Server with multiple Media Servers.

NetBackup Master with a Single Target

The most basic configuration is that of an environment with a single target for media and a single Storage Domain. This single Storage Domain would consist of only a single NetBackup Master Server, which could act as a both a Media Server and NetBackup Master Server simultaneously. This configuration provides a very basic environment in which to implement a Storage Domain, and is a microcosm of all the elements of a Storage Domain. However, this type of implementation is typically only found in very small environments as the ability of the Master Server to ingest data can be rapidly overshadowed by the performance requirements of the backup management portion of the unified platform. For most implementations, the additional cost of a separate Media Server will save costs of expansion as the backup need grows. This need can be in environments with client counts as low as 30 servers, depending on the amount of data or number of files that are contained within the Storage Domain. Figure 7–2 shows the relationship between the Master Server and the Media Server.

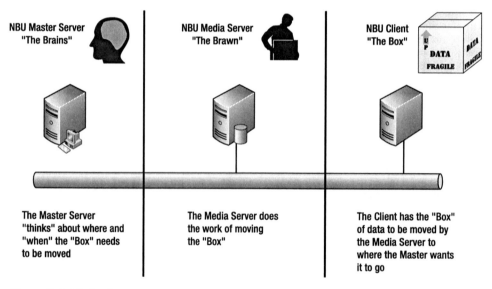

NBU Master Server "The Brains"

NBU Media Server "The Brawn"

NBU Client "The Box"

DATA FRAGILE

The Master Server "thinks" about where and "when" the "Box" needs to be moved

The Media Server does the work of moving the "Box"

The Client has the "Box" of data to be moved by the Media Server to where the Master wants it to go

Figure 7–2. NetBackup components

NetBackup Master with a Single Media Server

This is the most common environment in most NetBackup configurations. This configuration consists of a NetBackup Master Server and a single Media Server that provides backup services to the Storage Domain. This configuration also forms the basis for all other environments to follow.

The configuration provides the basis for horizontal scalability. Horizontal scalability is the core of any good architecture, regardless of product. This is the ability to provide increases in capacity without the necessity to add additional control mechanisms, such as a NetBackup Master Server. There are several reasons to avoid creating additional Master Servers:

- Clients backed up in one Storage Domain cannot be restored in another Storage Domain without an extensive client migration process.

- Media created in one Storage Domain cannot be used in another without a time-consuming scanning process.

- Client, media, and duplication policies are unique to the Storage Domain.

Creating additional Storage Domains to solve scalability problems actually creates many more scaling problems than it solves—it is simply that the scaling problems now become operational instead of technical or performance-based. The use of Media Servers avoids these issues by simply placing a system that does all the heavy lifting, removing that load from the Master Server, while maintaining centralized management of policies and clients.

As with CommVault MediaAgents, additional Media Servers may be deployed to support general-purpose uses, such as growth in the number of clients that need backup at a particular time. Alternatively, a standard NetBackup client may be "promoted" to also have Media Server functionality to allow the client the ability to move data directly to media instead of through a general-purpose MediaAgent. This combination of a NetBackup client and Media Server is referred to as a *Dedicated Media Server*—a Media Server that is dedicated to serving only one client—itself. This dedication is enforced at the Master Server via licensing and policy, so other standard NetBackup clients cannot be accidentally configured to use the Dedicated Media Server as a general-purpose one.

Here's the good news: the same tuning and configuration that will be described here applies to either general-purpose or Dedicated Media Servers. So regardless of which type is the first Media Server deployed, there is no configuration difference between them. As the environment grows, there will be a collection of both general-purpose and Dedicated Media Servers within the environment, so it is important to understand where to deploy them. In the section regarding multiple Media Servers, the deployment rationale for Dedicated Media Servers will be discussed in detail. In most cases, the first Media Server is a general-purpose one, so that is the context in which the single Media Server deployment will be discussed.

Storage Units

The intent of scaling environments by adding a Media Server is to provide an alternate point to which the backups can be written, offloading this task from the Master Server and freeing it up to manage the environment as a whole. But how does the Master Server ensure that backups are not directed to itself for backup, instead of to the new Media Server? This is done through the use of logical containers called Storage Units. A Storage Unit contains a group of devices with that can be identified as backup media targets for different policies to use. Figure 7–3 shows you how to configure a Storage Unit.

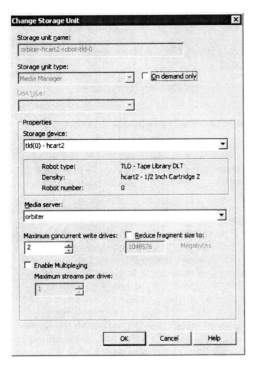

***Figure 7–3.** NetBackup Storage Unit configuration*

When creating Storage Units for a single Media Server configuration, it is important to ensure that separate Storage Units be created for the devices attached to the Media Server from those attached to the Master Server. Any existing policies, as well as any new ones, should only use Storage Units associated with the Media Server and not those created for the Master Server. Configuring the Storage Units and policies in this way will force client backups to the Media Server, reserving any Master Server Storage Unit for the Master itself.

Forcing the backups to go to the Media Server in this manner allows the Master to take on its role as operational manager of backups, not providing primary backup services. As the environment grows, the Master will not have the overhead to deal with performing backups as well as managing the Storage Domain. While it is relatively straightforward to shift policies to use storage units on Media Servers instead of on a Master Server, in order to avoid unpredictable performance as the environment grows and load increases.

From an overall construction perspective, the Media Server should utilize a Disk Storage Unit (DSU) if the primary backup is to remain on local disk, or a Disk Staging Storage Unit (DSSU) if the disk is only intended to be used as a temporary, staging area, for the backup image on its way to permanent storage media. If a DSSU is used, the backup is purged from the Storage Unit media once the copy is made on the intended storage. (See Figure 7–4.)

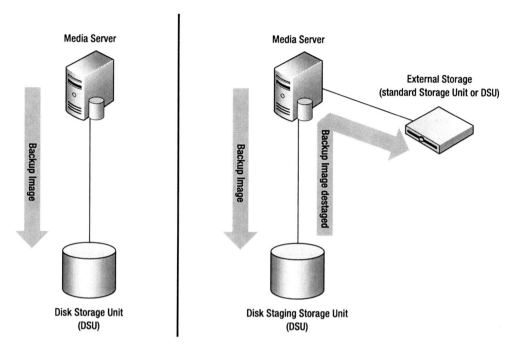

Figure 7–4. Disk Storage Unit versus Disk Staging Storage Unit

Storage Unit Media Selection

This configuration implies that there are two types of media when using a DSSU or, in the case of a single Media Server, a DSU. This is correct—in this configuration, the Storage Domain should have two types of media present: disk and some other external storage. The external storage configuration can be physical tape, virtual tape library (VTL), or disk storage, but it must be a type of media that is intended to provide a low-cost, alternate copy of the media, freeing up the more expensive disk-based storage for use in other backups. This also provides secondary protection against failure of the Media Server, particularly the disk storage associated with the DSU or DSSU associated with temporary storage. Simply having a DSU may seem effective and can be useful; however, it provides a risk of having all backups be dependent on the Media Server. If the Media Server fails, it is far easier to simply reattach a library or external storage and re-inventory than it is to try to move physical disks or to re-create backups.

When looking at the growth scenario, simply having all the backups stored within a single set of internal disks does not provide a mechanism to easily move clients and their backups between Media Servers without extensive copying of data between the "new" and "old" Media Server. When looking at this type of configuration, it is important to identify how to grow such an environment. If this type of configuration represents a small environment without potential to grow out of the single Media Server, simply providing internal protected (RAID) storage for the DSU, adjusting the DATA_BUFFER variables for optimal performance, and directly connecting the external storage is the appropriate solution.

The exception to this is if the DSU is using disk storage that is attached with CIFS or NFS, such as a NetApp filer, a Windows file server providing a CIFS share, or other types of TCP/IP-based storage. This effectively creates both a primary and secondary mechanism as it separates the storage of the backups from the physical Media Server. (See Figure 7–5.) The separation has the effect of allowing the primary to still have locality versus the physical server that the Media Server resides upon, but allows the ability to easily recover from a Media Server failure or to a growth scenario. In this case, a secondary copy would *not* need to be created; this also implies that the storage unit would be a DSU (permanent) versus a DSSU (staging) as there is not a secondary copy. *However, it is still may be prudent to create a secondary copy for use as an offsite copy, or for further protection.*

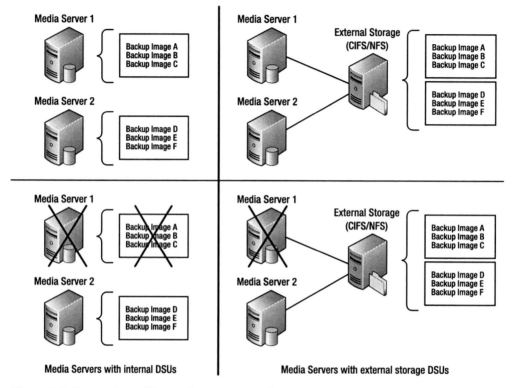

Figure 7–5. Comparison of internal versus external storage

Regardless of connection type, any external direct connected types of storage—disk, VTL, or physical tape can be connected to other servers via various connection mechanisms, primarily the sharing of connections to the storage types via Y cables, SCSI-3 reserve/release protocols, Fibre Channel, or combinations thereof. The mechanisms for device sharing were discussed at length in Chapters 2, 3, and 4, and should be reviewed when considering this type of method. Direct connect sharing methods limits the number of servers that can share the resource for growth, typically to no more than two, so if growth is slow, this type of connection may last the lifetime of the backup solution.

Unless the environment is completely static, represents a remote office location with extremely limited space, or have other constraints that severely limit the hardware that can be installed, it is strongly recommended that small tape libraries be deployed instead of multiple tape drives, even in the case of a single tape drive being required for the backup. This avoids the necessity to remember to physically insert/remove tapes from drives and provides a small cache of tapes that can be used in the case of a backup overrunning a single tape and an operator not being present to switch tapes.

In addition, the small tape library also provides the ability to grow easily as described, effectively doubling throughput simply by adding connections, but not doubling the management overhead of now inserting tapes (correctly) into different drives. The small library also aids in media management by providing the ability to insert/remove tapes in a bulk basis (say for weekly offsite storage or tape rotation) versus managing individual tapes that can be more easily lost. Costs of small libraries are typically not significantly higher than the cost of two drives, plus the costs of losing that first organizationally critical backup, and provide a much better level of protection than the single tape drive.

Advanced Storage Unit Media types

For environments that have a potential for faster growth, it is desirable to implement more dynamic types of storage connectivity: iSCSI, CIFS/NFS, or Fibre Channel–based storage. A shared storage environment, such as a low-cost drive array that acts as an iSCSI target, makes an excellent, low-cost option to provide storage to a single Media Server, with the option of adding additional Media Servers to account for future growth. iSCSI provides the ability to have a common platform, with a relatively efficient protocol, that can provide storage services to both Storage Domain needs as well as other application needs. This can be accomplished with a minimum of cost and a high utilization of storage resources. If you are considering iSCSI as a storage platform, there are a number of excellent resources available that can cover the advantages and disadvantages of this protocol for general use; they should be consulted prior to making any decisions regarding the implementation of this storage model.

NAS Storage

A CIFS/NFS implementation also provides an inexpensive method of implementing a DSU that can be expanded for use easily from a single Media Server. Storage utilization is high as the CIFS/NFS share utilizes common storage and manages the storage platform as a single entity, not as discrete LUNs as does the iSCSI solution. CIFS and NFS are also mature protocols with well-known limitations regarding their implementation, many of which are discussed in Chapter 3. The major limitation that should be considered when planning for a growth model is that of the protocol overhead. CIFS in particular typically has a very high overhead requirement that can impact the amount of performance that can be provided. While this overhead is not necessarily visible in a single Media Server model, it can become visible once more Media Servers are added to the share. Another factor to consider is the management of the storage on the CIFS/NFS provider and its impact on the overall performance of the storage being provided for use by the Media Server. Again, a simple storage layout (for instance, a single RAID 5 group shared as one "lump" of storage accessible by all shares) may be sufficient for a very small number of Media Servers; such a layout will quickly lose performance as more demand is placed on it. When considering a CIFS/NFS-based approach for the Media Server storage, even in the single Media Server model of this section, you should account for this type of issue as it is difficult to change if the environment grows and you want to utilize this common storage for multiple users and applications, including NetBackup-based ones.

SAN Storage

For those environments that are starting small but anticipate very fast growth and high performance requirements, Fibre Channel is the way to go. However, as the most expensive and management intensive option for Media Server storage, it is not to be considered lightly, and there must be preparations made in terms of training and expectations prior to implementation. Fibre Channel provides the highest speed storage, up to 8 Gb/sec in current implementations, and can be shared between servers at the LUN level. Since Fibre Channel uses a dedicated network, known as a storage area network (SAN), to provide storage services, it is typically not subject to the same type of issues that iSCSI and CIFS/NFS implementations suffer from. But such specialization comes at a cost, both in terms of capital outlay and additional administration.

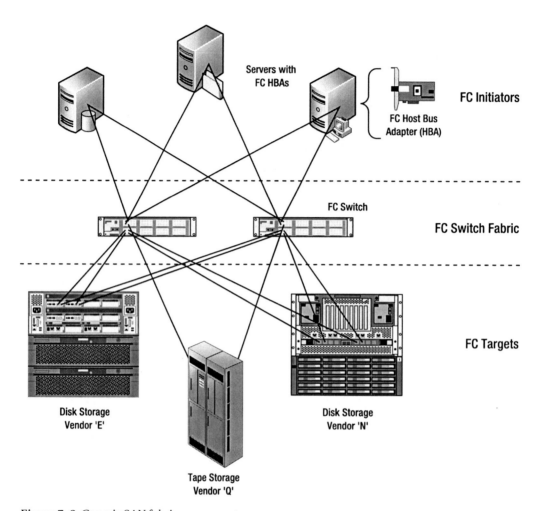

Figure 7–6. *Generic SAN fabric components*

SAN implementations do require a number of specialized components that make them a choice for single Media Server implementations only in situations where growth will be accelerated and performance is at a premium. Media Servers participating in a SAN environment require specialized HBAs to connect and access the storage offered on the network. Storage arrays also must be attached to this network, which may remove the array from other types of connectivity, depending on the array vendor and model. The SAN itself requires connectivity management that is completely separate from that provided by standard TCP/IP networks, which in turn requires specialized knowledge to design and maintain, which begets higher administration overhead for the environment as a whole. Figure 7–7 illustrates the difference between NAS and SAN storage.

Single Media Server implementations with SAN-based storage typically utilize dedicated LUNs for DSU implementations in order to provide high-density, high-speed storage for use as storage targets. This storage is located on a common set of arrays that provides the ability to manage the storage from a single location, thus allowing storage to be effectively allocated, both from a capacity and performance perspective.

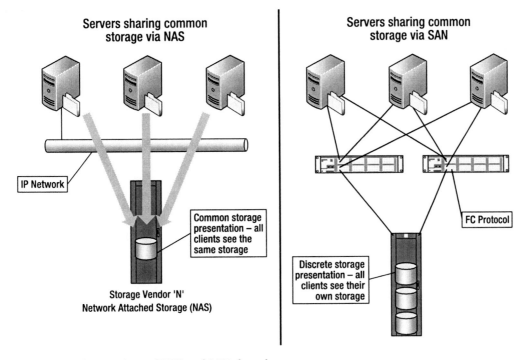

Figure 7–7. Comparison of NAS and SAN shared storage

This type of storage allows both the Media Server to be easily replaced in case of a failure, or upgraded while maintaining the storage contents, as they are externally located. SAN-based disk also allows for the utilization of more rack dense Media Servers. Since the server that contains the Media Server does not have to also hold all the storage associated with the particular Media Server as the critical storage resides externally, there only needs to be enough storage to hold the operating system plus the NetBackup software. Servers implemented this way still do not share storage in the same way as a CIFS or NFS share does, but do share storage array locations.

NetBackup Master with multiple Media Servers

Once the single Media Server environment has grown beyond its bounds, the next logical expansion point, as defined by a horizontal capacity model, is to add additional Media Servers to provide potential capacity from both a storage and throughput perspective. These two areas are not necessarily dependent on each other, and a shortage on one does not imply a shortage on another. Frequently one of the resources is consumed far quicker than the other, which forces a decision to move to the expansion via addition.

Network Resources

Network resources are consumed with every backup, but are released for reuse at the conclusion of every backup—when a backup starts, it sends network traffic in the form of backup data to the Media Server; when it completes, that traffic ends and any bandwidth consumed is freed for use by other clients performing backups. As more clients utilize the existing connections on a single Media Server in parallel, less and less bandwidth becomes freed per unit time. At some point, the network interfaces becomes used at its maximum capacity (saturated). At saturation, no additional traffic can be added to the interface at a particular time without impacting the performance of all other users of the same interface.

Just as with CommVault, network performance discussions center around two items:

- Network performance views are centered around point-in-time measurements.

- Network saturation can occur periodically, but can be recovered from by removing traffic.

So again as with CommVault, before adding additional Media Servers or network interfaces to solve network performance problems, look at the overall traffic pattern and compare it with the backup schedule. Most of the time network performance issues can be solved simply by moving the time when backups start to times when other backups are finishing. Not to belabor this point, but schedule adjustments are the most overlooked solution to performance problems, particularly those involving network utilization. This is because while network utilization is measured as point-in-time snapshots, the tendency is to think that because a network interface has reached saturation during one snapshot or window, the entire interface is therefore saturated at all times.

NetBackup administrators do not tend to schedule backups any differently than do their CommVault counterparts: the backup window starts at a particular time, all backups start at the very beginning of the window, or may be staggered within a few hours of the backup window. The now familiar traffic pattern is generated by this burst of backups (see Figure 7–8).

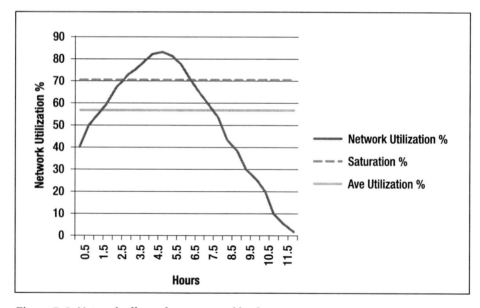

Figure 7–8. Network effects of concentrated backup starts

Note that all the work comes during the beginning of the backup window and rapidly tapers off after the first half of the window. In this particular case, the maximum (saturation) utilization is at 70 percent of the theoretical maximum—any activity that happens above this saturation value will degrade in performance globally over all connections. Said another way, there is a traffic jam—too much traffic on too few lanes. After the middle of the window, the traffic rapidly declines because the shorter-running backup jobs have completed, leaving the longer-running jobs to have the remaining bandwidth. But notice what the average utilization is for the entire window—it is well below the saturation value. But most administrators design for the first half of the window and create an ever-increasing requirement for network bandwidth that does not necessarily need to be satisfied—there is still plenty of bandwidth available, but it is being inefficiently utilized throughout the backup window.

If a client starts at the beginning of the windows, but finishes within a couple of hours, then why not move the client start time to after the longer running backups complete, but still allow it to finish within the allotted window? This may be possible, given that there are no business or technical requirements that the backup run at a specific time, and no windows that are specific to particular applications or business functions. If this is undertaken, it will introduce some additional administrative and operational overhead into the environment as the backup administrator will continuously have to reassess the environment looking for new "imbalances" in the client backup times. However, if the effort is put into this analysis, the result is to effectively remove network traffic from the interface and allot it to jobs that need to run for longer periods of time. In an ideal world, the long-running backup jobs would be balanced with shorter running ones, creating networks that would vary around an average utilization point that was well below the saturation point, such as the performance curve shown in Figure 7–9.

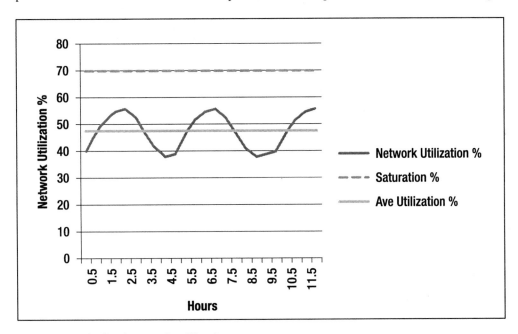

Figure 7–9. Idealized network utilization curve

While the average and saturation points are roughly the same, the load when distributed across the window never reaches saturation at any point during the window. Longer-running jobs are still started at the beginning of the window, and there are peaks and valleys depending on other factors, including starting new batches of jobs, but overall the exact same workload will actually complete *faster* with the same amount of resources because all jobs are not competing for the same network bandwidth, thus allowing all jobs to get as much bandwidth as they can consume and be able to transfer data faster. This is referred to as an increase in work per unit time—the individual jobs may or may not run any faster, but overall the backups complete faster because the bandwidth bottleneck has been removed. The best way to apply this approach to solving network saturation issues is to first characterize jobs in terms of *window required* not *performance*, *size*, or *type*. Once this characterization is complete, assign like *performing* jobs in terms of the window size to the same start time, taking into account the length of time each set of jobs take to complete. This should produce performance that resembles that discussed previously.

As jobs grow longer, more clients utilize the Media Server; the average utilization begins to reach saturation and/or the peaks cross saturation and stay above the line for longer periods of time. It is at this point when additional resources should be considered. Additional resources still do not imply a second Media Server…yet. Adding an additional network interface to the same physical Media Server may extend the life for some period of time, without the addition of a physical server. The network interface provides additional bandwidth for use by the collection of clients.

Network Interface Teaming

In situations where the amount of bandwidth that a single network interface can provide is not sufficient for a single client or set of clients, a hardware/operating system–based solution, interface bonding/teaming, is appropriate. This method uses drivers within the operating system to take like network interfaces, combine them together, and present them as a single network interface with X times the amount of bandwidth, where X is the number of discrete interfaces that have been combined together. (See Figure 7–10.)

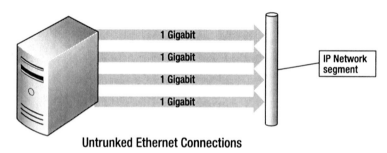

Untrunked Ethernet Connections

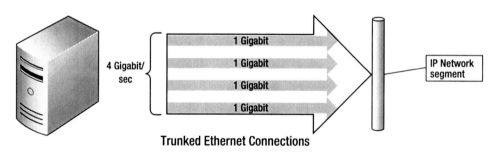

Trunked Ethernet Connections

Figure 7–10. Untrunked versus trunked Ethernet connections

While it is not exactly a linear increase in performance, teaming does provide a significant increase in available bandwidth available for use. To the Media Server software, the teamed interface appears to be a normal network device, and the clients simply sees a IP connection point, and does not have any knowledge of the device types, at least from an TCP/IP perspective.

There are several different methods of implementing teaming, none different from those introduced in Chapter 6, but are summarized here:

- Active/passive

- Link aggregation (802.3ad)

- Load balancing

Adding an additional network interface will create load effects on the other areas of the Media Servers: CPU, memory, bus type, and disk I/O capacity. If any one of these components is near maximum utilization, or even hovering around 60 percent when using a single interface, the addition of additional network resources will not have the desired effect and may actually decrease performance overall. As with the MediaAgent in the CommVault environment, this can be attributed to new interface adding additional load to these other elements. When this type of performance reduction is observed, that is the time at which additional Media Servers should be considered.

When Do You Add a Media Server?

The addition of a Media Server is a judgment call as much as a technical call. The point of decision may come prior to the Media Server not being fully utilized, but beginning to exhibit some of the performance behaviors discussed previously. When the Media Server continues to be loaded in the same manner at this point, additional load cannot be placed on it without reducing overall performance. This effectively strands backup media writing resources in an unused state. Using the same rationale as with the CommVault MediaAgent decision, the judgment call is made from an organizational point of view regarding the tolerance of the extension of backup windows versus the cost of new hardware and software licensing. This question unfortunately cannot be answered definitively from any formulaic or technical point of view, and must be judged almost completely from a cost perspective. However, as the backup administrator, you can take the current performance, extrapolate out the growth, and present the case based on a datacentric approach when using this type of method to judge the need for additional Media Servers based on network utilization.

One advantage that NetBackup has over CommVault in this regard is the ability to simply add the new Storage Unit that would be created as a result of the new Media Server to another abstraction called a Storage Unit Group. A Storage Unit Group consists of a collection of Storage Units that can span Media Servers, grouped together so that policies can auto-magically and transparently distribute backup images across all the resources represented by the Storage Unit Group. When adding a Media Server to an environment that contains one, it is recommended that Storage Unit Groups be created to allow faster addition of Media Server resources in future deployments. (See Figure 7–11.)

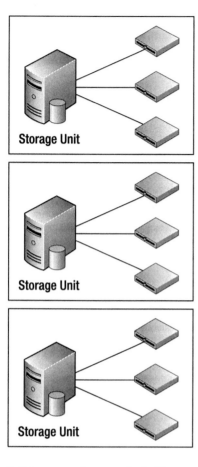

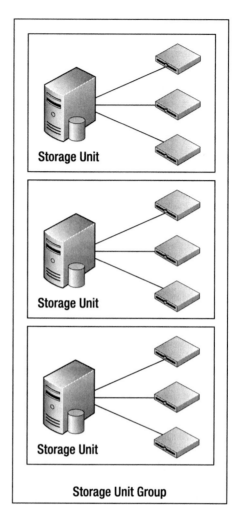

Policies can only use a single Storage Unit – resource can be wasted

Policies can use the Storage Unit Group – all resources of the individual storage units are available

Figure 7–11. Storage Unit groups

Storage Resources

Network performance is not the only factor that can be used to determine when to add a Media Server to the Storage Domain. The performance of the back-end storage can also drive the installation of a new Media Server. Storage performance is driven from a number of different variables, all of which are interrelated and make a determination of performance issues a complex process. The assessment of storage performance for NetBackup Media Servers does not differ radically from that performed on

CommVault MediaAgents. The same process applies for Media Server when looking at storage performance to determine when to add additional resources:

- Assess storage last
- Ensure proper storage configuration
- Use multiple paths to storage
- Use multiple DSUs or DSSUs

Assess storage last

Assessing storage performance should only be undertaken once all other components on the Media Server have been addressed, such as network, CPU, and memory. This is because these elements are higher in the data flow "stack" than storage—with storage being the bottom of the stack. See figure 7–12.

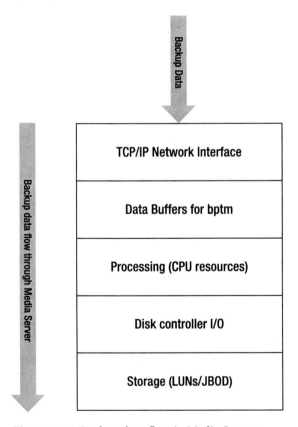

Figure 7–12. Backup data flow in Media Servers

Backup data flows into the network interface (the "top" of the stack), is buffered and processed on the physical server itself (CPU and memory—the middle of the stack), passed on through the bus to disk controller, and then to the physical storage itself. Any elements above the storage innately effect (limit) the amount of data that can be sent to the storage and thus the overall performance of the storage. However, incorrectly configured, laid out, or utilized storage has significant impacts on Media Server performance. While storage is the bottom of the stack and is affected by the upper layers, storage is also the slowest and least flexible component of the stack, so even incremental changes to poorly conceived storage can have large positive impacts. The difference: it becomes increasingly difficult to achieve performance gains once the storage is properly configured. NetBackup Media Servers, when using DSU/DSSUs, require an optimal disk layout for best performance. As DSU and DSSUs are functionally the same when it comes to configuration and performance requirements, for the purposes of this discussion, any reference to DSU configuration will also apply to DSSUs as well.

Microsoft Windows Storage Features

Before we discuss the hows and whys of multiple DSUs, this is a good time to quickly review mounting features within Microsoft Windows. Prior to Windows 2003, the only way storage could be attached to the operating system was to assign a drive letter to the file system. On Windows 2003 and above, Windows borrowed from *NIX operating systems and added the concept of mount points—the ability to attach storage at any point within a directory tree below the root of a drive letter. With this ability, drive letters can be expanded transparently, or specialized storage configurations can be added simply by creating a directory under the desired drive letter and "mounting" the storage at the directory.

Windows 2008 took this further by introducing another *NIX concept: links. A *link* is a pointer from a file or directory to another, creating an alternate path, or link. Think of links simply as shortcuts (that is actually how they appear in Explorer). Within Windows there are three types of links:

- *File*—There are two types of links: file symbolic and file hard. The *symbolic* link is effectively a shortcut that looks like a regular file to the file system. The *hard* link can be thought of as a zero space clone copy of the file. Changes to a hard link breaks the link to the original file, but keeps the changes made in a new separate copy of the file that is now stored in place of the hard link.

- *Directory*—A symbolic link for directories instead of individual files.

- *Junction*—A hard link to a directory. The advantage of a Junction link over a Directory link is that Junction links can point to entirely different mount points or drive letters, whereas Directory links must stay within the mount point of the original directory.

So whenever the term *mount point* is used in the discussion, if the environment is a Windows-based environment, a mount point could refer to a drive letter, a directory on which additional storage is mounted, or even a Junction link. (See Figure 7–13 for examples.) How you logically organize the storage attachments is completely a judgment call of what makes operational sense to the backup administrator and the team who will be responsible for maintaining the backup infrastructure. Whichever path is chosen, *document the rationale and naming standard so that future administrators understand how the storage is managed!*

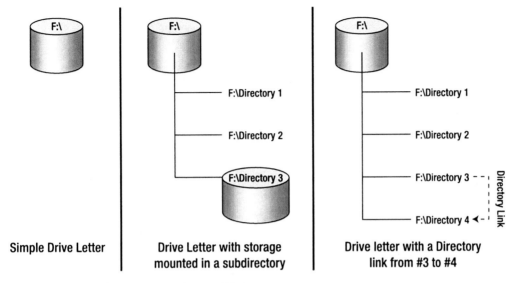

Figure 7–13. Windows mount points and links

Ensure Proper Storage Configuration

When configuring disk storage for use as a DSU on a Media Server, the tendency is to lump all the available storage into a single mount point and simply have the largest single DSU for use. While this may provide a seemingly straightforward way to manage the disk storage space, it is not particularly efficient nor does the configuration provide the best possible performance. When looking at the design of storage layouts for Media Servers, it is better to split the storage into multiple drive letters or mount points. Each mount point that is created will become a DSU with settings applied that will regulate the maximum number of backup images that can be written on it at the same time. This spreads out the I/O load between different physical drives represented by the mount point.

Why is this the case? Just as in the CommVault case, when working with multiple controllers or external drive arrays, the smaller multiple mount path method is preferred. Configuring disks into multiple LUNs works better for a number of reasons, even given the same number of disks. When creating a single large LUN, there is a trade-off between optimizing the performance within the storage array and creating larger LUNs. This was discussed at length in Chapter 2 as well as in the Storage section in Chapter 6, but to summarize here, drive performance of RAID-based storage is far better than that of single disks. The potential IOPS available for any particular drive operation is greater when combining a set of disks that any single disk can provide.

But remember to minimize the amount of RAID set wrapping that happens—the more wrapping that occurs, the higher the likelihood of performance problems. (See Figure 7–14.)

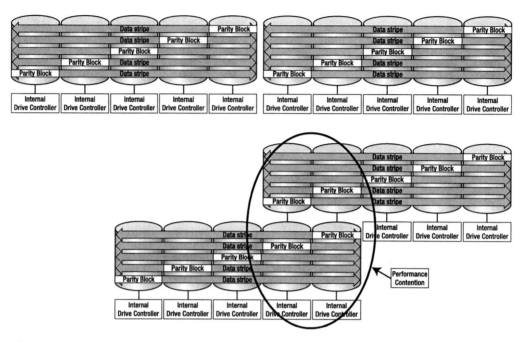

Figure 7–14. RAID group "wrapping"

The exception to this rule is when a single internal controller is used with a small number of drives. Since the number of drives is limited on internal storage, it is best to create RAID groups that span the drives, giving the best possible performance for the LUN. This allows localization of I/O to specific sections of drives and also provides the benefits of the combined IOPS potential of all the drives working together. The advantages of this configuration in a small drive set outweigh any performance issues that may be seem by trying to breakup drives into either individual LUNs, or LUNs that may contain only two or three drives.

Great! The problem of having a single large LUN seems to be solved, but what happens if you have to grow that LUN? Since the data is likely spread across multiple drives in a structured format, namely a RAID stripe, you cannot simply add drives to the configuration at the array level. The striping mechanism is set up with a set number of drives; most arrays cannot simply extend a stripe to another drive—and those that can require extensive time and I/O to move all the data around in order to restructure the stripes to contain the desired number of drives.

Simply adding a drive to a volume at the operating system layer can be worse. A *volume* is a logical container that provides a way to encapsulate a number of LUNs and presents it to the operating system as a single LUN—it is operating system–based RAID. While the focus of this book is backup, operating system RAID has some drawbacks for managing storage and should be carefully considered prior to implementation.

Having said that, using volume management to extend storage space will indeed provide the desired extension, but at a price: inconsistent performance. Extending volumes in this way uses a method called *concatenation*—basically "stick the drive to the end of the chain". (See Figure 7–15.) LUNs that are concatenated together work as a chain: I/O is written to the first member of the chain and then to the second member once the first is full. This also means that I/Os will be concentrated on the first member of the chain until it reaches capacity, and only then will I/O reach the second member.

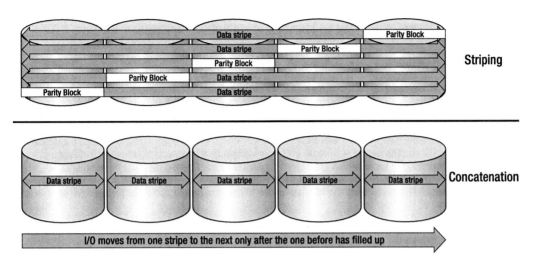

Figure 7–15. Striping versus concatenation

Concatenation will provide an unbalanced configuration that will not perform predictably or consistently because any particular I/O may have different performance, depending on which LUN in the volume the I/O is destined for. In order to grow the group, the RAID configuration across the LUNs has to be torn down or migrated using storage array–specific products. Either way, new RAID groups are required to be created using available storage. The storage used to create the new RAID configuration needs to be equal in size to the amount required to create the desired LUNs size—potentially requiring a doubling of storage capacity to simply add a small amount of storage to an existing LUN. *If the addition of this quantity of storage is not possible, the only way to expand the RAID configuration is to deconstruct the existing group, add the incremental storage, and reconstruct the group. This works great except that deconstructing RAID groups destroys the data on the group—effectively erasing any backups that were on the LUN.*

The solution to the problem is to use RAID LUN configurations that are smaller and present multiple LUNs to the Media Server instead of a single large LUN. When additional storage needs to be added, simply create a new RAID group configuration and present it as a new mount point to the Media Server, adding it to the existing DSU, if desired. Setting up the storage in this way also provides optimal performance, both from the operating system and NetBackup perspective, by using multiple DSUs to parallelize backup operations.

Use Multiple Paths to Storage

There is one other physical configuration piece to consider before moving on to setting up the DSUs. Unlink network connections that can only combine connections into a single logical connection, storage can actually have multiple distinct paths to the storage target. This ability to have multiple connections has several benefits:

- *Bandwidth management*—As the bandwidth to a particular piece of storage is consumed, additional paths can be added to seamlessly increase the bandwidth. Just as with network teaming, not all the bandwidth added is available for use.

- *Increased resiliency*—One of the best benefits of multiple storage paths is the ability to survive an outage on one path. The caveat is that any bandwidth demand that was consumed on the failed path is placed on the surviving path(s), potentially driving down performance.

It is not generally a native ability of the operating system to detect multiple paths and it requires specialized software. Multipath I/O (MPIO) drivers are specialized drivers, typically provided by the storage provider to interrogate the external storage about the LUNs being presented to the particular system. If the MPIO driver determines that the same LUN is being presented down the multiple paths, it will present the multiple paths as a single path to higher layers within the operating system. In addition, most MPIO drivers provide the ability to schedule I/O operations to the external storage that has multiple paths, so the overall I/O bandwidth is increased and more I/Os can be sent than would be possible using a single path. Again, the more paths, the more bandwidth—with the limitation being the bandwidth ingestion rate of the array and the ability of the LUNs to absorb the I/Os being sent to them via the multiple paths.

Use Multiple DSU/DSSUs

Once the LUNs are created on the storage, they can be used as DSUs on the Media Server. The creation of multiple DSUs provides multiple targets that can be used by NetBackup to store the backup data. This optimizes the Media Server throughput in two dimensions:

- *Spreading I/O*—More disk targets equal more potential IOPS and a probability of lower physical drive contention.

- *Reducing process bottlenecks*—Spread the processing of the backup streams across as many individual processes as possible to maximize CPU and memory resources.

Distribution of disk I/O has been discussed at length in other sections of this book, so we will not revisit the specifics here. This section will focus on the advantages of reducing the process bottlenecks that can be created by having single large DSUs.

Each DSU is managed by a bpdm process—simply a bptm process created to manage the I/O to DSUs. Multiple bpdm processes are also created by the inbound backup streams, all competing for resources on the Media Server—in this case, disk resources. If a single bpdm is created to manage all inbound processes, it will eventually become a bottleneck—there will simply not be enough time for bpdm to process all the data streams. The creation of multiple DSUs solves this problem by spreading the inbound connections across multiple bpdm processes, thus spreading the load across more processes. (See Figure 7–16.)

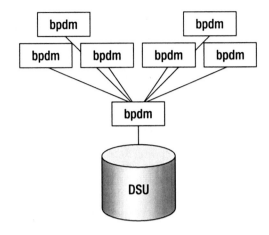

Single DSU

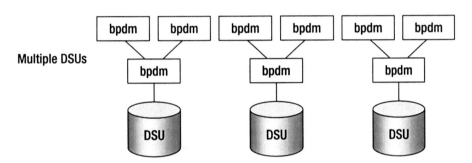

Multiple DSUs

Figure 7–16. Comparison of single versus multiple DSUs

However, this cannot be extended indefinitely. Each child bpdm process consumes system memory and CPU time. The amount of memory consumed is based on the settings of SIZE_DATA_BUFFERS and NUMBER_DATA_BUFFERS that were discussed in the beginning of this chapter. The CPU time consumed is a variable based on what the bpdm process is working on and the speed of the backup stream. Since system memory and CPU time are both fixed resources and are used for all other functions within the operating system, there is a limit to the number of bpdm processes that should be run at any one time and, by extension, a limit on the number of mount points that should be created on a particular Media Server. The recommended number of mount points can determined by looking at the amount of CPU time and RAM consumed by a single mount point on a particular Media Server during a backup operation. Project this out for both resources—one of the resources (memory or CPU) will be exhausted first. That will represent the maximum number possible—take 50 percent of that and it will be the recommended number of mount points. This number should be somewhere fewer than 10 mount points per Media Server—any more than that becomes difficult to manage operationally.

So given all these factors in storage RAID configuration, multiple mount points, DSU mount point counts, multi-path I/O drivers when do you add a Media Server based on an analysis of storage? The answer is this: when any one of the areas described exceeds 70 percent of available capacity or bandwidth, it is time to consider adding an additional Media Server to absorb the load. Note that this is *not* based on the capacity of the storage or the performance of the array. If the capacity of a particular LUN or mount point is becoming full (80–85 percent or greater), it is time to add another. If the overall ability of the array to absorb additional IOPS is being reached, it is time to look at the addition of an additional array or to upgrade the existing array to be able to process more I/O. Neither of these conditions necessarily warrants a new Media Server—neither space nor array performance additions simply imply the potential of an additional device within a DSU.

However, when the addition of devices causes any one of these issues, it is time to consider a new Media Server:

- *CPU utilization* Increase in CPU or memory load that would exceed 70–80 percent of utilization overall or cause a noticeable decrease in the overall performance of the physical server providing the Media Server services. This could be due to either the number of processes or (much less likely) the number of file systems to manage is pushing kernel performance limits.

- *Throughput drops* No increase in throughput or a decrease in throughput at the disk layer when an additional mount point is added. It can indicate that the controller is becoming saturated with work. In this instance, the addition of a second controller that is pointed to the same storage may help. However, if this occurs in an existing multipath system, the addition of additional paths may have no effect (there comes a point of diminishing returns for path addition): the Media Server simply may be running out of resources to move the data over the controller. In this case, it is simpler and cheaper to acquire an additional Media Server.

The decision to add another Media Server becomes more of a cost/risk decision than a technical one. For instance, if a Media Server has two paths to storage, with multiple mount paths then it may be that the controller is simply overloaded. In this case, the addition of another set of controllers (controllers should always be added in pairs to maintain symmetry of operation) may offload enough of the traffic to rebalance the load and allow the Media Server to keep functioning. The downside is that the addition of the addition I/O path may expose CPU or memory weakness that was not detected because due to masking by the throughput issue—thus requiring an additional Media Server to solve.

The combination of both network and storage factors, as reflected in overall system performance and server utilization, provides indicators as to how and when to deploy additional Media Servers in the general case. However, what if a server is so large, or transfers data over the network at such a slow rate, that it is not practical to back up to a Media Server? In this case, a Dedicated Media Server may be the solution. In most installations, the client sends backup data to the Media Server for storage on the appropriate media. In the case of the Dedicated Media Server, the client self-references the Media Server target and sends data directly to backup media that is locally attached, not to an external Media Server.

Since the throughput to the storage can easily exceed that available to the network, especially given the shared nature of the network interfaces (see Figure 7–17).

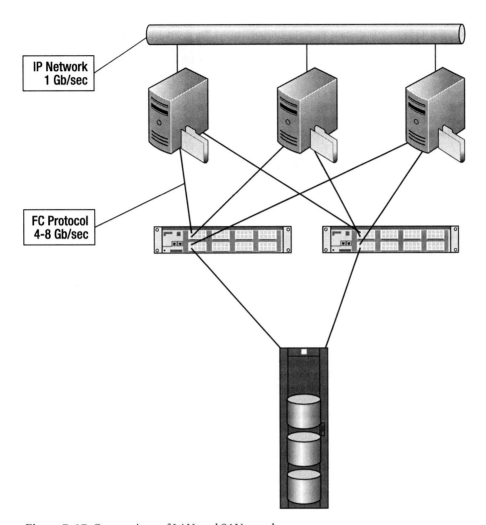

Figure 7–17. *Comparison of LAN and SAN speeds*

The overall performance of the backup is increased and the network and storage load of a long-term backup is removed from the general Media Server with the potential net effect of all backups increasing in performance. Some situations in which a Dedicated Media Server may be implemented are the following:

- Data to be transferred is too large to be transferred using the network speed available, within the backup defined backup window.

- The client is behind a firewall, located on a slow network link, or at the end of a WAN. These three situations represent slow or impeded networks that can prevent backup data from being transferred.

- The general Media Server is becoming overloaded due to the particular client load. In order to prevent the purchase of a completely new piece of hardware, the client causing the issue is converted to a Client/Media Server, thus offloading the backup load back to the client and freeing resources for the general Media Server.

The combination of both general-purpose and Dedicated Media Servers allows the administrator to balance the needs of both large and small clients, crafting a solution that meets the needs of the enterprise as a whole, but is tailored to meet the needs of individual clients. But what happens with the limits of an individual Storage Domain are reached, and when are new Storage Domains required?

Multiple Storage Domains

There are limits to a single Storage Domain. The conditions that would trigger consideration of the creation of additional Storage Domains are the following:

- Unreliable network links

- Locations separated by long network distances

- Legal or organizational needs

- Multiple large data centers

- Performance degradation on the primary Storage Domain

When placing Media Servers at remote locations, it is important to be able to have reliable communications back to the NetBackup Master Server in order to ensure that clients are properly scheduled and contacted, as well as to ensure that the metadata regarding the client backups is properly stored. If the network separating the NetBackup Master Server and the clients is either unreliable or has noise that causes a number of network packet losses or retransmissions, the communication necessary to make sure that clients are properly started and tracked either may not happen or happen in such as way as to slow the backup process down. If the network issues cannot be resolved, by placing a secondary NetBackup Master Server at the remote site, the communication becomes local, thus bypassing the issue. For instance, if an organization has a headquarters in Seattle and a remote office in Singapore, the connection between the two sites may (and in many cases will) have a significant amount of loss and noise. While many applications can tolerate this, backups run locally against a Master Server located in the Seattle headquarters will run very slowly, even if the Media Server is local to the clients. In this case, a separate NetBackup Master Server would be recommended to ensure maximum backup performance.

An additional effect of distance is the network latency that is induced. As distances between points on networks increase, the round trip time of packets to travel between the sites also increases. This is simply a law of physics problem—the speed of light is a fixed value, and it takes time for a signal to traverse long distances. While there may be plenty of network bandwidth available, if the distances that the network packets have to travel grow, the net throughput of the network will drop. The drop in performance will slow the transmission of metadata from the remote site, thus reducing the overall backup performance. While this may not be noticeable for small data backups, for larger backups, particularly those consisting of large numbers of files, this increase in metadata transfer time becomes apparent quickly. Again, the addition of a Storage Domain at the remote site avoids the distance problems, localizing backups.

There also may be legal issues that force the use of multiple Master Servers. Different legal jurisdictions place different requirements on the ability of an organization to store certain types of information. This may be for a variety of reasons, with the net result being that it may expose the organization to legal sanction if backups are even administered from outside of the jurisdiction. In situations such as this, the only option is to place a NetBackup Master Server at the site and manage backups remotely for that area. A common Storage Domain could not be used, as even the metainformation regarding the backups can be construed as sensitive information because it can convey the nature of the content or provide information regarding particular files or file types that would contain the sensitive information that is to be protected.

Client Density also has an effect on the decision to install additional Master Servers, just as in the CommVault case. NetBackup Master Servers are even more affected by Client Density for two reasons:

- *Nondistributed indexing¯* CommVault uses a distributed index, stored on each MediaAgent to track the location and contents of media. This allows each MediaAgent to take some of the processing load from the CommServe, thus reducing the overall impact of large numbers of clients. NetBackup Master Servers contain all the indexing information for all clients under its control—centralizing that processing requirement in a single location on a single server. This may mean that Master Servers would have lower thresholds for client/file counts than their CommVault equivalents.

- *Lack of catalog database¯* CommVault uses a combination of SQL Server on the CommServe and binary indices on the MediaAgents to provide end-to-end tracking of backup images. NetBackup, on the other hand, uses a directory catalog structure with binary files to accomplish the same function. While this approach has its advantages and disadvantages, at scale it disproportionally slows down with the increase in the number of clients and files that it is required to manage.

The other effect of Client Density arises when managing multiple large centers in a single Storage Domain. The client effect described previously is now compounded by any latency introduced by the network linking the large remote sites back to the central one. The amount of metadata that is transmitted by the clients over a WAN link that connects the central to the remote site can consume large portions, sometimes more than 50 percent, of the link. If enough of the link is consumed, the overall performance of the WAN link decreases, thus decreasing the transmission rate of the metadata. The ultimate effect of the reduction in the rate at which metadata is transmitted is a corresponding decrease in the throughput rates of the client backup that rely on having fast, reliable metadata transfer rates.

In either Client Density scenario—simple client count or convergence of large data centers the number of clients will drive the requirement to deploy additional Storage Domains. There is no theoretical number of clients that will drive such a decision. The inflection point that helps determine the point at which a secondary Storage Domain could be created is the overall performance of the backup environment, as compared with the performance of the NetBackup Master Server with regard to CPU and I/O capabilities. Once either of these details approaches 80 percent of utilization on a regular basis, it is time to consider adding a secondary NetBackup Master Server.

When considering adding an additional Storage Domain, you need to consider how to migrate existing clients from the original Master Server to the newly created one. NetBackup does not provide a straightforward method to move clients between Storage Domains. The policies, schedules, and client information can be exported via command-line interfaces to files and then reimported using custom scripts. While this migration of client policies and connections is relatively straightforward, it is by no means trivial. Once reimported into the new Master Server, the policies and schedules will need to be reviewed to ensure that configuration information regarding the old Master Server has not been transferred into the new. In addition, each client that was being backed up by the old Master Server will need to be manually reregistered with the new Master Server so that the client recognizes the new Master Server's "authority" to perform backups.

The migration of previous backups is much more involved. There is not a good way to bulk migrate images and media targets previously used by the original Master Server into the newly created one. Most organizations undertaking this process simply allow the old backups to expire and reconnect individual clients back to their original Master Server if restores from that time period are required.

■ **Note** If a Master split is being considered, it is *very strongly recommended* that Symantec professional services be engaged to assist with this process, at least from the planning and scripting perspective.

Summary

NetBackup has a number of elements to consider when deploying or upgrading a Storage Domain. From the smallest combined Master/Media Server to large deployments of multiple Masters, items such as network performance and configuration, storage design, and client counts must be continuously considered and evaluated. It is important to take the recommendations and guidelines presented here, as well as the experiences and idiosyncrasies of the specific backup environment into consideration when making decisions regarding any change in direction.

CHAPTER 8

■ ■ ■

Application Backup Strategies

So far, we have discussed the methods of backing up data. This chapter will explore some strategies for backing up specific applications. It will address three general types of data that are backed up in all environments: file system, database, and mail server. In addition, some general strategies regarding how to attack the backup of other types of applications will be addressed as well.

General Strategies

For all types of applications, there is a set of general questions to ask to determine when designing a solution to provide backup services:

- Does the application need to be stopped or the data quiesced in some way prior to backup by the backup software?

    - If so, how is the application stopped or the data placed into a state where it can be effectively backed up? This ensures that issues similar to those faced by non-quiesced databases, namely the inability to utilized non-quiesced data in a restore situation.

- What is the impact of putting the application into a mode where backup can be performed? Does the application stop processing data or does it slow processing? What other impact is seen?

- What other applications are dependent on the state of the application being backed up? Do they also need to be placed into a particular state as a result of the backup?

- How does data recovery happen? Can data recovery happen? What are the steps to recover the data back into the application? How often are restores tested to verify backups are actually happening as expected?

- How is the data being backed up stored on the server? Is it stored in a small number of large files? If the application stores data in large numbers of files, does it qualify as a high-density file system (HDFS)? Is the directory structure a horizontal directory structure or vertical directory structure?

- Can the application also be backed up with the data? Is this a requirement for the backup or recovery?

These questions will provide the basis for determining how to approach the backup. The answers could lead toward a backup solution that looks like a file system backup, a database backup, or a combination of both. Simply take the responses and look at the descriptions of backup environments provided in the previous sections. There will be similarities between the application being analyzed and one or more types of standard applications, which will lead to methods in which the application can be addressed in terms of putting together a backup solution.

File Systems

File systems represent the most common and most basic type of data that is backed up. As simple as they may seem, file systems come in two general types: normal and High Density (HDFS). The distinction between the two is not exact, however. Normal file systems are what are typically found on file servers. HDFSs represent a special type of file system.

■ **Note** An HDFS is any file system that contains greater than 1 million files per TB.

Most file systems contain relatively small numbers of files, fewer than 1 million files per TB. However, beyond this measure, both NetBackup and CommVault begin to suffer from performance degradation—not due to the size of the files, but due to the number of files that need to be processed. Why does the number of files cause a decrease in performance? As the number of files is increased, processing each file against the file index, whether in a catalog (NetBackup) or in a database (CommVault), becomes the limiting factor when performing the backup. The time a backup takes to complete is actually dependent on two factors: the amount of time to transfer the data, and the amount of time to scan the file index and insert updates. During normal file system backups, the amount of time to transfer the data becomes the limiting factor as the size of the backup, relative to the transfer rate, is the determining factor. However, with an HDFS file system, because there are so many files, the time it takes to scan the file index, update the index with new information regarding new backed-up files, or new metadata regarding existing files, will take a large amount of time relative to the amount of data backed up. The same effect takes place in everyday use—while modern drives can transfer upward of 250 MB/sec, the effective transfer rate drops dramatically as the number of files increases, due to the overhead introduced by the file system processing all the file entries. Interestingly enough, however, the strategy for backing up large amounts of file system data is very similar to that needed to back up HDFS systems, as you will see shortly.

Normal File Systems

The normal file system is the most straightforward to back up—it can be as simple as installing the backup client, selecting the ALL_LOCAL_DRIVES directive (NetBackup) or using the default subclient for CommVault. Performing the backup in this method will back up all the file system data on the servers without any additional configuration. Since this method captures everything on the file systems, it also may capture data that is either not necessary to back up or not usable in a restore, such as database log files. This is not an issue in smaller environments—this model can be used until the length of time the backup begins to get near the window available to complete the backup. In order to keep a simple file system backup, but not capture everything on the system, specific items can be identified in the backup policy, or storage policy, that will allow for more selective filtering of the file systems to be backed up.

Selective Backup

This filtering or include/exclude generally starts at either the drive letter (for Windows-based systems) or at the root (/) directory (for *NIX-based systems. While the Windows systems are straightforward, doing the same type of splitting at the root of a *NIX system can be less so. The approach in these situations is to look at standard directories, such as /usr, /opt, /etc that can be separated out, and to also look at additional file systems mounted on directories on the root file system, as separate entries into the backup items or into a standard storage policy.

As this level of indirection reaches the limits of meeting backup windows, the next level of splits are applied. These splits are made by determining the size of each of the original mount points/drive letters, looking at the directory structures under the root of each of the drive letters, and then creating additional policies based on groups of directories. These directories should be grouped according to equality of size—each additional grouping of directories should be roughly equal in size, as much as possible. (See Figure 8–1.) This is to ensure that no one backup consumes all the resources of the backup service, and that there no backup causes the backup of the entire system to exceed the window. In addition to filtering out items that are not necessary to be backed up, it also allows for a simple method of establishing multiple streams of specific data for multistreaming/multiplexing operations.

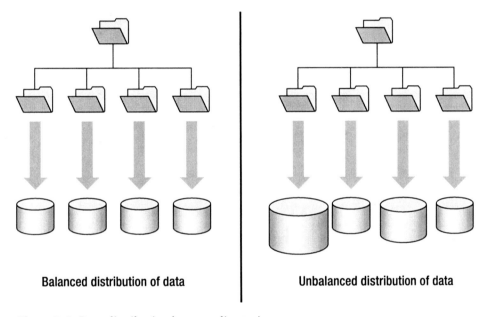

Balanced distribution of data   **Unbalanced distribution of data**

Figure 8–1. Data distribution between directories

Here's an example of how this can work from a real situation: A backup administrator has a server with more than 4 TB of data to back up. Using a simple ALL_LOCAL_DRIVES directive, backups were exceeding the backup window. When the administrator looked at the data being backed up, he discovered that 3 TB of the 4 TB of data were located in three different subdirectories, each located off of the root of the file system. The data was spread equally between the three subdirectories. Since the directories were all under the same file system, NetBackup could not identify the directories explicitly using the automatic multistreaming supplied by the ALL_LOCAL_DRIVES directive.

Solution: The backup administrator created a new policy that contained the following entries:

```
<subdirectory #1>
NEW_STREAM
<subdirectory #2>
NEW_STREAM
<subdirectory #3>
```

By creating the policy in this way, and forcing the split of the directories along the subdirectory boundaries and creating a stream (NEW_STREAM directive) for each directory, NetBackup started three backups for the same data for which one was originally started under ALL_LOCAL_DRIVES. Using this policy, the backup time was reduced by 30 percent.

The previous example illustrates how by looking at the structure of the data being backed up and the distribution of the data across the file systems, significant gains in backup performance can be gained by creating policies with discrete listings of directories. The downside of this solution is that it requires regular maintenance and coordination with the application owner. In the previous example, the backup administrator had regular meetings with the application owners, through a standard change control meeting, to ensure that any changes to the environment were propagated to the backup configuration, if necessary.

When looking at directory structures to split, it is important to understand the two general types of directory structures: Horizontal and Vertical. (See Figure 8–2.) All directory structures have characteristics of both; however, it is the top-level structure, as viewed from the root directory of the file system, which is important when looking at backup structures. A *horizontal directory structure* is one that has the majority of the directories at the same level, forming a peer relation between the directories. A *vertical directory structure* is the opposite—a set of directories that have a hierarchical directory relationship. When splitting file systems into directories to back up, it is preferable to have a horizontal structure instead of a vertical one. A horizontal structure allows for easier splitting of directories into logical groups that can be grouped together. Since the directories are all peers to each other, no special exclusion rules need to be written to ensure that no backups overlap.

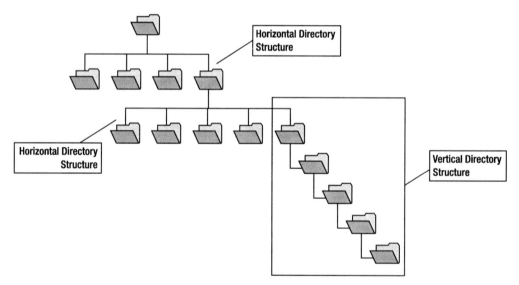

Figure 8–2. Horizontal and vertical directory structures

Backups Split By Schedule

In some cases, backup sizes do not drive the separation of backups, but external requirements dictate that the specific file systems be backed up on specific days. For example, five different Windows systems have three drive letters that are backed up by policy: E:\, G:\, and H:\. However, due to business and capacity requirements, each drive must have a full backup independent of the other drives, and each system must have its full backups done on different days. Without the requirement of having the backups on different days due to the business policy (the separation of the full backups), all these servers could be backed up using a single policy. However, in this situation, separate policies have to be created, with different schedules that reflect the requirements. Table 8–1 illustrates these differences.

Table 8–1. *Example Backup Schedule*

	E:\	G:\	H:\
Server 1	M-Full	T-Full	W-Full
	T-Sun Incr	W-M Incr	Th-T Incr
Server 2	Th-Full	F-Full	Sat-Full
	Fr-W Incr	Sat-Th Incr	Sun-F Incr
Server 3	Sun-Full	M-Full	T-Full
	M-Sat Incr	T-Sun Incr	W-M Incr
Server 4	W-Full	Th-Full	F-Full
	Th-T Incr	Fr-W Incr	Sat-Th Incr
Server 5	Sat-Full	Sun-Full	M-Full
	Sun-F Incr	M-Sat Incr	T-Sun Incr

The table shows the distribution of full and incremental backups for the example. The backup schedule type illustrated here is what is known as a *staggered full schedule*. The staggered full is applied both between servers and within servers to minimize the amount of resources on any particular server that are used and also normalizes the amount of data transferred from all servers on a particular day. For instance, Server 1 does a full on Monday, Tuesday, Wednesday; Server 2 on Thursday, Friday, Saturday; Server 3 on Sunday, Monday, Tuesday, and so on, with incremental backups as the difference.

In a NetBackup environment, this would require separate policies for each combination of schedules and drives, adding the clients to each one. For example, a policy would need to be created for E:\, with scheduled Monday full/daily incremental backups, and would only contain Server 1 as a client.

Schedule-based splits do not preclude the creation of capacity-based splits, however. As the data grows, the backups then need to be further split, using the directory method listed previously. As these additional directories are added, they are simply added as entries in the backup selection area, separated by the NEW_STREAM directive. This will force new streams to be created for each group of directories, thus creating the ability to better balance the resources used during the backup cycle, while still maintaining the original cycle for the drive letters.

Should individual drive letters still have issues completing backups even after splitting using directives within the same policy, new policies should be created that reflect the directories that were previously grouped together in a set. At some point, however, this creates such a large number of NetBackup policies that it can become impractical to manage. Using CommVault is much simpler in this situation. With CommVault, you can create individual subclient policies for each set of drive letters and directories. Then create a backup set and add the subclient polices for each client. The individual schedule policies can then be created and applied to the resulting storage policy.

In this situation, file systems that are common to a group of clients can be placed together in the same policy, in the case of NetBackup, or created in common subclients, in the case of CommVault. This allows for clients with similar backup structures to be backed up with a minimum of management. As clients are added to the environment with similar structures, they can simply be added to the same policy or storage policy. Backup files or subclients in these policy configurations are usually at the drive letter or mount point level, but are also contain common directory structures, depending on operating system. Some common examples of these types of directories are C:\Documents and Settings on Windows server systems, and /usr/local on *NIX type servers.

High Density File Systems (HDFSs)

High density file systems (HDFSs) present a challenge that is similar to large file systems. However, instead of dealing with the amount of data to back up, HDFSs deal with the problem of large numbers of files. While there is no formal definition of what an HDFS is, in general it is any file system that has more than 1 million files per terabyte or greater than 10 million files on a particular file system. The challenge with HDFSs is not the quantity of data—with the density of data described, HDFSs are smaller than most—but the amount of time required to process the data within the backup software itself.

There are two problems.

- *Scanning*: In order to determine which files to back up, during either a full or incremental, the software must determine which files are on the system and, in the case of an incremental, determine which files to back up. This scan time is performed in different ways on different operating systems, but increases proportionally to the number of files to scan.

- *Indexing*: Both NetBackup and CommVault need to track which files have been backed up and what versions are being maintained. This requires that the backup software maintain a catalog of files that can be referenced by end users so that which version to restore can be easily determined. When large numbers of files are encountered, however, this insert process is very system-intensive, both in terms of CPU and of disk I/O for the Master Server or MediaAgent. With normal numbers of files or small numbers of large files, the cumulative effect of this insert time, as compared with the total time of the backup, is small or insignificant. However, when very large numbers of files are required to be inserted, the cumulative effect of the insert time becomes greater than that required to actually transport and store the data.

The strategy applied to HDFS environments is similar to that applied to file system backups as they grow: split the file systems into smaller chunks. But instead of basing the splits on the size of the backup stream, the split is based on the number of files under the particular directory. This can be very effective as it forces parallel streams of processing on the Master Server/MediaAgent side of the equation, pushing the ability of the system to perform multiple parallel inserts into the catalog.

Why the MediaAgent instead of the CommServe in this situation? In CommVault, the MediaAgent performs the tracking of the file status in the Index Cache, not the CommServe. This is one of the reasons why the MediaAgent must have very high speed drives assigned to the Index Cache. The CommVault architecture also allows the multiple streams that are created to handle the HDFS to be spread across MediaAgents as well as having multiple streams. Since the subclients can be assigned to different storage paths, there can be multiple MediaAgents assigned to the different subclients, further spreading the I/O and processing load between multiple systems.

Block-Level Backups

So when the backup policies become more complex, in the case of NetBackup, or the Index Cache cannot keep up in CommVault, even when spread across multiple MediaAgents, what is left? This is where the *block-level backups* are useful. A block-level backup tracks changed blocks within file systems and provides backups of only those blocks, instead of entire files. (See Figure 8–3.) Restores of files are made through the reassembly of blocks into files, transparently to the end user. The backups are faster than file-level backups since the only things backed up are the blocks and the associated metadata, such as what files the blocks belong to.

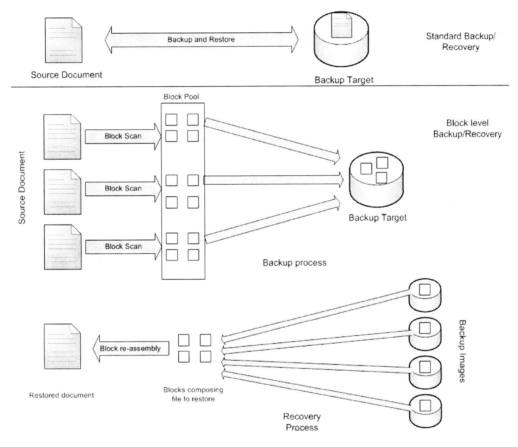

Figure 8–3. Block-level backups

Block-level backups speeds backup times for both file systems with large amounts of data, as well as for HDFSs. For large file systems, only the changed blocks are moved during the backup, thus reducing the amount of data moved during a backup to the changed blocks that were created between the backups. The amount of data required to be moved can be much less than even an incremental backup. During an incremental backup, the changed files are identified and moved during the backup. However, these files contain both blocks that have changed and those that have not, forcing the backup software to move blocks that have been repeatedly backed up. In a block-level backup, only the portion of the file that has changed is backed up, which can represent a significantly smaller amount of data.

In the HDFS scenario, the block-level backup reduces the processing time by not having to perform the file scan prior to backup. Since the block-level backup tracks the blocks and the associated files, the time required to perform the scan is removed since the backup already knows which "files" to back up. However, the time required to perform the insert into the catalog, whether on the Master Server or the MediaAgent, is still unaffected by this, so the amount of time to back up the HDFS is not reduced to the point of the data transfer, but is still much reduced.

Restores of files backed up with block-level backups are identical to those backed up with standard backups—the only difference is how the data is retrieved. With standard backups, discrete files are backed up and stored as a complete unit. During restore, the file is simply retrieved from the backup image and transferred back to the requesting client. With block-based backups, the backup software identifies the required blocks, determines the media location of the blocks, and then reassembles the blocks back into the requested file.

This reassembly process illustrates why block-level backup is not a panacea for all backups or backup problems. Since only the change blocks are backed up, in order to reassemble an individual file or set of files, the location of all the blocks that make up the original file must be located. These blocks will be spread across multiple backup images. Restores of individual files under a block base backup method can take significantly longer than discrete file backups due to this location and reassembly process. The time to locate and recover blocks grows disproportionately faster than the amount of additional blocks backed up. The recovery time will eventually grows beyond any reasonable expectation of completion due to the location and assembly process with large numbers of blocks to scan.

Source-Based Deduplication

An alternative to a block-level backup is to use source-based deduplication. This type of backup is particularly effective on larger file systems, but can also have some effect on the backup of HDFS file systems. Remember from earlier chapters that source-based deduplication is the ability of NetBackup and CommVault to look at blocks of data, and only send the blocks that have not been already sent during previous backups. This method can reduce the data sent as part of the backup by 80 percent and above. While there is time in processing the blocks on the client system, this time can be much less than that is required for moving a large amount of data. However, as was also shown in previous chapters, source-based deduplication also requires specialized software and servers, and thus may complicate the backup environment.

An additional benefit of this source-based deduplication is a significant reduction in the amount of data that is sent across network links. The source-based deduplication scans the source backups and identifies unique blocks to send to the backup storage. This scanning and identification process happens prior to the transmission of the backup to the backup target, so any quantity of backup data sent to the target is simply the sum of the unique blocks identified by the deduplication process—a number significantly smaller than the size of the source data. This effect is particularly useful when backing up large amounts of data over small links, such as a file server located in a remote office.

Source-based deduplication can also assist with HDFSs in the same way as block-level backups assist. However, the effect may not be as great as with block-level backups, as scanning still must occur at the time of backup, not as changes are happening as with block level. However, in cases where the number of files is very large and there is a large amount of data to move, source-based deduplication can be a very effective means of providing effective backup.

Real-world example: a software developer stores large quantities of individual files, comprising their source code and other development-related files on a single file server. The file count had become so great that backups would fail due to timeout issues. The backup administrator reviewed the file counts in the file systems being backed up and discovered that the collection of 5 file systems on the server had a total of 10 million files stored. Due to the nature of how the applications stored the files, the file counts were relatively evenly distributed between the five file systems. Additionally, the file systems were structured in a horizontal directory structure, which the backup administrator attempted to take advantage of by splitting backups along the directory lines. However, the backups still took too much time to complete due to the scan and indexing times required by the large quantities of files.

Solution: the company acquired a source-based deduplication backup solution to perform the backup. Once the initial deduplicated backup was taken, the backups were completing nightly, well within the required backup window.

File Systems Summary

While file systems are the most common type of backups performed, they are not necessarily simple to accomplish. Strategies such as splitting file systems and block-level backups can mitigate large file systems and file systems with massive numbers of files. Source-based deduplication can also provide some assistance, but can require a large amount of extra infrastructure to implement, but should be considered in larger environments.

Databases

There is one cardinal rule when designing backup solutions for databases: database administrators (DBAs) always want local copies of their database backups, so it is important to understand why. DBAs, as custodians of the databases they support, need to have total control of many aspects of the systems on which they run, backups included. Part of that responsibility is to ensure that the databases are restored as quickly as possible or as frequently is requested; the data needs to be restored "instantly". When DBAs talk about restoring data, they are speaking about having the data back in the database structure and available to end users, including all the steps required to re-integrate backups provided by the backup service back into the database in question. Frequently, DBAs only need to restore small portions of the database, not entire sections. They are restoring data as a result of mistaken entries to the data, not typically corruption of the database as a whole.

DBAs, especially ones who have more career experience, have had poor experiences with external backup software, either in terms of ability to restore small pieces of the database, performance impacts on the databases during backup, and availability of backups from which to restore data. Given all these factors, many DBAs prefer to have native database tools perform local backups of the database(s) onto local disk and then have the backup tools back up the resulting file set. From the DBA perspective, if there are problems with the backup or resulting restore, the DBA only needs to engage the database vendor not a group of people consisting of the backup administrator, backup vendor, and database vendor to solve any problems.

While this is one strategy, it is important to understand that while it may seem efficient from the DBA perspective and solves the tactical issues at some level, as the backup architect, your view must be more strategic. Modern backup software does not impact the database any more than native tools, and in many cases simply uses the same API as the native tools for backup. Additionally, while backup software does not provide record-level recoverability of databases, both NetBackup and CommVault provide the ability to perform incremental and differential copies of databases, providing the ability to not have to restore entire databases.

Local backups to disk also consume large amounts of resources. The disk space alone will require at least as much space as is required for the database as a whole, and may actually require more space, depending on the rotation schedule that would be required to maintain active copies available during backup operations. Native tool backups also create compressed copies of the data in order to consume as few resources as possible. The compression techniques used are no different from those used by standard folder compression, and come with all the CPU, memory, and I/O overhead. So, by running the native tools, it is possible to actually introduce more load on the server than using the backup software, when running in a compressed mode. In addition, the compression hinders the ability of the backup software to make copies of the native tools backup. Both NetBackup and CommVault use the hardware compression on media tape drives. However, having compressed source data defeats the hardware compression on the media and actually slows down the media transfer rates and increases the media that is consumed. *If the target media is a deduplicated target, then the ability to perform deduplication on compressed data is effectively turned off.*

Database Log Backups

Local backups do have alternatives. Both Oracle and SQL Server maintain records of the transactions that have been committed to the database over a specific period of time. These records are called *transaction logs*. Oracle has two types of these logs: redo logs and archive logs, and SQL Server has transaction logs. These logs can be replayed against a database to bring the database back to the last transaction within the database. As will be shown later in the chapter, it is strongly recommended, and in some cases required, that these logs be backed up as part of a regular backup scheme.

If the database logs are backed up more frequently than the database, the logs can be used to restore the database to a point in time between normal backups. This effectively provides the equivalent of an incremental database backup, occurring between regular backup cycles. So instead of committing the disk space to a local backup, a database could be backed up daily by the backup software and then provide periodic backups of the transaction logs, which can then be replayed back. This provides a roughly equivalent functionality to the local backup plus record restore functionality enabled by a local backup methodology. Discuss the option with the DBA as an alternative to local backup.

Locally Controlled Database Backups

If DBAs do not want or need local backup, many times they do desire a locally controlled backup. This type of backup is essentially a user-initiated backup and provides control of exactly when the backup occurs. While both NetBackup and CommVault provide scheduled backups, they are not deterministic schedulers, meaning that they only provide a window in which the backup may be executed, not an exact time of execution. This may not work for certain environments in which data processing occurs on the database during specific hours and when backups cannot be run. Locally controlled backups may go to disk, followed by a backup software pass, or may directly execute the backup software. A locally controlled backup typically requires some level of scripting to integrate the native backup tools and the backup software into a single process. Since the process is controlled locally, the backup can inject a load into the backup system that may not be accounted for in the normal scheduling process. This load may actually delay the database backup further—the backup job is waiting for resources that were not "scheduled" for use or may impact the performance of other backup jobs by competing for resources that were originally allocated for use by scheduled backups.

Pre- and Post-Scripts

The alternatives to locally scheduled database backups do not completely solve the problem. Both CommVault and NetBackup provide a means to execute pre- and post-backup scripts. Pre- and post-backup scripts are optional components that can perform tasks prior (pre-) or after (post-) the execution of the backup. This ability of the backup software to start a script before the backup actually runs gives DBAs the ability to control the exact time that a backup will run through the use of a *trigger*. A trigger script is one that is executed and waits for a specific event before stopping, known as a trigger. DBAs will use their own scripts to place the database in the appropriate state and issue the trigger. The pre-backup script will then stop and the backup will begin. The post-backup script then puts the database back into normal operation at the conclusion of the backup.

In general, a trigger could be designed to function in response to a number of items: time of day, completion of processing, and so on. The trigger script would be included in a pre- and post-backup process that would be executed well before the window in which the application is required to be backed up. While this solves the problem of not a deterministic scheduler executing a backup at a specific time, these types of script commit backup resources and idle them until the trigger is pulled. If the script fails then the resources can be committed until the error is detected, many times well after the backup was supposed to have been completed. Additionally, these scripts have to be maintained—if there are changes to the backup software, database software, or both, the scripts have to be revalidated to ensure that the process and functionality remain after the software change—a process that can be time-consuming and fault injecting. When looking at local control of database backups, balance the ability to forecast resources for the backup against the need to have scheduling around critical business processes. If the business process requires non-backup time to complete the tasks, local control may be the answer. Simply plan around the resource constraint as best as possible and monitor the backups of both the database and other jobs around that time to ensure that there are not issues introduced by using this method.

Snapshot Backups

But what if you could have the best of both worlds—have the ability to provide a local copy of the database, but be able to control the backup environment? Split-mirror and snapshot backups provide this type of functionality. A split-mirror backup is one where a mirror copy of the disks are created, most often at the disk array level, and made available for use independently of the original source disks. The split mirror is a full clone of every block, on every physical disk, that is used for the database and participated in the mirror split.

Snapshots

A *snapshot* backup is similar. Snapshots can be created on the operating system, using products such as VSS or FlashSnap, or on the disk array with TimeFinder or NetApp Snapshot. Instead of creating a full clone copy of every block, the snapshot starts at a point in time, tracks the blocks that have changed by making a copy of the changed blocks onto a separate set of disks, and then references the unchanged plus the changed blocks to make a usable, presentable copy of the disks. The snapshot process, in most instances, uses a method called *copy on write (CoW)*. A CoW snapshot, unless carefully managed and used for only a short period of time, can have a significant impact on performance. CoW intercepts all writes to a set of disks and makes copies of blocks that have changed since the start of the snapshot session. These blocks are then copied to a separate set of disks, while the original blocks are committed to their intended location on disk. The write is not acknowledged back to the host until *both* copies of the block have been fully written—introducing a second write, thus introducing time to write. When the data is read from the snapshot, the data from the blocks that have changed during the duration of the snapshot session are read from this separate location in which they were written, but the unchanged blocks are read from the original location. If another process is attempting to read the same block at the same time as the process reading a snapshot, a deadlock occurs, and one process must wait, introducing latency to the other. While this may seem like an unlikely occurrence, in a relatively small number of blocks, with only a moderately active database, such deadlocks can occur frequently enough to slow the overall performance of the database.

Split Mirror

The split mirror/snapshot backup works by using a combination of operating system and/or array functionality that creates this point-in-time copy of all the files on the disks occupied by the database.

This point-in-time copy can then be backed up independently of the database, at a time of the backup software's choosing, and without impacting the database as a whole. This copy could even be backed up by an alternative system that would completely offload the whole backup process from the database server—effectively making the backup look to the database like it was almost instantaneous, depending on the requirements of the database. The process looks something like this:

1. The database is quiesced and/or placed into a backup mode. This mode may allow the continuation of processing during the backup.

2. The snapshot is created from the quiesced database. This snapshot represents a full point-in-time copy of the database at the point at which the database was placed into the backup mode. The snapshot must include all portions of the database that allow it to run, such as transaction logs, trace log, and the like.

3. The database is then taken out of backup mode. This effectively ends the backup cycle for the database.

4. The snapshot is then available for backup, offline processing (as another database), or restore purposes (record-level restores—just like a local copy). All this functionality can be local to the source server, or operated on a secondary server, set aside for such purposes (such as a Media Server or MediaAgent).

However, as with all things backup, there are trade-offs. In using this type of backup method, there still can be a significant amount of disk required. The storage requirement can range from a full copy of the disk space, in the case of a split mirror, to the amount of change that occurs between backups—the requirement for a snapshot backup. The process described previously is not automatic; in order to function in a scheduled backup environment, it must be automated. This automation can be in the form of a set of scripts that implement the functionality or in additional agents that need to be installed to extend the backup software capabilities to include integration with the split mirror/snapshot provider. Additionally, if it is desirable to back up the mirror/snapshot on a server separate from the source, shared storage is required, and additional servers of the same OS type and level need to be in place to host the mirror/snapshot. This secondary server is known as a *proxy server*. Finally, if any database operations are desired to be performed on the proxy server, such as record-level restores, a copy of the database software must also be installed and maintained on the proxy server. Depending on the database vendor, this proxy server may need to be isolated from the production network as the database may try to advertise itself as the primary database. This is most often the case when working with SQL Server—SQL registers itself with Active Directory at start time.

The previous discussion talked about the need to put the database into a "backup mode" prior to making copies of the database. Prior to backing up, all databases need to make sure that pending transactions are committed to the database which creates what is known as a consistent database. This is necessary to ensure that all data that is in the database is correctly stored and referenced by the internal database structures. If this process is not performed, the resulting database copy can be unusable. There are generally three methods of preparing a database for backup: shutting down the database completely ("cold"); placing the database into a log tracking–only state where new transactions are placed only into the transaction log and not committed to the database until the backup mode is exited ("hot"); or through the use of an data arbitrator or API specifically designed around database backup ("programmatic"). Mirror/snapshot backups operate using either the cold or hot database backup methods; native backup tools use the programmatic method (sometimes in combination with either the hot or cold), and the backup software can use a combination of all three.

So what are the differences? A cold backup requires that access to the database be suspended and that all transactions that reside within the transaction logs be fully committed to the database. This process usually requires the complete shutdown of the database software to complete. Obviously, this represents downtime for the database during which time end users cannot perform any work. However, a cold backup is useful as a baseline copy of the database from which to work, and is the easiest to back up: simply make a copy of the data files that are part of the database. Once the copy is made (which can be made via a mirror/snap, as well as a simple direct backup of the data), the database can be restarted and brought back online. This method is great for databases that do not have any off-hours activity or only require periodic backups as they represent archive copies of structured data.

A hot backup, on the other hand, allows for access to the database during backup. During a hot backup, the database software is commanded to place the database into a specialized mode, commit any pending transactions, and capture all further transactions exclusively in the transaction logs until the database is removed from hot backup mode. This mode provides the ability for end users to continue to query, insert, and update records from the database, while maintaining consistency of the database files for backup. Table 8–1 shows the differences between cold and hot backups.

Table 8–1. *Comparison of Cold and Hot Database Backups*

	Advantages	**Disadvantages**
Cold backup	Provides complete, guaranteed consistent copy of database.	Database is offline during backup.
	Easiest to execute.	Largest backup; backup is a full backup every time.
	Does not require any special configuration of database to run.	Only full database restores are possible without proxy servers.
Hot backup	Database continues to function during backup.	Performance of database can degrade during backup.
		Records are not committed during backup, so database is not truly updated.
		Transaction logs are of fixed size and can quickly fill during backups, causing database outages.

A hot backup sounds like the perfect solution; however, it comes at a price. Since all new transactions are placed into the transaction logs, and not committed to the database during hot backup mode, the database is in a state where there two records of the same data at the same time can exist— one in the transaction logs and one in the database. This is reconciled after the backup mode is released, as the transaction logs are replayed against the database, making the records consistent again.

Additionally, the transaction logs are of fixed size, and only occupy a small amount of fast disk space. (See Figure 8–4.) If the backup mode is maintained for too long, the transaction logs can run out of space and the database can crash, requiring DBAs to perform database recovery and possible restoration. Therefore, it is important to keep a database in backup mode for only short periods of time—just long enough to get a backup copy. Enter mirror/snap backups. By combining the hot backup mode with a mirror/snap, backups of very large databases can be accomplished, at least from the database perspective, in a matter of minutes by using the hot backup mode in the mirror/snap process.

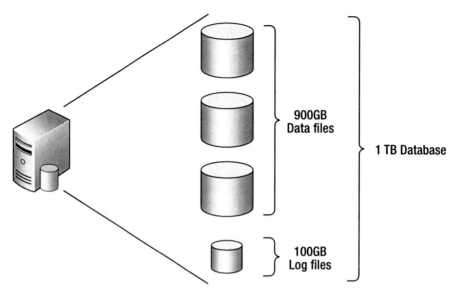

Figure 8–4. *Size comparison between data and log files*

The programmatic method of creating backups is used by software vendors and scripting authors to create customized methods of backup. The database vendor developers use these programmatic methods to selectively ensure that parts of the database are consistent during backup and that the individual records, or in some cases database blocks of data, are retrieved and backed up in a manner that will allow for selective or full restores. These methods can be in the form of software APIs that allow for standard methods of database access at a low-level or vendor-provided tools that provide access and backup outside of the traditional cold and hot backup methods. Third-party software providers such as SQL Lightspeed use these methods to provide optimized backup methods outside of both the "official" SQL Server backup tools as well as NetBackup and CommVault—as will be discussed later in the chapter.

Of course, the reason why backup software providers have database agents is to provide an automated, controlled, and tracked method of backing up database data. Both NetBackup and CommVault have several database agents that cover a number of different databases, such as Oracle, SQL Server, and DB2; and even some smaller database types such as MySQL and Postgres. The two most commonly found databases will be review here in detail: Oracle and SQL Server.

SQL Server

SQL Server has the advantage of only running on Windows platforms and is able to take advantage of several features of the OS that make backup easier. SQL Server has the ability to perform both hot and cold database backups using native tools, and has several ways that allow for backup application integration.

SQL Server Terminology

Before we get into the specifics of how to back up SQL Server, let's talk about terminology. Like all other software, database software does not necessarily use a common lexicon to describe the different pieces that make up a database. SQL Server is no different. SQL Server is installed on a physical server and creates an instance of SQL Server. The instance is the highest level of granularity on a server. Within each instance, there may be one or more databases contained and managed within the instance. The database will consist of multiple filegroups, which are exactly what they sound like—groups of files that contain the data structures that are created within the database to store the data: tables, triggers, indices, and so on. (See Figure 8–5.)

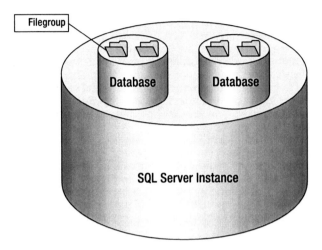

Figure 8–5. SQL Server hierarchy

The simplest method that SQL Server uses for backup is the native dump. This provides a local, point-in-time copy of the database, and can either be a simple copy of the required files within the filegroups of the database, or can be a data-level backup, essentially an export of the data contained in the database into a SQL Server specific backup format. When backing up databases within a SQL Server instance, the method of performing backups is guided by a "recovery model" that is specified during the database creation. This model can be changed after the database is created, but the model guides both the method of backup and the ability to recover data. The recovery model can be one of the following:

- SIMPLE—Transaction logs are automatically managed (truncated) during normal database operations. Since the transaction logs do not necessarily contain information since the last backup, no backups of the transaction logs are taken. This means that the database can only be recovered to a specific point in time— the time of the last backup. This model can be used for either file-/filegroup-level backups or database-level backups.

- FULL—Transaction logs are only truncated after a completed backup, and as such maintain all transactions that occur in the database between backups. Because of this, transaction log backups are taken along with the database. Can be used for either file-/filegroup-level backups or database-level backups. Allows for point-in-time recoveries of data at any point between backups by replaying transaction logs. This is typically the most common and recommended recovery model for SQL Server.

- BULK_LOGGED—Only minimal transaction logs are created during normal operations. This model is designed specifically for databases that have data loaded into them all at once, not over time. Such databases are called *bulk-* or *batch-loaded* databases. This recovery model also requires that transaction logs are backed up.

SQL Server also allows for the concept of full or differential backups, both at the database and the file-/filegroup-level. The "full" backup stated here should not be confused with the FULL recovery described previously. When *full* is discussed here, we are referring to the level at which the backup is taken taking all the data and backing it up, not the method of maintaining transaction logs relative to the backup (the recovery model). A full backup at the database level contains all data that resides within the database. In a differential database backup, only the data that has changed since the last backup is put into the backup container. A full backup is required to have been taken prior to a differential to act as a baseline. While this may seem like a trivial activity, it is important to understand that SQL Server does not automatically assume that a full backup has not been taken, and actually has no way to determine differential data without a full being previously taken.

SQL Server also allows for full and differential backups of files or filegroups within a database. This can be useful as it creates a simple method of protecting databases simply by copying files. However, do not be fooled—restoring the database can be complex because multiple files from multiple backups may be required to bring the database back to a consistent state. File-level backups are also larger than their database counterparts as the file will contain an unallocated database area in addition to the live data. This unallocated space within the database files, depending on your DBA's level of paranoia, can be more than 50 percent of the total size of the data files—effectively doubling the amount of data required to be backed up.

SQL Server also can take advantage of a Windows–specific operating system feature for backups: Volume Shadow Service (VSS). VSS provides a native operating system–level ability to create snapshots of file systems or *volumes* on a particular server, and make these snapshots available for use by backup or other operations. The VSS snapshot is effectively a full copy of the database at the point in time of the backup, but only contains the blocks that have changed since the initiation of the VSS session. This method is good for full backups under the SIMPLE or FULL recovery models.

SQL native tools are good for providing local backup to disk, but both NetBackup and CommVault provide management of backups over time and can utilize different methods of backing up the data within the database to make recoveries more straightforward. NetBackup and CommVault both use another feature of SQL Server, called the Virtual Device Interface (VDI), to accomplish database-level backups. VDI is a command data interface to the databases that allow NetBackup and CommVault to request specific streams of data to be generated and send through a "device" which is read by the backup software and re-directed back to the backup media. While this backup method does not allow the ability to track specific row/records, it does allow the ability to playback data to a particular point in time. CommVault and NetBackup also allow for file-based backups using the VDI interface—the interface places the database into a quiesced state which allows for the backup of all files within the database, or just specific files that have changed since the last backup.

NetBackup and CommVault also have the ability to use VSS as a backup method as well. While this method is not as granular as the VDI method, it can be a faster method of backup from the perspective of the database. During VDI-initiated backups from both NetBackup and CommVault, load is placed on the database as both pieces of backup software are essentially executing database-level operations while regular operations are occurring, thus competing for resources along with regular queries. VSS backups, however, work at the operating-system level to create a snapshot copy of the database. The only time the database sees any interaction is when the VSS service quiesces the database long enough to create the snapshot—an operation that is measured in minutes or seconds, not hours. From there, the backup software can take a backup of the database directly from the VSS snapshot without any further impact, other than OS-level impact, on database operations. While VSS snapshots do not have the ability to play back data as does VDI-based backups, they can be relatively small and taken several times a day, thus providing an ability that is analogous to log replays. Simply apply the VSS snapshot to the database, and the database is restored to the point in time at which the snapshot was originally taken.

In addition to the SQL Server native and NetBackup/CommVault-based backups, there also exists backup software that interacts directly with SQL Server and creates backups that allow row/record-level recoveries from backup stored locally on disk. The most widely used software for this type of backup is SQL Lightspeed by Quest Software. Lightspeed provides SQL Server DBAs the ability to do what they want—have locally controlled "backups" that quickly restore rows/records to a specific database without requiring external assistance, or obviate the need to have a second copy of the database software running to which to restore a native backup. Lightspeed is a powerful tool, but when used for creating backups that will be protected by either NetBackup or CommVault;,there are some issues to be aware of.

SQL Lightspeed

Since Lightspeed does not interact directly with either backup software, NetBackup and CommVault will essentially treat the backup of a Lightspeed backup as a full backup, regardless of what Lightspeed has generated. This is because to NetBackup or CommVault, the new backup generated by Lightspeed is simply a collection of files—there is nothing inherently different from a backup perspective of the Lightspeed backups from any other type of file. This means that the amount of data actually backed up by the backup software can be much greater than is really required from the database.

Secondly, there is an inherent assumption that the Lightspeed backup actually backed up data that was different from the previous backup. Said another way, there is no way for either NetBackup or CommVault to track what data was actually protected within a Lightspeed backup. This has two implications:

- **Backup levels‾** Every backup of a Lightspeed database dump is by definition a full backup. To both NetBackup and CommVault all files in a Lightspeed backup are new, so all files need to be protected.

- **Restore levels‾** There is no real way for either piece of backup software to determine which backup contains the necessary Lightspeed backup when restoring to a point in time, without intervention/documentation from the DBA(s) performing the Lightspeed backup.

This exposes the data protection method as a whole to the ability of the DBAs to manually maintain a record, either within Lightspeed or externally, of which backup corresponds to which point of recovery.

Finally, LightSpeed by default creates compressed copies of SQL Server backups. While this is very efficient for storing backups on local disk, it can play havoc with backups to media via either NetBackup or CommVault. Both pieces of backup software, when using tape media, use the compression that is native to the tape drive. When compressed data is backed up to a tape drive that is using compression, the drive does two things: it slows down as it is attempting to recompress already compressed data and it stores two to three times less data since no compression is possible on the data set. Under normal file system backups, this is not significant because in most cases the amount of compressed data as a percentage of the total data type is not great. However, with a LightSpeed backup set, 100 percent of the data is compressed, making for media storage that is greatly expanded from that which would be normally required. This issue is even more pronounced when using deduplication—compression can cause 10–20 times more storage requirements and performance degradation over uncompressed data.

When deciding which backup method(s) to use, discuss with the DBAs for the database their assessment of how often the data would need to be recovered, and to what level of granularity. Generally, a combination of approaches will cover the requirements of the backup administrator to provide detailed, long-term storage of data for protection; and those of the DBA to provide granular, short-term operational backups of data available for immediate restore. If the DBAs are using

LightSpeed or a similar product, work with them to understand the reasons for use. If the DBAs are simply using LightSpeed as a pure backup (they do not require the ability to quickly do record-level restores), work with them to implement a backup based on the backup software modules.

If a local backup is required due to operational or business concerns, then a separate backup, either using VDI or VSS, should also be made daily, independent of the LightSpeed backup. Why not just back up the LightSpeed output? There are several reasons. First, as was discussed previously, since the backup software does not interact with the local backup, there is no way to determine the point in time at which the backup was taken. While this may not seem like an issue at the point of backup, it can become critical at the point of recovery, particularly when recovering offsite.

Take the following scenario: backups are taken of the local backup onto the backup software. An offsite recovery is required to allow for auditing of the database at a particular period of time in the past, which lands between backup cycles. There are two LightSpeed backups that have been tracked by the backup software, which bracket the point in time required for the audit. Which one is required to restore? The only way to tell is to restore both, restore the databases from the resulting LightSpeed backup, and make the determination at that point. If a NetBackup or CommVault backup of the database had been taken in addition to the LightSpeed backup, the determination of the point of backup and the restoration of the database to satisfy the audit is a single restore process, with the ability to determine exactly which backup version is require.

If the backup software modules from NetBackup or CommVault are acceptable to the DBAs, determine their true needs. If the needs require a granular level of restore throughout the day, perform VSS backups of the transaction logs with daily VDI-level backups of the database, with the FULL recovery model having been implemented for the database. This will enable the DBAs to recover the database to a particular point in time, while having the continual record of transactions available for recovery on backup media. This will require moving data to the backup media throughout the day, however, since only the transaction logs will be moving, the amount of data actually backed up will only represent the amount of change since the last log backup. The daily VDI backup will roll up all the changes during the business day into a single backup. The VDI backup would be implemented on a standard full/differential schedule, as determined by the retention requirements of the business.

If a lower level of granularity can be utilized, either a VDI- or VSS-based backup can be taken of the database. Either the FULL or SIMPLE recovery model can be utilized, depending on how much granularity is required during restores. If the FULL recovery model is used, a VDI backup should be used. While this places more load on the database during backup, it allows for a smaller amount of data to be moved during a differential backup because only the changes within the database, not the whole database file, is backed up. However, if it is acceptable to only take a daily snapshot of the database, or if the SIMPLE recovery model has been implemented, using a VSS-based backup of the database at the file-/filegroup-level should be considered. This will still allow for a full/differential backup scheme, but since the SIMPLE recovery model does not allow for the capture of transaction logs, there is no reason to gather database blocks directly—the file or filegroup has already captured all the data needed for a restore.

Native tool backups should be avoided unless there is a very specific operational need. The SQL native tools provide no benefit over the use of the backup software tools, and the resulting backups can consume large amounts of disk space and system resources. The recovery method of native tool backups, while appearing to be simpler than the backup software–based backup, can actually require more steps than using the backup software client into SQL Server. In addition, native tool backups also suffer from the same nondeterministic identity problem described previously for LightSpeed backups. If there is an absolute requirement for local backups, a backup software–based backup should also be taken to mitigate the issue.

Oracle

Where SQL Server operates on a single platform, Windows, Oracle operates on Windows and multiple flavors of *NIX operating systems. While this may seem to present an issue in crafting a backup methodology for Oracle, there is a good set of common tools, both from the native Oracle backup and the NetBackup/CommVault sides to make backups across platforms look very similar.

Oracle Terminology

Oracle, like SQL Server, has its own set of terms to describe the various pieces of the implementation. Oracle databases are implemented on physical servers, with instances of Oracle representing the global memory structures and in memory elements required to run a database. The data within an Oracle database is placed in containers on disk called a *tablespace*. A tablespace can consist of one or more data files that hold the data content. Oracle also maintains transaction logs, but there are two types that can be generated, depending on the mode in which the database is currently running. In standard, or non-archivelog mode, the Oracle database generates only REDO logs. These logs are used to replay transactions that have already occurred—hence the name. In function they are very similar to the transaction logs in SQL Server. Oracle provides a second mode in which the database can operate: ARCHIVELOG mode. In ARCHIVELOG mode, Oracle generates *two* types of transaction logs: the REDO log and ARCHIVE logs. While the function of the REDO logs remains the same, the ARCHIVE log is used to capture transactions *before* they are committed to the database. This allows for not only roll back of the database to a point in time but also a roll *forward* to a point in time after the application of REDO logs. This is a very powerful tool and is required for hot backups, as you will see.

There are several other types of files that are extremely important to Oracle backups: control files and configuration files. Oracle control files are binary files that essentially store information for the database that tells the various software binaries critical information about how to start and maintain state within the database and stores the current state of the database in a static area. There are usually two copies of the control file created: a primary and a backup copy. If the primary copy of the control file is corrupted or missing, the backup can be substituted. Without a control file, the database will not be able to be started, or *mounted* in Oracle terminology.

■ **Note** It is *exceedingly important* to back up the control files along with the backup of *any* Oracle database.

Oracle also maintains configuration files that provide information to the binaries regarding options that can be utilized during binary startup and maintains information regarding licensing of the options to the database being maintained. The primary configuration file within a database is the init.ora file. This file contains information regarding the database name, the location of the primary and backup control files, and other configuration information that is critical to identifying the database to the instance. Additionally a secondary file, sqlnet.ora, may be present. It defines connection parameters for the *database*. The sqlnet.ora file contains information regarding the network interface on which to listen for connections, the physical server name and DNS domain, the external name of the databases, and the security method to be used on the databases specified. While not as important as the control files, the init.ora and the sqlnet.ora files should always be backed up as part of any backup created.

Oracle has two basic methods of preparing the database for backup and several methods for local backup. When using a manual or external method of backing up the Oracle database, using a backup of the data files as the way to back up the database, the database must be quiesced, just as in the SQL

Server process. Oracle can be quiesced by shutting down the database, but this imposes the same issues on Oracle as it does on SQL Server—namely that the database is unavailable for use by end users.

Oracle Hot Backup

Oracle can also be placed into hot backup mode, or online backup mode, depending on the documentation set being referenced. In this mode, the ARCHIVE logs act as the primary target for transactions while the database is being backed up. In Oracle version 10g or greater, each individual tablespace, which consists of one or more data files, can discretely be placed in hot backup mode and backed up independently. Prior to 10g the entire database had to be placed into hot backup mode and backed up as a unit. Why is placing the entire database into hot backup mode an issue?

During the period of time that the database is in hot backup mode, the ARCHIVE logs are receiving the transactions and the REDO logs are receiving the complete applied transaction, not just the pointers to the changes as normally happens. Since the ARCHIVE and REDO logs are simply circular logs that are located on disk, they do not have the performance that the database as a whole has. So the overall performance of the database is greatly reduced during the period of time that the database is in hot backup mode. Oracle partially solved this problem by allowing individual tablespaces to be placed in hot backup mode. This means that only a select group of files, representing the tablespace being backed up, is impacted, thus allowing an overall better performance during backup of the database, although possibly at the expense of the speed of the backup.

The traditional Oracle hot and cold backups also provided a mechanism to perform quick snapshot backups. The ability to create a snapshot, after placing Oracle into either mode, greatly sped the backup process from the Oracle perspective, and also provided an instantaneous copy of the Oracle database that could be mounted, restarted, and used for other purposes. The snapshot could be VSS-based, in the case of Windows implementations of Oracle, or could simply be an array-based snapshot or clone—the functionality of which would apply across operating system types.

■ **Note** Using array-based snapshots or clones for Oracle database backups require that scripting to integrate both the Oracle and the backup application so that the snapshots can coordinate with the state of the database.

This also somewhat fixed the issue with the impact of placing all or part of the database into hot backup mode, by greatly shortening the length of time required for the database to be in hot backup mode to the time required to make the snapshot copy—typically measured in minutes, not hours. This method also had the limitation of requiring complex scripting to coordinate the change of database mode with the creation of the snapshot and then reversing the change of mode back to standard operation.

RMAN Backups

The hot and cold backup modes for Oracle have the limitation of only allowing data file-level backups of the database, especially using snapshots for the database copies, which effectively looks like a full backup to the backup software. While the traditional methods are still in use, Oracle introduced a native method that allows for a robust means to perform full and differential backups of an Oracle database: Recovery Manager (RMAN). RMAN is essentially an internal mechanism to track Oracle backups of the data within a particular database. RMAN has two methods of tracking this information: locally maintaining backup metadata within the database control file or globally within a Recovery Catalog—

essentially a separate Oracle database specifically set up for RMAN backup metadata. RMAN can perform online and offline (cold) backups of the database being monitored, and is the primary method of integration for both NetBackup and CommVault Oracle backup agents.

■ **Note** RMAN is *required* for agent-based backup, such as those provided by NetBackup and CommVault. The Recovery Catalog is required for RMAN and must be set up by the DBA prior to executing backups using the backup agent. For more detailed information regarding implementing RMAN, consult *RMAN Recipes for Oracle Database 11g,* by Sam R. Alapati, Darl Kuhn, and Arup Nanda (Apress, 2007).

RMAN provides useful features to the backup software that are not found with the traditional hot/cold file-level backup. Since RMAN maintains state within the control file, differential backups of Oracle data, not data files, can be created—significantly reducing the amount of data required to be backed up and thus the time required for completion. This is similar in function to the VDI-based backups that can be used for SQL Server—a mechanism to track the individual database blocks and only back up those blocks that have changed. If the global Recovery Catalog is used, this metainformation can be maintained for longer periods of time and can cover multiple databases, across multiple servers—providing the ability to manage an entire enterprise and maintain multiple levels of RMAN recovery points, all from a single location.

RMAN can be operated from several points. First is the Database Control graphical user interface (GUI). This provides an interface that is very similar in functionality to what standard backup software would look like, except that it is specific to Oracle. Secondly, RMAN provides a command-line interface (CLI) to allow for command-line execution of backups, along with all configuration features. Lastly, and most important for this discussion, is RMAN's ability to run as a scripted utility. RMAN scripts form the basis for both local Oracle backups, as well as for backups controlled by both NetBackup and Oracle. The RMAN script contains all the configuration and command information necessary to execute the backup. By scripting RMAN, it is possible to consistently back up a database multiple times—which again provides a repeatable mechanism that can be used for backup software. It is by using these scripts that both NetBackup and CommVault can perform automated Oracle backups.

One of the more interesting features provided by RMAN is the ability to natively multiplex Oracle database backups through the use of RMAN channels. An *RMAN channel* is a data pipe through which the backup data flows to be written to the defined backup media.

■ **Note** Just like the relationship between the maximum amount of streams allowed from either a NetBackup or CommVault file system client, the RMAN channel specification must be tuned to the capabilities of the database from which the backup is taken.

For instance, if you have a database with 10 data files, you may want to open 10 channels, one for each data file. However, there may be limitations for performance—the system may have I/O limitations, or the number of media targets available for backup is fewer than the number of channels that are created. In order to throttle the number of channels backing up at the same time, RMAN provides the PARALLELISM parameter within the RMAN script to artificially limit the number of channels that can be operated in parallel.

RMAN Interfaces to NetBackup and CommVault

RMAN provides the interface for both NetBackup and CommVault through the installation of special binaries, called *libraries*, into the Oracle software. These libraries provide the software "pipe" through which the output of RMAN backups flows to the backup software for tracking and storage onto the backup media. In default configurations, Oracle DBAs create RMAN scripts and run them by using either the Oracle default library to create a local, disk-based backup or the provided software libraries to seamlessly provide backups to the backup media. Here is where the differences between NetBackup and CommVault implementation are seen. NetBackup *requires the manual creation of RMAN scripts* by the DBAs, which are then called by the Oracle agent to be executed at the time of backup. CommVault, on the other hand, *generates RMAN scripts based on the parameters specified* during subclient configuration. The RMAN script is generated at backup time and executed using the native RMAN tools.

There are advantages and disadvantages to each approach. The NetBackup approach allows for a great deal of customization and tuning, using the large number of configurable parameters within RMAN to optimize the backup stream or to provide a method of quickly altering how the RMAN backups are completed, simply by changing the RMAN script being used. The CommVault strategy takes the opposite approach. When a subclient is created within CommVault, the backup software already knows what common parameters are changed within the RMAN script and allows for an easy method of adjusting the parameters without physically logging in to the client and manually adjusting the script. CommVault also allows for a script "preview" where the backup administrator or DBA can take the generated copy of the RMAN script and make changes.

This feature of CommVault brings up some interesting side notes:

- If the RMAN script is essentially running the backup, with only minimal involvement from the backup software, what would prevent the script from being run at will from the database server?

- If RMAN is so powerful, why use backup software at all to capture the backup output?

To the first point, there is absolutely nothing that inherently prevents the RMAN script used by either NetBackup or CommVault from executing manually, except any exclusion windows for backup that have been created on the Master Server/CommServe that restrict times in which backups can run. In fact, this feature of RMAN is what is used to run the RMAN scripts for CommVault that have been manually altered in the preview process. The power of RMAN is to provide a very flexible method of performing backups of Oracle databases, run either from the backup software or the client as a user-initiated backup.

But why run backup software at all? RMAN has a scheduling utility, a method of tracking the backup status of the various databases under control and is able to restore quite well. The answer goes back to a subject that was discussed in the SQL Server discussion above: the ability to track backups from an enterprise level, not just from a tactical level. While RMAN does have all these abilities, the backup administrator must be concerned with protection of data in the entirety of the enterprise, not just within the specific set of clients that represent the Oracle databases. The backup software provides a means by which backups can be tracked and recovered external to that provided strictly within the purview of the DBA. Using backup software to perform the Oracle backups also provides the ability to restore servers that may be related to the particular Oracle databases that are *not* backed up by RMAN. Just as with SQL Server, a variety of approaches that depend on the needs of the DBA(s), including RMAN scheduled backups, is entirely appropriate.

Again, just as with SQL Server, it is important to assess the needs of the particular database and make some determinations regarding the criticality of the data, the requirement for granularity in restore, and the required RPO/RTO (recovery point objective/recovery time objective). Fully automated, RMAN backups to local disk may be a good solution for DBAs who require the need to very quickly restore data to a point in time, without waiting for backup media. After this type of backup is taken, it is possible to perform a backup software backup of the resulting RMAN backup. However, the same issues of the ability to track the backup and its status as it relates to other issues in the environment remain, if the second pass method is used.

RMAN provides a solution to the problem. Instead of having RMAN define the backup target and provide the interface, create a local backup disk target within the backup software (essentially make the database server its own media writer) and allow user-directed backups to the disk target. Then duplicate copies of a now backup-software-tracked backup can be made by either using Vault/bpduplicate (in the case of NetBackup) or an AUX copy process (in the case of CommVault). Very short-term retention periods can be set using this method, again working with the DBA(s) to determine how many copies they are required to keep, which allows the backup software to automatically maintain the backup space, offloading that task from the DBAs as well.

During a restore, the backup media is always available (it is the local disk). If not, RMAN will seamlessly request the backup from the backup software. It will provide the appropriate media stream if it is currently available or throw an alert to the backup administrator to retrieve the media and make it available for recovery.

However, this is an expensive process—there are additional licenses required for the media writer implementation, along with the disk storage required to physically store the backups that are generated by the process. So this method should only be used for critical systems that really require very tight restore timelines.

Sounds great! So, why can't this process be used for SQL Server? While it could in theory, the integration between the SQL Server and either NetBackup or CommVault is as seamless as RMAN—a restore call from the native SQL utility only recognizes backups generated by SQL Server—the restore is not seamlessly passed to the backup software for restoration, regardless of location. The RMAN interface allows for this seamless interface through the use of the software "library"-level integration—that pipe that moves the data from RMAN to the backup software for tracking, storage, and retention maintenance.

The alternative is to simply have RMAN back up to the standard backup media, as defined with the backup software. While the backup is not "local," it is still fully accessible from the RMAN recovery methods, it is simply located on media that is not on the same physical system. There are several issues that DBA(s) cite when presented with this method:

- The performance of the restore will be slow—it *may* be slower than the local restore, depending on a number of factors on the Media Server/MediaAgent side and the network connection used to perform the backup/restore of the database. If the initial backup is stored on a Disk Storage Unit (DSU)/magnetic library (MagLib) and duplicate copies are made for longer-term storage, then the overall performance will only be gated by the network.

- The backup will not be accessible because the tape will be inaccessible for some reason. One way to avoid this argument is to use disk storage as the backup target instead of tape and then make a copy of the backup image to external storage. Since the backup will remain on storage that is directly attached to the media writer, the backup will be accessible for use at any time. As a side benefit, potentially more RMAN backups can be accommodated by more effectively using the total storage allocated for RMAN backups and centralizing it on one or two Media Servers/MediaAgents.

- Backups/recoveries cannot be done at a specific time due to batch processing, database maintenance, and so on. Since the backups are running to disk, which the backups will then be duplicated to longer-term media as a secondary step, essentially the backups can be scheduled at *almost* any time. However, this does present challenges for the backup administrator in terms of resource allocation and network congestion.

Using standard media on a "remote" Media Server/MediaAgent provides the ability to fully manage the complete backup process without sacrificing DBA direct access to the backups for operational purposes.

An alternative to using RMAN backups is to create a snapshot copy of the database. This requires that the database and all related files, including control files and configuration files, reside on disk that has the ability to have snapshots. These snapshots can be array-based snapshots, volume manager–snapshots (through the use of software on the operating system), or (in the case of Windows) a VSS snapshot. The procedure for taking backup copies based on snapshot is as follows:

- Quiesce the database, either as a hot or cold database.

- Create the snapshot.

- Restart or remove the database from hot backup mode.

- Mount the snapshot database.

- Perform the backup.

The advantage of doing Oracle database backups in this way is that a complete copy of the database is made during the backup process. This copy can be used for reporting, testing, and development; extraction for data warehousing; and just about any other means needed to have a replica database available. The disadvantage is, of course, the requirement for a relatively large amount of storage to perform the snapshot—either the amount needed for the change when using snaps or the complete size of the database when using a clone.

Oracle provides a great deal of flexibility when it comes to protection of the data within the database. Through the use of RMAN, Oracle can both meet the needs of the DBA for operational protection and the needs of the backup administrator in strategic protection of the data over time.

Mail Servers

Backing up mail servers is possibly one of the most complex, yet most important tasks required of the backup system. E-mail is the main transport of information, communication, and data distribution in most, if not all, organizations today. A mail system is a combination of file server, database, and network communicator, all of which have differing backup requirements and methods. Since there are so many differences and requirements, this section will focus more on how CommVault and NetBackup perform data protection than the native tools available to do the backups. This approach is taken as with most mail servers; backup of the data was never really built directly into the product. There is, and was, always the assumption that external methods would be used to protect the mail server, and the mail server was historically viewed as a transport mechanism, not a storage platform. More to the point, the users' mail was intended to be stored locally on their workstation, and was not the responsibility of the person administering the mail server. While there are many different types of mail servers and systems in use, we will look at the two major mail servers in use today: Microsoft Exchange and IBM Lotus Notes, or Domino.

Exchange

Microsoft Exchange is a database that stores and forwards mail. The core of Exchange runs on the Microsoft Jet database, the same engine on which other products such as Access are built on. The various versions of Exchange use increasingly sophisticated interfaces to the backup software to make backups of the underlying mail data and be able to subsequently restore data with many different options. In versions prior to Exchange 2010, Exchange utilized structures named storage groups to group data and make engine searches and management of the mail server. (See Figure 8–6.)

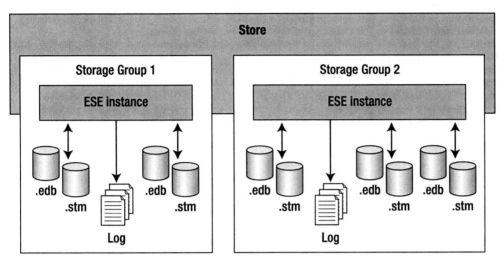

Figure 8–6. Exchange 2003 storage group architecture[1]

The storage group is a group of databases within an Exchange server that contained a subset of the mail being managed by the Exchange server as a whole. The storage group represented the most granular level of backup and restore, other than mailbox-level recoveries that could be attained. However, in Exchange 2010, there have been a number of improvements in the overall structure of the Exchange system, which have been reflected in some structure changes, namely the removal of storage groups as a construct within the Exchange server. Exchange 2010 now maintains the mail store in entire databases, not in separate databases related in a group, as were the storage groups. This change in architecture drives some differences in the backup methodology used by both NetBackup and CommVault when backing up Exchange.

There are three ways backup software performs backups of Exchange: VSS, data stream, and file backups.

- *VSS*: VSS backups work in a similar way as backups of SQL Server using VSS: the Jet database is momentarily quiesced, a VSS snapshot of the Exchange environment is taken, and the database is sent on its way.

- *Data stream*: Data stream backups use an interface similar to VDI. This data stream method allows for both full and "brick-level" (mailbox-level) backups and recovery.

- *File*: File-level backup is self-explanatory: makes a copy of the files that make up the Exchange environment.

There are also specific methods of Exchange recovery that are used to restore data that are implemented by the backup software. For pre-Exchange 2010, Exchange has the ability to recovery

---

[1] *Exchange Storage Architecture,* http://technet.microsoft.com/en-us/library/bb124808(EXCHG.65).aspx, accessed 18 December 2010.

storage groups to an alternate location within the same Exchange domain through the use of a recovery storage group (RSG). Normally, an Exchange storage group could not be directly restored to the same Exchange domain because it would create name conflicts within Exchange. The RSG solved this problem by providing a method of restoring the storage group to the environment, but also isolating the naming issues and allowing direct access to the data within the recovery storage group.

In Exchange 2010, the implementation of the storage group has been removed. As such, the RSG has been replaced with the Recovery Database (RD). The RD provides the same functionality as the RSG, allowing the recovery of an Exchange database to the same domain as the original backup was taken from. Exchange 2010 also has a new high availability feature called the Database Availability Group (DAG), as shown in Figure 8–7. The DAG allows for a virtualized Exchange database that appears to the Exchange environment as a regular database used by Exchange. Exchange RDs can be used as restore points for both standard Exchange databases and DAG-based databases.

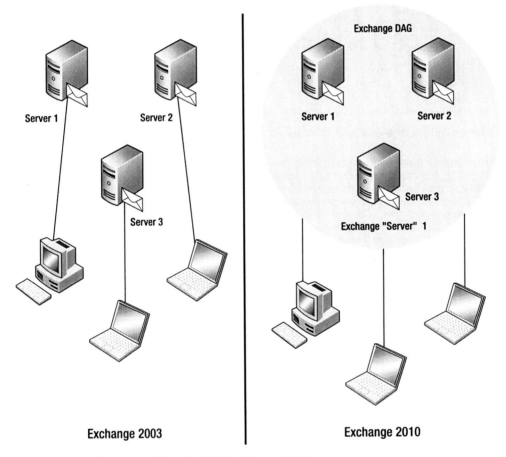

Figure 8–7. Exchange Database Availability Group (DAG)

Exchange can also use VSS snapshots to restore from. As snapshot, the VSS restore recovers entire databases or storage groups to Exchange, not brick-level recoveries. However, since VSS snapshots can be taken at several times throughout the day and only capture the differences between the snapshots, it is possible to provide somewhat granular recovery of Exchange. Array-based snapshots are also possible using the VSS interface, but will require the VSS provider for the array interface to be installed prior to use.

Exchange can also be backed up and restored using simple file-level backups. This can be accomplished by either creating a consistent copy of the entire Exchange environment with a cloning technology or stopping Exchange to allow for a file-based backup. This method of backup is very rarely used as it requires significant outage times for the Exchange server to complete the backup.

Both NetBackup and CommVault use the various backup and recovery methods to protect Exchange data and provide for the ability to recover data.

NetBackup has a number of methods to provide backups of Exchange:

- *Granular Restore Technology (GRT)*—This backup allows for brick-level backup and recovery of Exchange,

- *MAPI-level backup*—This backup is an alternative to GRT that can be used for brick-level recovery on Exchange 2007 and prior.

- *Full backup*—With this backup, all databases or storage groups are backed up using the data stream from the Exchange server. Transaction logs, which have the same function for Exchange as they do for SQL Server, are truncated during this type of backup. This means that during a restore, only the point in time contained within the backup can be applied to the Exchange server.

- *Differential incremental backup*—This backup captures all changes since the last full or differential backup. This backup also truncates the logs after the backup, creating a point-in-time backup. This backup only backs up the transaction logs and must be applied to a full backup of the database.

- *Cumulative incremental backup*—This backup also captures all the changes since the last full or differential backup, but does not truncate the transaction logs. This method allows the backup of the database to occur and the transaction logs to be replayed to any point in time. Note that this backup method can require the replay of large numbers of transaction logs during the restore process.

- *Snapshot backup using VSS or array-based snapshots/clones*—This type of backup creates a full point-in-time copy of the Exchange server, but uses a snapshot instead of the data stream to get a copy of the Exchange environment. This backup is at the file level and can be performed as either a full or incremental backup. This method can also be used for DAG backups of a selected replica database and to provide for an instant recovery option when using VSS—NetBackup can transparently reapply the snapshot against the Exchange server.

NetBackup uses a single agent to provide these options, which are configured when setting up the backup policy for the Exchange server on the Master Server.

Where NetBackup uses a single agent, CommVault uses a targeted Exchange agent to perform backup and recoveries, depending on the type of backup that is desired. The CommVault iDAs (Intelligent Data Agents) that are provided are the Database, Mailbox, and Public/Web Folder data agents. The names of the iDAs describe the function and level of granularity provided for the backup:

- *Database iDA*—Provides data protection at the Exchange database (storage group)–level. This iDA can provide protection with full, differential, or incremental backups. Differential or incremental backups are defined as "preselected" backups within the subclient configuration. By default, the Database iDA uses VSS to provide the backup data for movement to the media as defined by the associated storage policy. However, if an array–based snapshot module is installed that the Quick Recovery iDA can manipulate, the Database iDA can use it as the backup mechanism instead of VSS. Database backups can be recovered to the same storage group, a different storage group on the same server (such as an RSG), or a different storage group within the same Exchange domain.

- *Mailbox iDA*—Provides protection of Exchange data at the brick or mailbox level, and allows for recovery of individual pieces of mail directly back into the Exchange server being protected. This iDA backs up the mailboxes, folders within the mailboxes, and any attachments associated with the e-mail being protected. The Mailbox iDA can provide full, differential, incremental, and synthetic full backups of Exchange. The resulting backup of the mailbox or folder can then be recovered either in "append", "overwrite", or "skip" mode. *Append* adds information to the end of the mailbox, duplicate or not; *overwrite* overwrites the mailbox with the duplicate data; *skip* skips any duplicate data. The Mailbox iDA also enables installing an Outlook plug-in to users with protected mailboxes to perform self-recoveries of their mail, freeing the backup administrator from having to respond to continuous requests for deleted mail recoveries.

- *Public/Web Folder iDA*—CommVault is unique in making a distinction between private mailboxes (the mailboxes that end users use), and public and/or web folders (publicly accessible folders that are used for a group or organization common storage area of various items, including group e-mail). These folders are treated separately with CommVault to allow for consideration of the differences between the public/web folders and private mailboxes. Just as with the standard Mailbox iDA, however, the Public/Web iDA can provide full, differential, incremental, and synthetic full backup capabilities.

▓ **Note** CommVault has two unique functions with regard to Exchange backup: the ability to directly integrate the Database iDA with the array-based snapshots via the Quick Recovery iDA, and the ability to allow self-serve restores of individual mailbox items via an Outlook plug-in when the Mailbox iDA is installed.

While the iDA provides different levels of backup, recovery types can span the particular iDAs, depending on the recovery model that is desired to retrieve the data back to the Exchange server. Just as with NetBackup, the CommVault Database iDA can either be a file-level recovery or a data stream-level recovery, both of which can use the transaction logs to replay all mail transactions to a particular point in time.

Exchange can be recovered at the file level using a point-in-time restore or a VSS direct restore. These types of restores recover the files and then replay the transaction logs to bring the Exchange storage group(s) or database(s) back to a consistent point in time. The VSS restore obviously utilizes the VSS snapshot to quickly perform the recovery of the data files back into Exchange, with the execution of any transaction logs occurring after the data file restore.

Exchange can also be recovered using the replay of logs to perform a recovery to the last mail transaction committed to the server. This type of recovery is called a *no loss restore* within CommVault. However, this restore type makes the assumption that all logs required for a replay from a particular point in time are available and online, ready for use. But why would the logs not be available—shouldn't all the logs simply be on the backup? Not necessarily. If a database backup was taken at 10 PM, and a failure happened at 10 AM the next morning, in order for the database to be recovered using a no loss recovery, the logs that were generated from the time of the backup until 10 AM would have to be fully available and uncorrupted. While this may often be the case, in the case of server failure or accidental deletion/truncation of the logs, a no loss recovery is impossible.

The last type of Exchange-level (database-level) recovery that is possible using CommVault is the *one-pass* restore method. This method rebuilds the Exchange server from scratch—simply wiping out all existing data files within the Exchange server and replacing them with the files on the backup media. This is strictly a file-level restore; not even VSS is available in this type of recovery.

With the multitude of backup and recovery options, how is a selection made about which is the most appropriate for the environment? Basically, backup and recovery in Exchange can be broken down into the three types previously described: file, database, and mailbox. The solution to most environments is a combination of the three, all applied to a particular issue. The File backup and recovery method is good in environments where e-mail is important but not critical, or where business operations are limited to standard business hours. Said another way, if the organization in question can afford to lose the mail generated between backups, the file-level backup is entirely applicable. However, this is the rare occurrence. The file-level backup is typically used to make cumulative, static backups of Exchange that can be stored for long periods of time, or to provide fully auditable copies of the Exchange server for offsite or extra-domain recovery and study.

The database-level backups are the most common. The database backups of Exchange in NetBackup and CommVault capture the transaction logs as part of the backup process. This allows the recovery of the database to the point of the backup or any point prior. Since the database-level backup does require some level of quiescing of the Exchange system, it can impact the delivery of mail during the time of the backup; however, if the mail backup is performed at a period of low activity, typically at night in most organizations, the impact is manageable. Of course, other e-mail maintenance activities such as defragmentation and compaction may be running as well during these off hours, so care should be taken when scheduling backups to not interfere.

Since the database-level backups for both NetBackup and CommVault can perform full, differential, and incremental backups, the amount of data that is required to be moved on a daily basis can be managed and balanced with other data being protected using the same data traffic analysis patterns described in other areas. This is generally the type of backup to implement for regular backup of the Exchange environment.

With the ability to back up and recover mailboxes, why would you not implement that for all users and simply use a data stream method of backup? The answer lies in how the mailboxes are determined to require a backup. Since Exchange does not maintain tracking of individual items as candidates for backup, the backup software must scan all parts of the Exchange server and determine whether a particular item requires backup or whether the backup of the item has already occurred. This places a great deal of load on the Exchange server, which in turn drives down the performance of the Exchange server as a whole. Additionally, this scanning process takes a great deal of time, many orders of magnitude greater than database backups. So mailbox-level backups, GRT or MAPI (depending on the Exchange version) should be applied with great care—generally only protecting user mail that represents a significant legal or financial risk to the organization or must be protected by statute. Mailbox-level backup and recovery can, and should be, combined with database-level backups to provide full coverage of the Exchange environment.

Exchange is a complex mail system with a great number of capabilities, but also introduces a number of problems into the backup administrator's life—possibly more than any other piece of software in the environment. With the flexibility of both NetBackup and CommVault to support the various methods of backup and recovery, and to provide these methods in a consumable way, the backup of this complex animal is made much more simply, especially over older methods of protecting Exchange.

Lotus Notes

Like Exchange, which uses a multidatabase model to store mail, IBM Lotus Notes uses the DB2 database to provide a mail store for users of the mail subsystem. However, Lotus Notes (or Domino as it is also known) provides a full office and document automation system in addition to the mail system. As such, other databases within Domino can be created and protected. They are completely unrelated to the mail system, but are equally important to be protected during a backup. Since these databases can be custom created, when protecting a Domino environment, it is important to understand the individual needs of the database(s) added to the environment, over and above the standard ones created during the installation of a Domino environment. Since there is no way to anticipate the needs and structure of the custom database environment, this section will only deal with the standard databases that are created.

Within Domino, every user entry created is treated as a *data document*—more succinctly, an entry in a database. Mail and attachments are no exception. Mail is simply a user data document with references to other documents, depending on the contents of the mail, the relationship to other data documents in the databases, and the context in which the document (e-mail) is received.

Domino has two types of databases that are created as part of this process: logged and unlogged. *Logged databases* are those that maintain transaction logs as part of their storage process; *unlogged databases* are the converse: no transaction logs are maintained, or logging has been turned off. Transaction logs in Domino can have three different states:

- *Circular*—The transaction logs have a fixed file size, which limits the number of transactions that can be rolled back/forward during data recovery operations.

- *Linear*—The transaction logs have a variable size and can extend in fixed amounts from the initial size, and can grow to the limits of the file system in which they are created. Linear transaction logs require manual truncation to control their size and to limit the number of transactions maintained.

- *Archive*—The transaction logs in an archive mode are varied in size, both in the size of the file and the size of the extension of the log, and are truncated as part of the backup process of the particular database.

Only Archive transaction logs can be protected as part of a Domino database backup, are required to be protected by the backup process, and provide the ability to have incremental backups of databases within the Domino environment. Once archive logs are backed up, they are truncated, marked as "recycled," and available for reuse for the database.

Both NetBackup and CommVault provide simple and granular methods to protect databases within a Domino environment. NetBackup can protect all types of databases and allows for online, offline, and transaction log–only backups. The NetBackup type of recovery is only at the database level, and provides only file and transaction log replay to recover the database to a particular point in time. NetBackup does provide a feature called Fast Recovery that attempts to recall all required transaction logs for database recovery to the specified point in time, prior to the recovery. This is different from the normal recovery method, which is sequential in nature: recover the log, apply the log, rinse, and repeat. The Fast Recovery restore method requires that there be enough recovery disk space available to recover all necessary transaction logs, which can be a very large amount of space on a database with a large transaction rate. Individual mailbox recoveries in a NetBackup recovery scheme must be accomplished by recovering the database to another location and then performing manual migration of mailboxes and information from the alternate location to the target destination of the recovery.

CommVault provides more in-depth functionality when performing Domino backup and recovery. As with everything CommVault, there are two iDAs available for Domino that cover different types of backup and recovery: the Database iDA and the Document iDA. As with the Exchange iDA, the Database iDA provides protection of the Domino database through the backup of the database and the transaction logs. This iDA has similar functionality to that found in the NetBackup Domino agent. The CommVault Database iDA has two types of database protection:

- *Subclient*—This allows the selection of a number of items to be backed up by defining separate subclients: the database only, the transaction logs only, and both the database and transaction logs. This allows for multiple types of backup and restores options at the database level, depending on the type and granularity of recovery required.

- *Partition*—This provides backups of all databases on a particular Domino server and provides only database-level backups. This type of backup is typically used for databases where Circular or Linear type logging is utilized.

Database recoveries can be applied in several different ways. During recovery, the database can be set to overwrite the existing database, to change the unique identifier of the database, called the *database id* or *dbid*, to allow for restore onto the same server as the original database, and to select whether transaction logs are replayed against the restored database or not. These options can be very useful, depending on what type of database is being recovered or how the data documents are intended to be reinserted back into Domino as a whole.

The Document iDA is where CommVault shows some differences. The Document iDA can provide protection of the Domino database by backing up and recovering individual data documents from inside a particular database. Document-level backup can be the following:

- Full backup

- Incremental backup

- Differential backup

- Synthetic full backup

The default subclient backs up all documents within a particular database, so secondary subclients should be created to target only those document sets that need to be protected. Why? For the same reasons as full mailbox backups for Exchange should be avoided: the load placed on the databases is very impactful on the overall performance, and the time required for full database scans can be many times greater than that required for database backups. Document-level recoveries, like database-level recoveries, can overwrite existing entries, possibly preventing duplicate entries within Domino.

By acting more as a true relational database, Lotus Notes Domino can make backup and recovery of the mail system easier and quicker. However, the lack of a standard mechanism to quickly access individual mail records, such as that provided by Exchange, can make recoveries less granular and require more manual intervention.

Other Applications

Thus far, only specific application types and applications have been discussed, but there are hundreds if not thousands of different applications in the IT ecosystem, each of which requires backup of the data generated/utilized, the application, or both. One of these applications is the protection of *virtual machines (VMs)*, which has its own set of challenges. Excluding VMs, there are also some general strategies that can assist with designing a backup solution for those applications that do not necessarily fit into the standard mold.

Virtual Machines

The new wave of deployment of servers is not to deploy individual physical servers into environments, but to provide a single physical server and deploy multiple virtual servers within the physical environment. The virtualization of servers allows better utilization of the resources within a physical system, as well as a typical reduction in the environmental resources required to run an equivalent number of physical systems.

Most VM environments have two essential components: a master control area called a *hypervisor* and a collection of one or more virtual systems or guest OS systems. The hypervisor is the main abstraction and resource allocation layer for all the virtual systems. It provides the allocation of CPU, RAM, virtual networks, and NICs; and disk space to each virtual machine that runs within the hypervisor. Virtual networks are typically attached or "bound" to physical network cards, which provide access to the LAN for TCP/IP access, just as with physical machines.

Disk space for a virtual machine is typically not allocated as individual physical logical unit numbers (LUNs), which the VM consumes as it sees fit (although this can be done under certain situations), but is allocated as a special file that sits on a file system within the hypervisor. This virtual disk is called by various names (VMDK for VMWare, VHD for Microsoft Hyper-V, and so on), but it is simply a file that the hypervisor reinterprets for the VM as a particular disk LUN that is attached to a virtual IDE or SCSI controller. This virtual disk (or multiple virtual disks) is where the operating system, applications, and application data for the VM are all stored. (See Figure 8–8.)

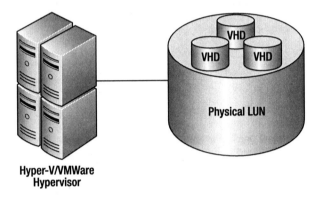

Hyper-V/VMWare
Hypervisor

Figure 8–8. LUNs and VHDs

When looking at this from a backup perspective, there is the question of what to back up. Since the virtual machines are running on virtual disks, and those virtual disks are simply files in the hypervisor, the backup software can treat the virtual disks as regular files and complete a backup of the guest OS and all applications and data in one fell swoop. However, since you are backing up the entire OS, application, and data in this case, the backup is probably capturing more data than is absolutely necessary and may not create a data backup that is usable. This is because as the backup is running, the guest OS and associated applications are also running, blissfully unaware that that the "disks" they are using are being backed up—thus creating inconsistent copies of data structures that may be created by the operating system and applications running within the virtual machine. As was shown earlier in the database and mail server sections, backups of inconsistent copies of this application type results in unusable data for restores as the data cannot be made consistent during the restore process.

Additionally, under normal conditions, there is no way to restore individual files from backups of the virtual disks. This is because while the virtual disks are indeed files from the backup software perspective, they are simply files that contain blocks of data—there is no inherent way the backup software can read a virtual disk and determine which files are contained within. This limitation can be overcome in specific situations, but in general the backup software only knows it has backed up a single file when backing up a virtual disk, not hundreds or thousands of files that happened to be embedded within the virtual disk by the guest OS.

Since each virtual machine is attached to a virtual network, and the virtual network is attached to a physical network, the backup agent, either NetBackup or CommVault, can be installed *within* the virtual machine and a backup taken just as if the virtual machine was a physical machine. But this configuration has issues of its own. Since there are multiple virtual machines connected to a virtual network, and this virtual network is typically smaller than the combined virtual network to which it is attached, any application that runs on a group of servers that generates a large amount of network traffic has the potential of overrunning the physical network. This is typically accounted for in the physical machine design for normal application traffic.

Backup, however, is typically regarded outside of the norm and can be expensive to design for by simply adding physical network ports to provide additional bandwidth. Backup network traffic is by nature a "burst" of traffic followed by long periods of inactivity. If more network interfaces are simply added to account for the backup traffic, on top of the normal application traffic, that additional bandwidth will be unused for large periods of time, increasing physical infrastructure unnecessarily. However, if this is not done, then the backup traffic can (and in most cases will) impact the application traffic performance.

Additionally, the load introduced by the backup software on the hypervisor also increases exponentially. Think of it this way: if a backup client is run on the hypervisor to back up all virtual disks on the system, only one copy of the agent is running for the entire set of virtual machines. If a copy of the agent is installed on each virtual server, there are the same numbers of backup clients effectively running on the physical server as there are virtual machines. Depending on what the backup agents are doing at any particular time, the load that is generated may affect all other virtual systems on the same physical system.

While the backup now can both back up and restore individual files—since to the backup software the virtual machine is simply a physical system—a great deal of duplicate data is generated from the virtual machine, needlessly increasing the amount of data backed up and consuming backup, network, and storage resources.

While these two perspectives seem like an insurmountable paradox, there have been solutions built to solve many of the issues around them. When a guest OS is installed within a virtual environment, there is a series of drivers and tools that also need to be installed, provided from the virtual environment, that allow the guest OS to communicate status to the hypervisor, and to allow the hypervisor to perform certain low-level tasks.

In Windows environments, both when using VMWare and Hyper-V, VSS can be used to momentarily suspend activities for running applications, such as SQL Server and Exchange, to allow for an *external*, or hypervisor-based, snapshot to take place. This snapshot can then be backed up using either a specialized client for the hypervisor (in the case of VMWare and other hypervisors) or using standard VSS methods built into the backup agent (in the case of Hyper-V). In addition, both VMWare (when run on top of a Windows server OS) and Hyper-V, when backing up Windows guest OS installations, can report on the individual file contents contained within the guest OS systems, and allow for file-level restoration of files. The snapshot functionality is also available for Linux environments under VMWare, but the functionality is limited to flushing file systems within the guest OS in an attempt to create a *crash-consistent* copy of the virtual disks. This is typically acceptable in most cases as the applications that run under Linux can usually be restored using crash-consistent copies, but this needs to be verified on a per-application basis.

■ **Note** Not only should VM backups be verified on a regular basis but all backups should also be tested and verified on a regular basis.

So when would the guest OS backup method be used? While the ability to perform the hypervisor-level backups can largely mitigate the necessity to perform guest OS backups by eliminating many of the issues, the guest OS–level backup can provide a level of granularity that can more selectively pick what is backed up and what is ignored. The guest OS backup still provides a superior method of performing VDI and data stream level backups of SQL Server and Exchange, where the VSS-based method of backing up via the hypervisor only provides a point-in-time granularity based on the last snapshot taken at the hypervisor.

Deduplication and VM Backups

One item that is common between both the hypervisor-based backup and the guest OS is that there is a great deal of common data that is shared between virtual machines, particularly between guest OS machines that contain the same operating system. A perfect solution for this situation, both from a hypervisor backup and a guest OS backup perspective, is to use either source-based or target-based deduplication. The use of a source-based deduplication solution, such as PureDisk in NetBackup or using the block-level deduplication feature of SILO storage within CommVault, allows the backup client to preselect the blocks that are common between all virtual disks (or virtual machines in the case of guest OS–level backups) and only send the blocks that either have not been already sent through another backup or do not already exist as a result of the deduplicated backup. This can significantly reduce the amount of data transmitted during the backup and thus reduce the overall time required for the completion of the backup.

However, source-based deduplication can require a significant investment in infrastructure and licensing costs that may be impractical for many environments. In addition, there are limitations on the amount of data that can be ingested per hour in either the NetBackup or CommVault source–based solutions—limiting the size of the environment that can be protected with a given amount of infrastructure. A target–based deduplication solution, while increasing the amount of data transmitted during the backup, can ingest data at rates significantly faster than source-based deduplication, and can provide a lower-cost solution for large environments as licensing and infrastructure requirements tend to be much less than source-based solutions. The target solution works by providing a backup target for either the Media Server or MediaAgent that is acting as the target for the backup of the hypervisor or guest OS–level backups. All data is routed to the target deduplication solution, effectively providing a global deduplication method that will only store unique blocks.

Virtual machines provide unique benefits to the physical infrastructure by reducing the physical infrastructure required to provide the same processing power and hosting ability. However, virtual machines present a number of backup issues that need to be addressed in order to protect the data within the virtual machines. Either hypervisor, guest OS level, or *both* can be utilized to address the various issues found when doing data protection. The addition of either source- or target-based deduplication to the solution can reduce either the amount of data transmitted during the backup (source-based) or the quantity of data stored (target-based).

Summary

Different types of applications have differing backup needs and requirements, depending on the type of data being stored, the application used, and the requirements of the data to be placed into a particular state prior to backup. The determination of these requirements is critical to ensuring that the data stored on the backup media is actually usable during recovery. Additional factors, such as the use of virtual machines and operating systems capabilities, are also factors that need to be considered when looking at application requirements for backup.

CHAPTER 9

Putting It All Together: Sample Backup Environments

So far, all the elements of a backup environment have been discussed: target media, backup software, and applications. Now it is time to put them all together into some sample solutions, based on backup architecture, specifically as they relate to the size of the environment. These sample environments take a number of different factors into consideration and build on the concepts and functionality that has been previously laid out. However, they only provide a starting point. The configurations of backup environments are as varied as the number of environments: everyone has specific considerations that need to be accounted for within the design. Additionally, as the sample designs grow, notice that the designs are not focused so much on adding capacity (that is accounted for in a horizontal scalability model), but more on adding features to meet specific needs.

Cloud/Backup as a Service

The use of offsite backups is not a new phenomenon. However, cloud or backup as a service (BaaS) takes remote backups a step beyond simple offsite backups. The BaaS offering provides a method of completely offloading the entire infrastructure required for backups to an Internet location, with a service provider ensuring that the infrastructure needed is available for use. These services are fully functional—on-demand backups and restores, ability to schedule backups, group policies application—all the features you would expect from a piece of backup software.

Great! So, why not replace all the backup software with a BaaS and call the backup problem solved? There are a number of issues with BaaS services. The primary one is that of scale. While backup services can handle a number of clients, the ability to ingest backups is largely gated by the connection to the Internet. As the numbers increase, so does the use of the bandwidth. While this is not typically an issues in sites with well-defined "off hours," it will impact other jobs or access because the BaaS services can take significant amounts of bandwidth otherwise used by regular client access. Additionally, BaaS clients also have a significant impact on the performance of the client on which they are run. In order for the backup to run quickly—as all of these BaaS clients use some type of either block-level tracking, real-time file tagging, or deduplication, the client software must consume a significant portion of CPU in order to work efficiently, thus dragging down any available CPU for use by normal operations. Most BaaS client software can be throttled, but this significantly increases the time required for the backup to complete.

A more basic issue is with access to the Internet. If this is placed in an environment with dial-up access only, metered Internet access, or generally a slow/unreliable link, the backup software may have issues with reliable completion. More important, restores may be made more difficult for the same reasons—if you cannot get to the Internet, you cannot get the files back. Some BaaS services mitigate that by providing a mechanism to request CD/DVD copies of files. But this requires you to know exactly what file(s) you need, the directory where they are located, and which version you require—a process that generally requires a paper or local electronic record of what was backed up when. Also, if the site has a slow link to begin with, there may be only enough bandwidth to deal with a very small number of restores in parallel. This will become an issue if there is a requirement to restore multiple files or file sets in parallel. For instance, if multiple desktops delete different files and request restores within the same time period, the restore requests will attempt to consume as much bandwidth as possible, slowing down both the restores and normal connections to the Internet. BaaS services are not free either—there is generally a significant charge for this, as well as the delay for the files to be recovered from the BaaS service, burned to CD/DVD, and then shipped to your site.

Security and BaaS

Related to the Internet access issue is one of security. When selecting a BaaS provider, it is important to determine the security that the BaaS service provides, from the client access, data transmission, and backup access layers. The service should provide strong authentication types, typically service signed certificates that would prevent access to the backup client by anyone except the service provider. Additionally, the backup should be encrypted as they are sent to the service. This prevents the use of the backup by unintended personnel who may have maliciously intercepted the backup stream as it was transmitted to the backup service. Finally, the backup service should have role-based access to the backups—levels of access for individual users that are based on what permissions they have to the backups, such as administrative or restore only types of access. This allows the backup administrator to have control over the environment, but provides for delegation of rights to individual users so that all requests do not necessarily require administrative intervention.

BaaS Costs

Most importantly, BaaS services have ongoing costs. While, from an accounting perspective, such costs may be able to be categorized as an operational expense (which is generally better to report than a capital expense), these costs can grow without bound and can quickly become more expensive over time than just buying a small backup infrastructure. Providers such as Mozy, Carbonite, and Backblaze all provide both personal and business-based pricing schemes, with the personal pricing models typically being a flat rate. This is because 90 percent of home users only back up a single PC—each additional PC is charged separately. The typical personal service also will generally limit the amount or type of data that can be protected, and will generally not protect any type of network attached storage (NAS) devices that may be utilized. However, each of these BaaS providers has a pro- or business-level product offering. Depending on the provider, these can be a flat rate per server, per month; a small flat fee plus a charge per GB protected; or simply a GB metered rate. While initially these rates can be very reasonable, it is important to watch these costs, especially as the number of servers and the quantity of data grows because there is not a cap applied to the amount charged, which can lead to some unpleasant monthly bills.

Having said all this, BaaS is a very effective method for small businesses or small ROs to have data protected without investing in the backup infrastructure or expertise needed to run backups. Understanding the BaaS client limitations in most RO situations, the client impact will be small as there are generally "off hours" times where backups can run freely, and almost all ROs have good Internet connectivity. Additionally, a BaaS can provide an excellent solution for protecting selected workstations and laptops—particularly for important members of the organization who have business-critical data on the workstation/laptop, or are part of a mobile workforce who rarely see the inside of an office. Business-level BaaS services also allow the backup administrator to run all RO backups, using a web interface, from a single location—simplifying the administration of backups. Table 9–1 shows the advantages and disadvantages.

Table 9–1. BaaS Advantages and Disadvantages

BaaS Advantages	BaaS Disadvantages
• Does not require infrastructure purchases • Complete remote management of backups • Can be deployed on desktops and servers • Backups can happen from anywhere—great for "road warriors"	• Does not scale well over time—each additional client consumes Internet bandwidth • Can impact client performance during backup • Ongoing monthly costs may outweigh infrastructure and administrative costs over time. • Restores can be slow, especially if multiple parallel restores consume available Internet access bandwidth

BaaS starts to become an issue when 200 GB of data or 30 servers, whichever comes first, need to be protected. At this point, the price of storing the data (especially if you are on a metered plan) becomes equivalent to simply buying some backup infrastructure and performing the backups yourself. Of course, this does add overhead to the organization, which for smaller organizations can offset the rising cost of BaaS. But if the BaaS is being used as a backup solution for remote locations, the additional infrastructure cost is negligible as an existing backup solution can be extended to meet the need, as will be described following.

From a technical perspective, the network bandwidth required to perform backups for BaaS also starts to become problematic as well, all of which can be absorbed by local resources versus Internet uplinks.

■ **Note** The addition of multiple application types, specialized nonstandard applications (something other than the standard Microsoft back office applications), or the addition of operating systems other than Windows (although some BaaS providers offer Linux support) will force migration from a BaaS in its current state.

Technically, the backup can be split between the two services, but from an operations simplicity standpoint, it is much easier to manage one backup application in a location than two.

BaaS offers a relatively inexpensive and easy-to-implement method of ensuring that backups are competed at small ROs. As with anything, there are limitations with the scope of such a solution that restrict its deployment to specific use cases. Beyond these limits, it is time to implement extensions of local backup systems or use commercial backup software such as NetBackup or CommVault to provide backup services for the environment.

Single Backup Servers

Where BaaS represents a solution that has fairly definite boundaries for use, the implementation of the single backup server, using commercially available software, provides a starting point that can effectively grow to meet the needs of very large environments (see Figure 9–1). Both NetBackup and CommVault are very modular and scalable in this fashion. Of course the first thing any datazone or CommCell needs is a control head—better known as a Master Server in NetBackup environments, and a CommServe for CommVault.

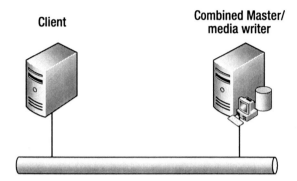

Client

Combined Master/ media writer

Figure 9–1. Single backup server

In previous discussions, the emphasis was placed on the implementation of a control head as a stand-alone device—one that should not do operations other than perform control and tracking functions, and should only do backups that are ancillary to the operation of the control head. This application of the control head works for environments that have already grown in size and need to back up a number of clients. But in smaller environments, the economics of implementing two servers to back up a small number of clients, in terms of the servers, software licensing costs, and infrastructure required, simply do not make sense. It is in these environments that the single backup server is the right solution.

The single backup server is a good solution for small environments that typically run over the 200-GB/30-client constraint discussed for BaaS solutions. It also just so happens that this also represents a good point at which a single backup server environment is best utilized, given a number of factors.

First off, there are large "off hours" windows in which backups can be run: smaller environments are typically not 24/7 operations, or if they are, they have only a small fraction of the operations running during the non–business-hour period. The single backup server can take advantage of this window to perform backups, taking on the additional load of processing the metadata in parallel to the backup stream, even if this processing represents a reduction in potential backup performance, as there is plenty of time to complete backups within the given window.

The disparity of platform types is small, most likely limited to a single server platform: Windows. By having a single well-known and documented platform, the backup environment, as the recovery procedures can be simplified and defined to the point at which almost any member of the organization in which the backup server is installed can operate the system. Most environments of this size, whether part of a large organization or a small operation, do not maintain any specialized, or subject matter expert (SME) IT staff to perform operations. Operating system (OS) and application issues are managed by the "computer guy"—likely someone who is a power user and works on his own environment as a hobby outside of the work environment. As such, *the support of the backup environment must be very simple and straightforward—thus requiring a simple architecture.*

Retention in these environments is simply driven by the need to be able to recover individual files from backups that happened within a short time span. This generally means that backups are only kept for a few days or possibly a week. This tactical approach is driven by two items: the cost of media and backup, and the need to get specific files back from a recent backup. Such a cost/short retention model makes traditional tape a good choice for a backup media target.

Selection of Backup Targets

As was discussed in previous chapters, tape provides a low-cost barrier of entry to performing backups. Tape targets can be individually purchased and attached directly to the Master/CommServe; or in environments that want small amount of automation, small libraries—one or two drives and a small number of slots—can be utilized with a small investment up front. The difference is simply a decision regarding how much is available to buy equipment (small library approach) versus the need to manually switch tapes on a daily basis (the cost of not automating and potentially overwriting backups inadvertently). Ongoing backup costs can be controlled by simply varying the length of time that the backups are retained, thus controlling the number of cartridges that need to be purchased for the environment. Many environments of this size are able to fit an entire full backup onto one or two individual cartridges.

Disk targets are not usually candidates for such small environments. The initial cost of purchasing enough disk storage to hold a cycle of backups is generally more expensive than simply purchasing a tape drive. Once the storage is purchased, it needs to be continually monitored and upgraded to ensure that sufficient space remains to perform backups—once it begins to run out, new space needs to be added. Unfortunately, the addition of disk space is not a straightforward process. Extending file systems, adding more disk backup targets, and moving backups around between simple disk targets requires more advanced knowledge of how the operating system in question, again typically Windows, works and potentially how to physical install hardware within the server. Tape drives, once installed, provide an "infinitely" extendable storage environment in terms of space. As has been discussed, this "infinitely" has definite limits, but from the perspective of a small environment, this much simplifies the storage management equation. Tape is also easy to send offsite—environments of this size, especially when operating independently, will generally have tapes stored in such varied places as someone's garage or in an offsite storage locker.

However, with the advent of target deduplication appliances, the disk/tape discussion starts to shift in favor of disk. In many small environments, the vast majority of data to be backed up is simple file type data, with a few locally created databases (Microsoft Access and similar desktop databases) stored on the server. These media types deduplicate very well, with expected day over day deduplication ratios of 10:1 or greater. This means that for every TB of storage purchased, typically 10 B of storage will fit on the devices. When applied to a small environment where retentions are relatively short, the purchase of a target deduplication device, while higher in initial cost, will pay for the difference in the long run. Why?

While the amount of storage for tape backups can be grown quickly, each cartridge has a cost associated with it. As the size of the environment grows, the number of tapes required also grows. More cartridges are required, and the cartridges that are used will not be completely filled as tape backups, assuming a daily rotation, will typically not fill a cartridge to 100 percent every day. Deduplicated targets solve this problem. While the storage consumed does grow, it will grow at a rate that is much less than the growth of data. This is because the deduplication algorithm depresses the rate at which data grows below the overall growth rate by storing less data on the device with the most data that the device sees. (See Figure 9–2.)

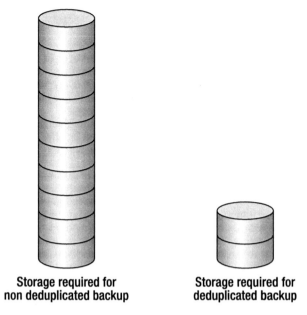

**Storage required for
non deduplicated backup**

**Storage required for
deduplicated backup**

Figure 9–2. Comparison of storage requirements for nondeduplicated and deduplicated backups

Remember that deduplication works based on only storing the data blocks that have already not been uniquely stored by another backup pass. Once the initial backup is complete, the amount of changed data actually stored will not grow as quickly as the overall growth in data as the probability of the deduplication device having seen individual blocks of data previously is increased. Because of this, deduplicated targets have costs of dollars per data stored ($/GB) that begin to approach, and in certain cases can be equal or less than, the cost of tape storage.

Growth of deduplicated environments also is much simpler than simple disk. They are simple to attach to a backup environment—many use the same file sharing technology that Windows uses to share directories: the Common Internet File System (CIFS). As such, the expansion of storage on a deduplicated disk appliance can be as simple as plugging in new drives into the front of a unit—most, if not all, appliances autoconfigure new space and immediately make it available for use by backup clients—all without user intervention on either the appliance or the backup server. To the backup server, it simply appears as if the amount of space available has "magically" grown—all the mechanics of presentation are handled at the deduplicated appliance layer.

However, such space should *only* be used for backup storage—not for storage of the index/catalog files required for the backup server. Given the storage advantages of deduplicated storage, it is tempting to simply put everything on the deduplicated target and forgo the storage required on the backup server in an attempt to save costs. However, the overall performance of the backup server would be extremely limited as backup targets of this type are specifically tuned for backup workloads—write rates are favored over read rates—and even those write rates, when taking into consideration the network overhead involved, will be much smaller than can be achieved with standard internal disk. (See Figure 9–3.)

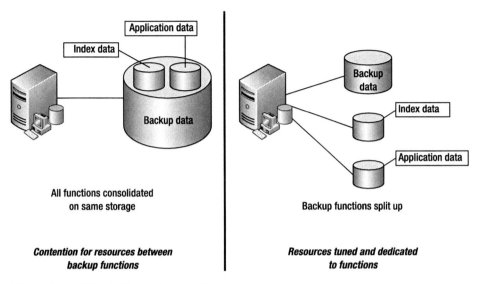

Figure 9–3. *LUNs dedicated for specific uses*

Deduplicate storage does not allow for offsite storage of backups. Even though they represent small sites, it is important to get a copy of the backup to an offsite location. This protects the organization's data even in the event of fire or theft of equipment. This is where tape comes back into the picture. Tape still is the only inexpensive, portable backup media that can be stored (for short periods of time) in many different locations. The issues of environmental controls for tape still exist—while storage in an garage safe is typically done, the life cycle of the tapes is typically very short—measured on the order of months and not years. However, the tape still represents a copy of the data that can be utilized in the event the primary backup contained on the appliance is not available. So, when looking at using deduplication appliances for primary backup, the cost of offsite protection using tape as the target should be considered as well.

There is an alternative: replication. If a central or other remote site is available, a second deduplication appliance can be placed and set up as an offsite location. This has the advantage of not having to handle or manage tape, as well as having the ability to automate the replication process. Deduplicated replication between appliances utilizes deduplication between the two appliances to minimize the amount of data that is required to be transmitted to only the blocks that are unique on the remote appliance—much in the same way as source-based deduplication queries the target to determine which blocks to send. This reduces the bandwidth required to the absolute minimum and makes offsite replication viable for even single server environments. However, the solution requires that a second deduplication appliance be acquired, adding cost to the solution. The cost of this additional appliance should be compared with the cost of the tape solution over the lifetime of the solution.

When building the single backup server environment, NetBackup and CommVault take different approaches to this initial step into the world of backup. The main distinction: the type of primary backup media used within the environment. NetBackup takes the traditional approach, with designs favoring tape. Disk Storage Units (DSUs) are not typically self-managing and require a substantial amount of monitoring to ensure that they do not fill, as described previously. To ensure simplicity of management, standard SUs based on tape drives are recommended. DSUs can be used, but should only be provided for local catalog backups that occur as part of the NetBackup backup process, with the resulting catalogs duplicated to tape for offsite storage.

CommVault takes a somewhat opposite approach. While backups can be written directly to tape, the present of a mechanism to self-manage disk storage, in the form of a magnetic library (MagLib), makes the use of disk a recommended method of primary storage. The MagLib effectively acts as a caching mechanism for the backup, providing the positive benefits of disk target backups, without a majority of the drawbacks. However, the use of this architecture may make the initial purchase of a server to house the CommCell slightly more expensive, the benefits of a more reliable and potentially faster backup target outweigh the cost.

Performance Considerations

Regardless of which platform is selected, the performance within small environments is gated by two main factors:

- Backup server performance

- Client performance

While this may seem obvious, there are some implications that will drive when to increase the backup environment size to accommodate growth. In the single backup server scenario, the Master/CommServe is pulling double duty: the server must track the backups as well as write them out to the target media. Both of these requirements compete for resources within the backup server during backup—particularly overall I/O requirements. While the backup server is trying to write data to the backup targets as quickly as possible, it is also attempting to write the metadata to the indices and catalogs as well. This creates a competition for the limited I/O resource within the server. (See Figure 9–4.) While in small environments the effect is negligible as the I/O competition will slow the backups, but not cause the backups to exceed the specified window, as the amount of data grows, the competition exponentially affects the ability to write both data and metadata in an effective manner.

CPU and RAM resources on the backup server are similarly affected. The processing of backup metadata requires a fairly substantial amount of CPU and RAM to identify, filter, and schedule for storage the metadata associated with the backup. However, the backup stream also consumes substantial portions of CPU and RAM. The backup stream is typically cached within the server RAM for eventually writing to storage. The management of the cache and the schedule of writes are performed by a series of processes that run on the server—which also consume additional RAM, as well as requiring CPU time to execute. As with the input/output (I/O) consideration, there are limited amounts of both CPU time and RAM available on the server to handle both types of loads. Just as with the I/O resource, at some point, the competition of both the backup stream and the metadata stream will overwhelm the resources available on the backup server, and will slow backups down significantly.

Interestingly enough, the LAN is not affected in the same way. Only data from the clients passes through the LAN interfaces to the backup server in the single backup server model. The metadata represents a very tiny fraction of the amount of data that is presented to the combined backup server/media writer and thus will not affect the overall amount of data that has to be consumed by the network interface, on a per-client basis. However, the network is governed by the number of clients backed up at the same time, which does take away from the overall backup performance. As the number of parallel backups is increased, the amount of bandwidth available for use by each individual client is reduced beyond a certain point. This was illustrated in the chapters regarding the configuration of the backup software. So while the backup server is not affected directly by the utilization of the network) the number and type of network interfaces on the backup server does govern client performance during parallel backups. As was just implied, this limitation can be solved, in some respect, by adding network interfaces or by increasing the network bandwidth, say from 1 GB to 10 GB to create more available bandwidth for use; however, this will simply drive the utilization of the other critical resources (CPU, RAM, I/O) more quickly by forcing the backup server to process more backup data/metadata during the backup window.

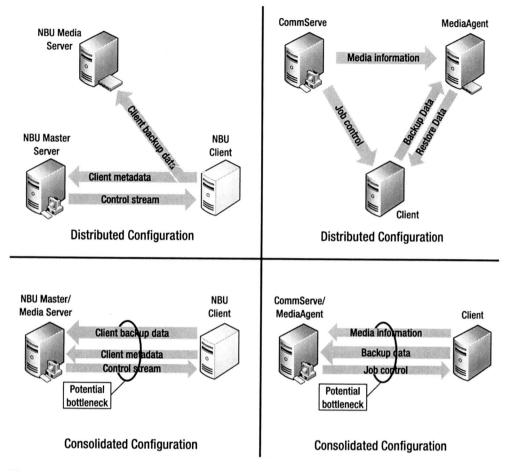

Figure 9–4. Potential bottleneck generated by combined server/media writer

Dealing with Growth

So how do you determine when to start the shift to a larger backup model? The rule of thumb is when any of the critical resources approaches 70 percent of the maximum value it is time to begin planning for a large environment. If it is difficult to measure this, due to either lack of resources or expertise, there is a simpler method. The amount of time that a particular backup takes is captured by both NetBackup and CommVault. A simple method to determine whether the single backup server is becoming overloaded is to look at the backup times of clients. As the load increases, the backup times will get longer until they reach a plateau—namely that the backup times will be growing faster than the backup data growth rate. At the plateau, start watching the amount of data that is being backed up. If the data size is growing, the backups may potentially be limited by the number of target media devices or may be limited to a network ingest rate. Adding network interfaces or a single media target may be a way to temporarily grow out the environment. If the addition of media targets and/or network interfaces does not help or only marginally helps, it is time to upgrade the backup environment to the next level.

However, if the data size is not growing or is growing very slowly, you have simply reached an equilibrium point at which in the current configuration, the data cannot be moved any faster. Backup times can be reduced at these points by different backup management techniques:

- Staggering full backups across the week

- Implementing client multiplexing and multistreaming

- Synthetic full backups

Client Performance Considerations

The second area where performance is gated in this environment is at the client level. While this is typical in any size environment, it is particularly noticeable at this size. Many times the backup clients are general-purpose machines, built for a variety of functions within the organization. This means that the applications that are installed on them, while having the ability to run with some measure of efficiency, do not find an environment that is tuned to their needs. Additionally, commodity equipment is generally used in these environments—equipment that may not be the best performing—selected as a trade of speed for cost. Both of these factors play into the performance of the backup. In all cases, the speed of the backup is ultimately gated by the ability of the client to initiate and copy the data as part of the backup stream. When using commodity equipment with lower performance characteristics, the backup stream is obviously limited to the performance characteristics of the equipment and the operating system that is run.

General Application Performance Considerations

The fact that the backup client application performance would gate client performance in this case is less obvious. If an application is tuned for best performance, it is able to process the data that is passed to it as efficiently as the operating system and system hardware is able to allow it to do. However, if the client application is simply installed on general-purpose equipment, it will run in suboptimal conditions, making the processing of data that much slower. The backup applications, especially backup applications that integrate directly with applications such as mail or database backups, rely on the ability of the application to push data at the backup at speeds that are as fast as possible, or at least to the maximum of any application backup throttle applied. If the application is hamstrung on performance for normal operations, this performance limitation will translate to the speed of the backup as well.

Taken in combination, the equipment/operating system performance, plus that of the application place a top end limit on any potential backup performance. But again, why is that a major gating factor for single backup server environments? As these environments start out, there are generally plenty of resources available for the backup to consume from the backup server side—CPU/RAM is freely available, I/O contention is at a minimum, and local area network (LAN) bandwidth is not compromised. Since all these resources are available and do not constrain the *potential* performance of the backup, backup times and windows can only be governed by the *actual* performance of the client itself. This fact can make adjusting backup windows for small environments difficult. *If the client is performing slowly, and the backup of the client is also performing slowly, then generally the only way to fix the backup windows is to fix the client performance in general.*

This leads to an interesting byproduct—an indirect measure of client performance based on the performance of the backup. We stated that the backup performance is gated by two factors: the potential performance of the hardware/operating system, and the performance of the client itself. However, the converse of this statement *may* also be true: the backup performance *indicates* the performance of the application. The reason for the caveat is that there are a number of interleaving factors that go into the performance of the application that are independent of the backup. However, clients that run slow for backups can be an early indicator of systems that may warrant investigation for overall client performance. Many times, the client performance issues are something simple, such as NIC autonegotiation settings.

Backup client applications in single backup server environments tend to be very limited: file server, mail, and potentially a database. File servers are the most common client type found within the small environment. These servers also will only require a basic installation of a standard client, with a simple backup directive (NetBackup) or Storage Policy (CommVault) applied to the client. Depending on the size and number of directories, it may be advantageous to start out with multistream backups, but in this situation it is not immediately required.

Ancillary client types to the file server within small environments are desktops. Many small environments run on a combination of centralized and desktop resources—making the backup of desktops critical to capturing the entire organization's backup. Desktop backups in this case can be treated as file server backups and configured as such.

Database Backup Performance

Database servers are less common. Many small environments do have databases, but these databases tend to be desktop-based databases such as Microsoft Access. More organization–centric database services, such as SQL Server and Oracle, are generally not found; however, as these technologies are embedded more within applications, backup considerations for them must be considered with looking at single backup server environments. Since these types of environment generally have off hours, when little or no activity is occurring, databases can be protected with the simplest of methods: cold backups. By using cold backups for database backups, the complexity of setting up database backup clients and the cost of the client itself can be avoided. This is at the cost of the ability to perform useful work against the environment during the backup period, as well as the ability to perform restores at a level no more granular than that of the entire instance. However, in most environments that only require a single backup server, this is an acceptable compromise.

Mail servers in single backup server environments are less and less common with the adoption of external mail providers such as Hotmail and Gmail for business use, but are still seen. When mail servers are present, they, like the database servers in the environment, only require the most simple of backups. This prevents dealing with setup and configuration issues that can be present. Microsoft Exchange backups should be made via VSS and simple file-level backups of the environment. While this does not allow for brick-level recovery, a standard full/incremental/differential style backup cycle can be applied for the backup. In Lotus Notes environments, the simplest backup possible should be used: NetBackup environments simply use the Lotus Notes agent, but without Fast Recovery; CommVault environments need only install the Database iDA and perform simple database-level backups.

The backup of mail servers in this fashion, both for Exchange and Lotus Notes, makes the assumption that the design goal is to provide the simplest, most cost efficient method of performing the backup. However, if the goal is to provide the most granular level of backup as a *feature* that is provided to the end users, then brick level (message level in Exchange/document level in Lotus) backups can work well in smaller environments. As was discussed in the previous chapter, brick-level backups, while providing a great way to allow for restoration of individual mail items, is very resource intensive on the mail server itself during the backup process. However, in small environments such as those served by single backup servers, there are two factors that work in favor of brick-level backups: the size of the mail store and the ability to run during off hours. Combined, these two factors allow for the ability to scan the entire mail store for changes in the environment and store them, as end users are not affected during an off hours backup. While the setup and maintenance can be time consuming, consider offering this ability to your users in smaller environments—it is a good way to show the value of backups and provide a very useful service to the users within the environment.

The single backup server model is a good starting point to build new backup environments and properly configured, provides the basis for growing the environment to meet the backup needs for a long period of time. Once the single backup server model is outgrown, it is time to add a new element to the environment: a Media Server/MediaAgent.

Single Server/Single Media Writer

As the environment grows, in terms of the number of servers supported by the backup server, the amount of data to back up, the size of the backup windows, or the number of different applications that are supported, simply using a single backup server as the focal point of all backups will not provide enough performance to handle the backups. At this point, it is necessary to offload the processing overhead on to a separate server and allow the backup server to concentrate on scheduling and monitoring backup jobs and processing client metadata. This specialized server that acts as a media writer is known as either a Media Server in NetBackup, or a MediaAgent in CommVault. (See Figure 9–5.)

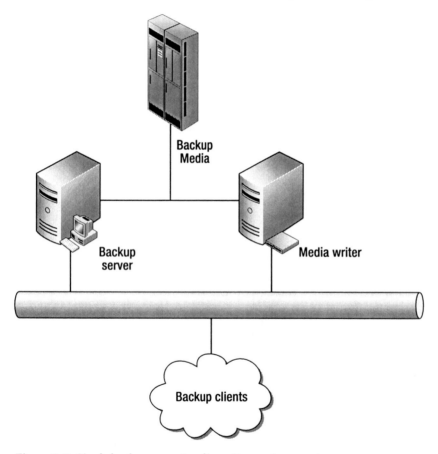

Figure 9–5. Single backup server/media writer environment

The implementation of a media writer provides more potential backup power not only by offloading the processing of the backup to the media, but also by providing method by which potential backup throughput can be scaled out, simply by adding additional media writers as needed to meet the needs. This works by providing the ability to add:

- *Additional network targets*: Adds potential network bandwidth by providing more points to which individual clients can back up to. This may reduce router traffic by localizing traffic to media writers on highly populated subnets or on subnets behind the firewall. The number of clients backed up is the driving point here—the more clients, more network connections. With an increase in network connections, the potential for network interface saturation increases as the number of packets transmitted increases.

- *Additional backup media targets*: Provides the ability to attach more media targets, thus creating the ability for more client streams to run in parallel, thus potentially speeding the backup process.

Note the "potential" caveat in each of the preceding points. The addition of the single media writer to the environment may not actually speed up backups. Its primary function at this point is to prevent backups from slowing down further due to load on the backup control head (Master/CommServe). The reason why the addition of the media writing server does not necessarily speed backups is that while the gating factor of the backup server performance is mostly removed from the performance equation, the backup performance of the client itself has not been. Client backup performance, in this situation, is now the main gating factor in overall performance within the environment—the client hasn't changed, the environment around has. So the addition of the media writer only adds potential performance, not necessarily actual performance.

Additionally, the operational environment in which the single media writer model is used also has not changed much. While most environments now have SMEs available to specifically support the IT function, they are generally not purposefully focused on the backup environment. There still may be off hours backup windows, but it is likely that these windows are beginning to become smaller as business processing may start to happen during these hours. Backups are mostly still viewed as a tactical necessity, used for day-to-day recoveries, not to meet any formalized retention requirements. Offsite storage of backups, if it exists at all, is most likely still a staff member's garage or non–purpose-built storage facility.

The media writer itself is fairly simple to implement from either the NetBackup or CommVault perspective. The Media Server in NetBackup is a simple server with media drives attached that has special set of software loaded in order to enable the Media Server function. The media drives can be tape, disk, or combination of the two.

■ **Note** The Media Server is typically built with an eye toward I/O—multiple network connections for inbound client and shared storage connections, and multiple block storage connections for attached block-level devices, such as tape or disk.

CPU and RAM are important in a Media Server, but only to the point at which

- There is sufficient amount of CPU to be able to drive the I/O interfaces as efficiently as the OS will allow.

- There is enough RAM to run the required software (a very small percentage of the total RAM) and to create buffer space for the device writer process—bptm/bpdm (it can be very large).

The Media Server software communicates with the Master Server and reports on the health of the media drives and of the status of the Media Server. The Media Server is effectively a fairly dumb server that simply serves as a point to which backups are pointed, which writes the backup to the designated media.

CommVault MediaAgent Approach

CommVault again takes a much different approach. The MediaAgent, the CommVault version of the media writer, is a smart server. The MediaAgent, the CommVault media writer server, not only writes the backups to the appropriate media but it also maintains a cache of information regarding what has been written on the media by server. This allows the MediaAgent to quickly access required backups during the restore process. The processing of the contents of the media requires a different hardware design from the NetBackup Media Server.

First of all, some amount of high-speed disk storage is required to hold the cache. The performance of the cache has a direct bearing on the overall performance of the backup, as the rate at which the metadata from each server is processed will be the gating factor in the overall performance of the MediaAgent. The storage required for the cache also should be separate from any disk storage used for MagLib storage—and therefore adds to the overall size of the MediaAgent hardware.

Secondly, because the MediaAgent performs this metadata collection and caching function, more attention must also be paid to the CPU and RAM utilization on the hardware selected. This is to account for the additional processing required, over and above that already being done to simply support the movement of the backups from the clients to the media. The MediaAgent processes require more CPU and RAM to perform this processing and ensure that the cache is quickly updated with the latest metadata while still moving the data to the media.

Using Disk for Staging Backups

In the single media writer environment the target media is still generally tape or a tape analog such as a target deduplication appliance. However, this again differs slightly between NetBackup and CommVault. In NetBackup, the tape target is generally set up as a direct target—there is not a requirement for additional storage to act as a caching mechanism. NetBackup does provide a special-purpose SU called a Disk Staging Storage Unit (DSSU) that provides the ability to have a temporary disk target for backups to be written to. Once the backup image is complete, it is moved or "destaged" from the disk to the tape target. In smaller environments, this is generally not required as the performance of tape is still sufficient to allow for backups to complete in their allotted time. Only as the performance drops as a result of tape drive contention between backup jobs do DSSUs become seen as the initial targets for backup. This begins to happen when the average throughput on a Media Server reaches 256 MB/sec.

The continued adoption of target-based deduplication changes this equation for NetBackup. As you saw in the single backup server model, the implementation of a target-based deduplication that either replaces or significantly augments a pure tape-based solution becomes economically possible as the effective cost per GB stored begins to reach tape prices. This is also true for the single media writer. More frequently, target-based deduplication solutions are being set up as DSU or Virtual Tape Library (VTL) targets for NetBackup Media Servers as the primary target for backup storage, with tape only large enough to allow for the generation of any *necessary* offsite copies. A single Media Server configuration, with a DSU using target-based deduplication should be the first choice over tape as the primary target if finances allow.

Why? The growth into a single Media Server environment represents the first step into providing a horizontally scalable backup model for the server environment being protected. Eventually the demands of the environment will force the growth of the backup environment to meet an ever-expanding demand for space. While with tape, this demand can be satisfied with additional cartridges and tape drives, this quickly creates an unmanageable environment with stacks of tape cartridges and quantities of discrete tape drives to manage within the environment. As the environment grows and requires additional Media Servers, either the existing tape drives must be shared using the Shared Storage Option (SSO), additional tape drives (and quantities of cartridges) must be purchased, installed, and maintained, or both. A target-based deduplication solution provides for a single point of attachment by one or more Media Servers, and only requires a single point of management—not multiples in the case of tape drives and cartridges.

In addition, one of the challenges associated with growing the multiple media writer environment is the potential for having a number of disparate media types, such as mixes between Digital Linear Tape (DLT), Linear Tape Open (LTO), and others. These media types may be spread across multiple robotic devices, each with their own inventory. By adding a disk solution, such as a deduplication appliance will allow the consolidation of backups targets into a single type—namely the disk target. Such a solution can either eliminate or significantly reduce the overall complexity of the environment, which will tend to increase both reliability and performance.

On a CommVault Media Agent, while direct tape targets can be created for primary backup, best practices recommend that MagLib storage be used for backup targets, with an AUX copy created to tape as a background job. Since MediaAgents require some amount of disk for the index cache, from a cost perspective it is generally not much more to account for additional disk needed to build an effective MagLib. In this configuration, the MagLib largely serves the same function as the DSSU: to cache the backup for writing to a tape target. However, the MagLib is really intended to be the primary storage media for backups, with AUX *copies* being created to support any offsite requirements. This is different from a staging mechanism as the backup is copied, not moved to the tape media. The two different copies are then subject to different expiration dates, if desired, and can be managed as two separate entities.

Target-based deduplication can also have a significant impact here as well. MagLib storage is not required to be internal storage; it can be a shared storage type, and is generally recommended to be shared storage to allow for growth within a particular CommCell. Shared storage used in this manner has generally been either in the form of NAS storage using NFS or CIFS, depending on the platform, or a SAN-based configuration in some more advanced environments. The index cache should also be shared and is also placed on NFS or CIFS storage—SAN storage is not available for this option. Target deduplication should not be used for the index cache. The index cache requires the highest speed storage for both read and write. While target deduplication performs well as a backup target, the performance in cases of read, particularly for random reads, is not optimized for performance for general purpose file system utilization.

Most environments start with standard NAS-type storage—it is inexpensive, easy to configure, and has relatively good performance. Standard NAS has all the advantages and limitations that were discussed in the media targets chapter: easily shared, good resource utilization, etc. When using a target-based deduplication platform for MagLib storage in place of the standard NAS, you not only get the benefits of standard NAS type storage but the benefits of deduplication also go along with it: the ability to globally deduplicate across all backup streams that run to the deduplicated storage—all without having to do anything more complicated than setup a share!

While in the single MediaAgent environment the effect of the deduplication may seem slightly trivial. However, as MediaAgents are added to the environment, the effect of the shared target is magnified. Since there are multiple MediaAgents writing to the target deduplication device, each stream is deduplicated to the same pool of storage no matter which MediaAgent wrote the backup stream. (See Figure 9–6.)

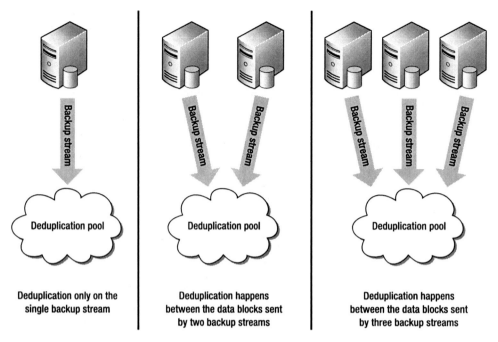

Figure 9–6. Effect of multiple backup streams on deduplication

The single media writer environment provides the basis for growth for the rest of the environment by allowing the scale out of the backup performance potential by offloading the backup streams from the backup server to the media writer. As the performance potential is consumed by the growing environment, additional media writers can be added to support the growing load.

Single Master/Multiple Media Writer

As more servers and data are added to the environment, at some point the capabilities of a single media writer, either a NetBackup Media Server or a CommVault MediaAgent, are not enough. Additional media writers can be added to ensure that the throughput of the clients is optimized as much as possible. (See Figure 9–7.) Typically when environments reach this size, a number of things begin to happen. First, a SME with a specialization in backup is added. This is to support the increasing complexity of the backup environment, ensuring that all backups are completed. The complexity is added by the addition of new backup servers, as well as the increasing number, type, and backup requirements of the clients within the environment as a whole. A general IT SME will most likely not have the knowledge or experience necessary to understand the interactions between application, operating system, network and backup, and be able to optimize for the best balance of all the elements.

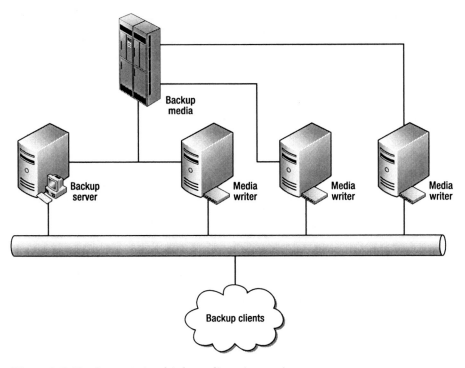

Figure 9–7. Single master/multiple media writer environment

There also tends to be an increasing emphasis on backups as a business function—the necessity of backups becomes driven by the need to be able to recover data in multiple areas, for reasons other than just accidental deletion of files. Backups become the means by which new servers can be created with old data or are depended upon to re-create whole environments in the event of the loss of a set of servers, potentially in alternate locations. Along those lines, retention becomes important—the age of data becomes a critical factor in determining usefulness, and/or data is required to be retained to meet operational, regulatory, or legal requirements.

In order to meet the backup and retention requirements, the ability to have alternate copies in an offsite location in a timely manner also becomes important. The addition of media writers implies that existing simple resources, such as tape devices, may have started to be outrun by the requirements of the backup environment. While the portability of such devices is important to the success of the business model, the limitations of the devices as a primary backup target are exposed. As such, tape starts to be moved to an ancillary device, with the movement and tracking of individual cartridges between onsite and offsite locations formalized through either local tools or those provided by the backup software, such as NetBackup Vault or CommVault VaultTracker.

While all these items influence the growth of the environment to a multiple media writer environment, the primary reasons for doing so have to do with the ability to expand the backup capabilities of the environment as a whole. The addition of the first media writer was to offload the backup streams from the backup server to a special-purpose system that is specifically built to handle this type of workload. The second media writer is generally built to handle the growth generated in the environment—again offloading further load and building potential backup performance potential into the backup system. However, media writer software can be added to application servers that normally perform production functions. Why would this be desirable? Doesn't the media writer function offload backups from the backup server as a mechanism to make backups more efficient?

In the general case in which client backups would be moving to the media writer, this would not be a desirable configuration—the additional load would adversely affect any application running on the server. However, in the case where the media writer software is installed on an application server, the intention is to not expand the potential backup performance bandwidth available. Instead, installing the media writer software is used to improve the backup performance of the server on which this is installed. As certain application servers grow, either their configuration or the amount of data prevents them from being backed up within their window. In order to maximize the processing and throughput during the backup of the application, the media writer software is installed along with the client software on the application to create a media writer dedicated only to that particular application. In a NetBackup environment this is known as a dedicated Media Server; in a CommVault CommCell, it is called a dedicated MediaAgent.

The addition of media writers, regardless of them being a dedicated or general purpose will start to expose weaknesses in the overall backup environment, particularly if tape is used as the primary backup media. As discussed previously, tape is useful as a backup media when used in simple backup environments—those with either a single backup server or a single backup/single media writer environment. However, as additional media writers are added, the number of devices in the environment is increased, the complexity of management is increased (or both) as they relate to tape drive management. In addition, the increased number of robotic arms, with their inherent mechanical complexity, also exposes the environment to outages through increased probability of failure due to robotic arm failure.

This is because the addition of media writers implies a need for more performance within the backup environment. This in turn generally drives an increase in the number of tape drives or the necessity to share tape drives between media writers. The addition of tape drives in this situation increases the number of cartridges, and will most likely decrease the effective utilization of those cartridges. If the number of drives is not increased or the utilization of the drives leaves some drives idle due to an imbalance in either backup scheduling or data rates, the in order to use all the drives to their full potential, they must be shared between media writers using either SSO—NetBackup or Dynamic Drive Sharing (DDS)—CommVault. Both of these sharing technologies involve the backup server (NBU Master/CommVault CommServe) scheduling the use of the discrete resources and are dependent on the media writer's ability to know when a particular resource is not available through the use of hardware-based, soft-locking protocols, such as SCSI reserve/release. This functionality requires additional licensing and thus additional costs to the environment.

This type of complexity quickly becomes difficult to manage, especially as the numbers of drives, media writers, or both increase. But what can be done about this? It is at this point that a serious look at a either a disk caching strategy using locally provided disk or a disk storage strategy using shared disk storage be reviewed (see Figure 9–8). A disk caching strategy, such as using a DSSU or a local MagLib, provides the ability to consolidate all backup streams into a single local device and then use a shared devices pool, such as a shared tape environment, as a back-end strategy to offload the backups for longer-term storage.

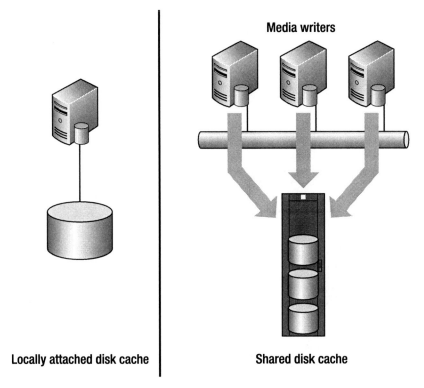

Media writers

Locally attached disk cache | **Shared disk cache**

Figure 9–8. Local cache versus shared cache

The local cache strategy has some advantages and drawbacks. It has the advantage of using local disk, which can have better performance, versus using shared disk storage, such as an NAS storage mechanism. The performance differential comes from the dependency of the NAS storage on LAN speeds and connectivity versus the typical bandwidth available for local storage. Local SAS/SCSI/SAN bandwidths are many times faster that than provided by the most common network interface, Gigabit Ethernet. Local disk also does not have issues with external contention as does NAS.

Where does the contention come from? In a shared storage environment, multiple connections are made to the same storage, through the same network interface or set of interfaces. If the NAS side does not have enough bandwidth to handle the data generated by backups through these connections, contention can result for the interface. Additionally, disk contention on the back side of the NAS can also occur if there are not enough disk drives to handle the combined IOPS that are being requested by the backup streams via the network interface.

Local caching is not without its drawbacks. Since the storage is local to the media writer, it must be managed as a discrete entity. While this may sound obvious, it has some deeper implications. Monitoring the disk space utilized by the disk target on each media writer becomes very important. The storage utilization should be viewed at the peak of utilization, not as a function of the average, because in the local caching method of disk-based backups, the most storage that is utilized during the backups is prior to moving the backups to external media. If the utilization is only viewed during off hours for backups, a false picture of the actual storage required will emerge. During the off hours, the backups have already been moved from the disk cache, freeing up a majority of space on the cache. However, the reverse is true during backups—the storage is at its peak utilization as all backups have been created on the disk storage, not yet moved to the external storage. (See Figure 9–9.)

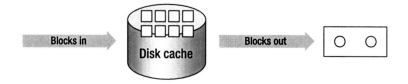

Blocks go into the cache and then leave, freeing cache for use

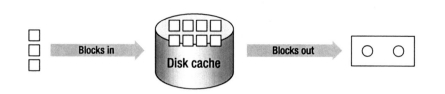

If cache fills, blocks cannot be written, so backups fail until cache empties out

Figure 9–9. Backup caching

Not having enough storage in a local caching mechanism can lead to backups not being able to be completed as the local cache runs out of storage during the backup. In a NetBackup environment, the failure of backups may appear intermittently at first. Since the DSSU is a true cache, backups are moved out based on a certain period of time, the age of the backup, or the amount of storage available in the DSSU. However, if the storage fills before the criteria are met, or if the DSSU is in the process of making space available when the backup is started, there is a possibility that the storage may fill as a result of the backup, be cleared as a result of the destaging process, and have enough space for additional backups to complete successfully.

In a CommVault environment, this is not as common, but can occur. The MagLib is treated as a primary backup target in most cases, not as a staging area. Most times, the MagLib backup has a short retention period, typically less than a week. An AUX copy is made of the backup on the MagLib during a scheduled time and is assigned a longer retention—one commensurate with the life cycle of the backup. The backup is then expired and the space reclaimed for use. While this appears to work like a DSSU, the difference is that the copy on the DSSU is strictly there for staging—while it is available for use as a restore target, the primary intent is to simply provide the attendant advantages of disk storage long enough to get the backup complete and then offload the backup to external media. Since MagLib storage is treated effectively in the same way as external storage, it is much more closely managed by the CommServe. This does mean that intermittent backup failures due to destaging schedules do not frequently happen. However, the size of the MagLib must always be sufficient to hold the size of the backups for the retention period designated.

This sizing issue illustrates the second limitation of local caching: a limitation in the amount of storage that can be provided. This limitation is only applicable for local storage—storage that is contained within the physical server that is running the media writer software. Local caching using SAN-attached storage or even external SAS–attached drive arrays does not necessarily suffer from this limitation at the onset, but there are always limits on the amount of disk storage available for use.

In the local or internal storage situation, there is a hard limitation on the amount of storage available for use, based on the number of physical drives that can be inserted into the server. For smaller environments with multiple media writers, this may not be an issue as the amount of storage that can fit into the front of a server can be significant. However, as the space requirements grow, it represents a hard limit. In addition, internal storage represents a potential failure point. If the server itself fails, the backups contained on the internal storage are most likely irretrievable.

Local storage is also subject to variable utilization as well. Unlike a shared medium, each media writer will have loads and storage requirements that are independent (to a large extent) of any other media writer. This means that not only can there be "wasted" or unutilized space on a particular media writer due to imbalances on utilization but there also can be imbalances in performance because some media writers may perform better than others due to the number of clients backing up to the disk storage as it relates to the disk performance itself.

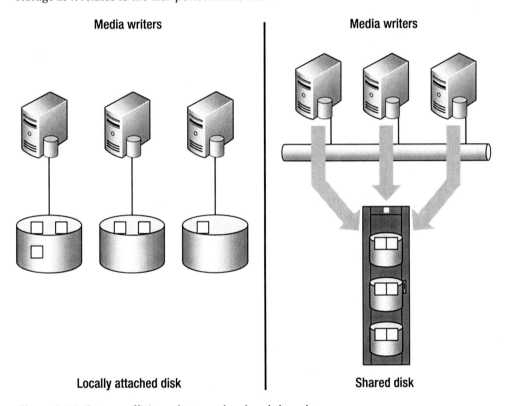

Figure 9–10. Storage efficiency between local and shared storage

NAS-based shared storage can take care of these types of issues. (See Figure 9–10.) Since the storage is a shared resource, it is not localized, and both consumption and performance are normalized across all users of the storage. Said another way, the NAS levels out the consumption issues by providing a

223

single pool of storage for all backup users to consume—eliminating much of the "waste" generated by the local storage model. Shared storage also provides a mechanism to level the performance of the media writers. Since all media writers have equal access to the shared storage, in terms of network access, the connection and load balancing algorithms in the NAS controller provide the mechanism to ensure that all requests are as close to equally serviced as possible.

So given the advantages of NAS storage, where does tape fit in? Although tape is complex to operate as a primary media type in the multiple media writer environment, as a secondary media type, it regains some of its luster. When used as a secondary media, tape is effective since the vagaries of tape targets are now masked from the client backup view by the disk-based storage, whether it is local or shared. From the client perspective, backups are complete once they hit the disk. However, as discussed earlier, new business requirements are added to the environment at this point that necessitate the movement of backups to offsite locations. Tape is a good medium for offsite due to its portability and relatively low cost of storage.

But wasn't it stated that tape management in a multiple media writer environment introduces a complex tape management problem? For the primary media, yes—backups were dependent on either having a device or set of devices available to complete backups. The devices needed to be shared, which required some type of resource arbitration on the backup server, or enough drive resources had to be purchased to handle peak load on each individual media writer—a situation that frequently leads to idle resources through lack of resource sharing. When using tape as a secondary resource, a tape sharing mechanism necessary for primary storage will still be required. This is because the tape drive resources are still better utilized as resources that are shared among all the media writers, rather than ones that are dedicated for specific use. This sharing ensures that the drives are fully utilized at any point in time (see Figure 9–11).

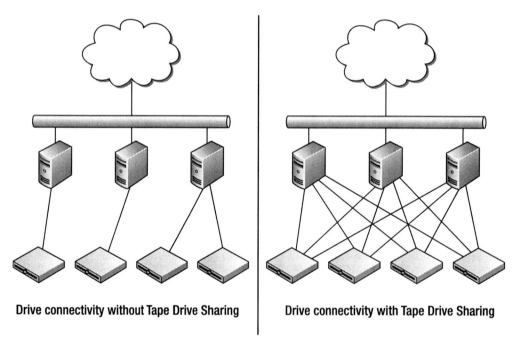

Drive connectivity without Tape Drive Sharing | **Drive connectivity with Tape Drive Sharing**

Figure 9–11. Drive sharing

Both from a performance and utilization perspective, tape utilization increases when used as secondary storage. On the surface this does not appear to make sense, but it actually works. When tapes are used as primary storage, especially within a multimedia writer environment, the individual cartridges are most often not fully filled at the conclusion of the backup windows. When the backups are assigned to the individual media writer, one or more cartridges are also assigned to contain that client's (or set of clients') backups. The backups that end up on the cartridge may not be enough to fill the cartridge, or even a large percentage of the cartridge. Once the backups are complete, the cartridge is removed from the drive and put back into the collection of available cartridge, ready for use on the next backup. When a new backup set is executed, there is no guarantee that the same cartridge, or even one that has been previously used, will be selected for use. The utilization of the cartridge is driven by the number and size of backups, as well as the total number of backups executed on the media writer in question.

This equation changes when using tape as a secondary media. In this situation, the cartridge will be packed as full as possible, as the cartridge will be used, assuming a common external retention, for all backups that are ready to be copied or destaged from the media writer. This process, known as *tape stacking*, provides the best method to ensure the most effective use of the tape resource for packing as many backup copies on a particular cartridge as possible.

Performance of tape cartridges is also optimized when using tape as a secondary media. In the primary media situation, the performance of the tape is largely governed by the combined performance of the clients writing to the tape at any particular time. This leads, at best, to performance that varies from optimal to virtually stopped, depending on the mix of client streams writing to the device at a particular time. However, when used as a secondary media, only a single high-speed (hopefully) client is writing to the device—the media writer itself. Since the media writer is taking backups that have been already complete and simply moving/copying them to tape from local disk, the data stream generated to the tape drive is both consistent and as fast as the combined effects of the disk performance and the processing power of the media writer. Stable, high-speed throughput ensures that tape drives write data as fast as possible as the tape transport speed does not have to be altered to match the data rate, a process that was discussed in some detail previously.

A combination of disk targets and tape would seem to provide the best solution for a multimedia writer environment to use, based on the previous discussion. But within the last couple of years, there has emerged a disruptive technology that completely alters the approach to take when looking at the issues of primary, secondary, and offsite capabilities applied within a multimedia writer environment: deduplication.

Deduplication in Multiple Media Writer Environments

As has been discussed, deduplication comes in two flavors: source and target. Source deduplication takes client data, deduplicates it prior to transport to the backup media, and then writes the resultant data stream, which is deduplicated and thus smaller. The target performs the converse: the data is written to the target media, where it is deduplicated in the process of physically writing data to media. While both affect the overall design of a multimedia writer environment, it is the use of target-based deduplication that has the most effect.

In the previous discussion, the use of NAS-based storage was discussed to provide a shared storage environment for the multimedia writer environment as a method to optimize the overall disk storage target utilization for primary and staging environments, across a number of media writers. However, one of the drawbacks listed was the need to manage the storage space and to ensure that one media writer did not dominate the environment. However, when using a target-based deduplication appliance as the primary storage, these concerns are significantly reduced. Storage management is much reduced because the deduplication reduces the amount of data actually stored on a particular device, and the effect of retention schedules effectively provides a method of reducing the overall growth rate of the device.

This effect of deduplication providing storage efficiencies across backups also ensures that a single media writer cannot dominate when storing data on a shared device. In the standard NAS environment, all backups are stored in discrete containers—either in a file format or in a file/directory structure mechanism that provides separation between backup images. The net effect is that all data is contained—there is no way to analyze the images for common data to provide storage efficiencies, so that if a single server writes the majority of images or has the largest amount of data, there is no way to look at any data contained within the backup image and make it commonly available across all images. However, in the target-based deduplication environment, this changes. As the data is written by any media writer, the *subimage* data (at the block level) is reviewed. Only data blocks that have not already been stored as a result of backups completed by *any other media writer* are stored as new data. The image file/directory is now simply a container that represents pointers to common data blocks.

If any media writer stores a large number of images or a large quantity of backup data, this actually enhances the ability of other servers to effectively store their backup data by providing additional data blocks for the deduplication analysis. The more potential data blocks stored to compare against, the greater the probability that the data has already been stored, and the greater common deduplication factor across all data being written from any media writer. A large consumer of a deduplication device can actually enhance the deduplication effect, thus reducing the negative impact that single large media writers can have on the primary storage environment.

Additionally, since deduplication appliances very effectively store data within the back-end disk storage, the requirement for destaging backups from deduplicated disk storage as a method of ensuring storage can potentially be eliminated, as long as some type of replication is set up to protect against device failure. The deduplication appliance can most likely provide storage for primary backups for the full retention period required, with the space simply being reclaimed for use at expiration. Tape can be eliminated for primary storage in this situation, thus reducing the complexity of the overall backup process by taking out the requirement to generate a secondary copy of the backup every time a new one is generated. This does have limits of course; if you have backups that have long retention times or have offsite requirements, it may still make sense to have a tape copy, but even that can potentially be eliminated using deduplication technology.

An additional feature of target deduplication appliances is the ability to effectively replicate backups over distance, using the same deduplication technology that is used to reduce the amount of data stored on the appliance. When replication is initiated, there is an exchange of information regarding the blocks that need to be sent from the source (primary backup storage) to the target (offsite replica): an indication from the target regarding what blocks are already stored as a result of other replication operations (see Figure 9–12).

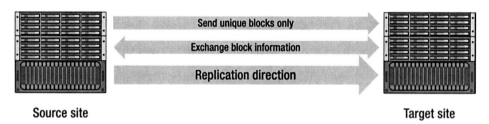

Source site   **Target site**

Figure 9–12. Deduplication replication

Based on this metadata, the source only sends the data that has not already been stored on the target, significantly reducing the amount of data that needs to be sent to the target site.

But how does this reduce or eliminate the need for tape for either offsite or long-term storage? If a secondary environment is available away from the site generating the backups, a target deduplication appliance can be placed at this secondary environment, replication enabled between the primary (site generating the backups) and the secondary site, creating an electronically created, offsite copy of the backup without generating a tape cartridge. This backup, whether the original was created using NetBackup or CommVault, can be utilized in much the same manner as a tape created as part of an offsite copy/destage policy.

NetBackup actually takes this ability one step further. Symantec has developed a backup storage protocol, OST, which allows for the creation of offsite copies that are fully managed as separate entities, simply by initiating a replication session between the source and target deduplication appliances. OST manages the process of replication, storage of the remote copy replication, and retention, which simplifies the management process of offsite copies, even beyond the simplistic method of tape cartridge management.

Here's an example: a software development company has labs in several different locations and wants to designate one as a central repository for all backups. The backups will occur locally on to deduplicated storage and then be replicated to the central site. Local backups would be held for 30 days, with the ones on the central site retained for 90 days.

Solution: create a central Master Server with a Media Server in each location. Install a deduplication appliance with OST enabled. Use Vault to create a replication policy that uses OST to replicate the data from the remote labs to the central site, changing the retention on the secondary copy.

While CommVault allows the creation of offsite copies through the use of replication, the process of managing the offsite copy requires the establishment of a MediaAgent and a shared index cache to effectively manage both the location and retention of the replica.

The replication of backups to offsite media, while typical for long-term retention requirements, is not a required mechanism to retain backups for long periods of time. Deduplication is applied in this case through the use of either migration to larger deduplication appliances, built for longer storage, which are sized to hold quantities of backups. This appliance can be located locally to the primary storage or remote in an offsite location, or it can be accomplished by sizing the primary to hold the backups for the period of time required by the retention period. The last method does not have much of an impact other than creating a larger target device and can have good net effects by providing the same common deduplication pool effect as was discussed previously regarding dominant media writers.

From the discussion thus far, it would seem as if deduplication or traditional disk plus tape solutions can be implemented, but not both. However, this is not the case. Whenever an additional media writer is deployed, a consideration must be made about which media type will be the primary type. If local disk storage was used for a staging area in the single media writer model, and an additional media writer is being added, there should be strong consideration given to using deduplicated storage versus the alternatives: local disk or NAS for a staging mechanism, plus tape for offsite storage. The introduction of deduplicated storage at this point is at a logical point because shared storage should be used in most cases when expanding to a multimedia writer environment in order to gain efficiencies of utilization across the two media writers, as well as preparing the environment for expansion in the future.

If deploying a second media writer in an environment where NAS is already used, the decision is slightly different. If the NAS has enough space to handle the backup needs for the initial deployment, the NAS storage should be retained as the primary storage. However, once the NAS storage needs to be upgraded, either in terms of capacity or performance, that becomes the point at which deduplication should be considered as a replacement for NAS-based backups. The decision at this point is largely about the cost—the initial acquisition cost of the deduplication solution may be higher that the NAS replacement or upgrade, but the length of time that the deduplication solution will last will be significantly longer under the same workload because the deduplication solution can store many times more data than a simple disk NAS solution.

Lastly, when expanding a multimedia writer solution, an assessment must be made about the number of storage resources that are available to the environment as a whole. Again, if the NAS solution will suffice for the time being, continue to use that solution. However, as with simply adding the second media writer, once the primary NAS solution is up for upgrade, then the same assessment needs to be made regarding the continued usefulness of the NAS storage type versus deduplication.

Of course, all this presupposes several things:

- Disk storage was used as a staging mechanism to tape—tape was/is not used as the primary storage target.

- If disk storage was selected as a primary storage, either for storage of the backup for the retention period, or as a simple staging area, the storage selected was NAS.

- If local storage is used, it is internal to the media writer and not SAN-attached storage.

The first two items are relatively obvious, but why does it matter if local storage is used and it is SAN attached? One of the big drawbacks of using internal storage is the lack of expandability—the amount of storage is inherently limited by the number of physical disk drives that can be physically installed into the server. The overall performance of the storage itself is very limited in its ability to expand to meet additional requirements, due to physical space limitations. However, if SAN storage is used for the local storage attachment, both capacity and performance limitations moved outside of the server as it relates to local storage, and placed on the disk array holding the storage presented to the server. SAN storage provides the ability to manage a central storage area, in much the same way as NAS storage, and quickly extend capacity, disk performance, or both, depending on the needs of a particular media writer.

If SAN storage is used, there should be strong consideration given to staying with the SAN-based storage as a primary data store, with deduplication representing the secondary target. In this configuration, multiple media writers still share the same storage pool, but have discrete targets as opposed to a single shared target. The SAN performance generally has exceeded that of NAS as connection speeds for SAN are at 8G/sec, with the NAS attachment (via the LAN) running at 1G/sec. This is changing with the introduction of 10G LAN connectivity, but server-based 10G is more expensive than equivalent SAN HBA cards, requires much more significant infrastructure upgrades and specialized cabling, and is not currently in widespread use. Deduplicated storage in this case provides the ability to house the backups for a longer term than the SAN-based storage, effectively providing the same function as tape did in previous incarnations.

This brings up a good question: what about tape in these situations? Tape still has a role in many environments, even augmenting deduplication in some instances. When confronted with a multimedia writer environment that does not have a secondary location into which a second deduplication device can be installed/managed, tape will still be required to provide an offsite capability. This is true whether using NAS, deduplicated shared storage, SAN, or local storage capabilities—the implementation of an offsite capability must be performed by tape in the absence of a secondary site to where backups can be electronically replicated.

Interestingly enough, CommVault provides a mechanism to eliminate tape, even in the situation where there is not a secondary site. Instead of using tape as the secondary target for offsite storage, CommVault provides the ability to use cloud storage as a target for replication. Cloud storage was discussed previously from an application backup perspective—a service provider was used to perform BaaS backups of local clients in small environments. What is being discussed here is different: using the raw storage capability of cloud service providers, such as Microsoft Azure or Amazon S3, as an offsite target for backup storage instead of shipping tapes to offsite locations and/or paying for pickup by physical storage providers such as Iron Mountain.

Cloud storage used in this manner provides the offsite capability normally afforded by tape, without the mechanical and management hassles of tape storage. Subclient backups are simply copied to the cloud target via an AUX copy process and maintained in much the same manner as backups to a local MagLib. A locally shared index cache will allow multiple MediaAgents access to the cloud backups, just as with any other shared media within the CommCell.

There are some things to consider when utilizing cloud storage in this manner:

- Cost

- Access

- Security

- Time to recover

First, cloud services are not free—there are charges for each access to the cloud, the amount of data stored, and other operations that happen as a result of backups. These charges are not one-time charges; they are recurring charges that must be taken into consideration when looking at a cloud storage solution.

Access to the cloud also must be considered. Since cloud storage is an Internet-based product, any backup stored there is only accessible if access to the Internet is available. In a situation where Internet access is down and access to an aged backup is required, that backup will not be able to be recovered until the Internet access is back online. Also, at the current time cloud providers are centered mainly in North America—sites that are remote from those time zones may not have access during business hours as they represent maintenance hours in North America.

There also are issues of security involved with cloud storage. Cloud storage providers, and the protocol—REST—used to communicate with the cloud storage, are based on standard HTTP web protocols and are inherently insecure. All data is transmitted in clear form and can be intercepted by unintended and/or unauthorized individuals, potentially exposing critical data backups. When looking at cloud storage, encrypting the backups prior to transmission is a requirement to ensure that if intercepted, the data would be effectively unusable. Fortunately, in addition to the cloud access mechanisms, CommVault also provides extensive encryption mechanisms to allow for encryption of the AUX copy prior to transmission to the cloud target.

Lastly, cloud targets are not designed for high-speed access. Since the cloud is an Internet target, retrieval speeds are dependent on the transfer rates of data from the cloud target back to the target system. While the speed may be acceptable for secondary copies of data, retrieval times may be unacceptable for operational use. Be sure to consider both in an analysis of cloud targets as secondary or tertiary media targets.

The bottom line when looking at media storage for multimedia writer targets is that removing tape should be a priority. With the advent of deduplication, efficient replication, and cloud storage, the necessity for tape as an offsite mechanism in environments that have enough backup capacity requirements to require multiple media writers is largely going away. The removal of tape from an environment allows not only better overall backup resource utilization but also removes a large amount of administration from the backup environment as individual cartridges of plastic and nylon do not have to be tracked, managed, maintained, replaced, and stored. Additionally, the removal of a highly complex piece of mechanical equipment, both in terms of the tape drive and the tape cartridge, will represent a significant amount of reduction in environment complexity and a corresponding increase in reliability and resiliency.

Once the selection of media targets is settled, the impact to performance must be analyzed. However, the analysis of the performance of the backup environment becomes much more complex and must take into consideration a number of other factors. While the speed with which individual clients can be backed up still is gated by the client, the overall capacity and potential speed of all backups is more difficult to assess. The performance potential of the environment as a whole is gated by the sum of the performance of the media writers installed in the environment. There are a number of factors that go into the relative performance of media writers, both with respect to the environment as a whole and between writers:

- *LAN connections*: The number and type of connections to the LAN in the reception of client backup streams as well as the output of the streams to shared storage media, if utilized.

- *System capabilities*: The ability to process and redirect streams, providing buffering as necessary—this is gated by primarily the amount of RAM available to the media writer as well as CPU power.

- *Disk staging performance*: In the case of the use of disk staging, the speed of the staging area will have a significant impact on the overall backup performance and will limit the number of parallel clients that can be serviced by the media writer.

- *Speed of the index cache*: When using CommVault, the speed of the index cache is also a significant factor. Since CommVault uses a distributed cache model, the index cache is critical to ensuring a fast backup platform. When using a shared cache, the speed of the cache is even more critical because if the cache is slow, all MediaAgents participating in the shared cache will be affected by the cache speed.

- *Client count*: As client counts increase, the amount of metadata generated increases exponentially. This metadata increases the load on the backup server, which in turn will eventually begin to slow down. The processing slowdown on a backup server will artificially drive down the overall backup performance of the environment because backups cannot complete until metadata is processed.

All these factors interact to ultimately gate the performance of the backup environment as a whole, and all interact. Increase the LAN ingestion rate, and the amount of metadata per second increases, driving backup server performance. Increases the number of clients running in parallel and potentially drives down the speed of the staging disk, reducing the overall throughput of all clients. It is a balancing act with no clear equation of relationship because of the number of factors involved. Adjustment of one factor will require monitoring of all others to assess the impact, potentially requiring the reversal of adjustments in order to try a different approach. Such is the nature of environmental tuning.

Another factor not listed here is the impact of how the applications are backed up by the backup software. In smaller environments, simple backup approaches could be used because there were generally still off hours backup windows, and backup SMEs were not available to analyze the environment and determine the best methods of application backup. However, once multiple media writers are introduced, most often there at least one person primarily responsible for backups, off hours backup windows are either small nor non-existent, and application backups need to be configured to allow for 24x7 operations.

Note While it may seem economical to only have a single person responsible for backups, it is important to have at least one other person crossed-trained in how to administer the backup environment. Backups do not stop just because the backup administrator gets sick.

Application Backup Considerations

Since it is generally not desirable to stop the application for backup, data stream–based backups for applications become much more prevalent at this point. The data stream backup allows for the backup software to interact directly with the application and determine the individual pieces of data to back up, as determined from the application perspective, rather than simply backing entire chunks of data contained within a file structure. Even if data stream backups are not used, file-level backups must use some sort of "hot" backup mode to keep the application running, with minimal performance impact, while the backup is occurring.

The determination about whether to use a data stream backup or a file-based backup in this situation is dependent on the capabilities of the application, the impact of data stream backups on application performance, the relative difficulty of recovery as assessed for both data stream– and file-based backup methodologies, and the quantity of data required to be backed up. As has been discussed before, while data stream backups can capture very discrete amounts of data, particularly the actual data that has changed within the application, this retrieval of information can have a large effect on the overall performance of the application during the backup. As a counterpoint, while many applications can tolerate the backup of only the changed files within their application, since the file may contain data that is unchanged as well as changed, particularly in database and e-mail applications, where individual records are updated, leaving both changed and unchanged data within file containers.

Data stream backups can also introduce complexities in the restoration of data as well. When restoring a file-based backup of an application, it is generally enough to simply restore the files, perform any application-level reintegration steps, and restart the application. However, in a data stream restoration, the blocks must be placed back into the application in such a way as to re-create the conditions that existed at the time of the backup. Since a number of blocks may have changed since the time of the backup, additional blocks may be required, over and above the original backup.

Why? Consider the following example: if I have a database with a single file (a contrivance, but used for the simplicity of the example) and create a full backup. For a first incremental backup, 10 changed blocks from the file are backed up. In the next backup, I change 10 additional blocks, 5 of which are the same blocks as the original backup stored. In the third backup, 10 additional blocks change, all but one is a different block from the original backup. (See Figure 9–13.)

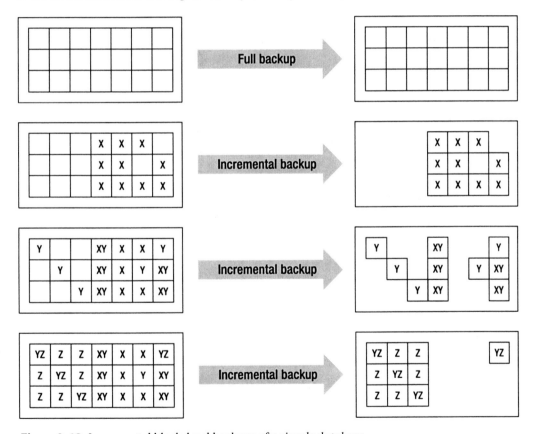

Figure 9–13. Incremental block-level backups of a simple database

Now, if the restore is executed, and the second backup (the one immediately following the full backup) is the desired point of restore, simply restoring the backup to the current state of the database will create a file that will not match the desired point as some of the blocks do not represent the state the database was in during the point of the backup. In order to restore the original state at the desired point, additional blocks will need to be restored from the full backup to overwrite any other blocks that changed since the desired backup from which to restore. Once the backed-up blocks plus the original blocks are restored, only then is the database back to the original state. This example illustrates the complexities introduced when performing and restoring data stream–level backups. Take this example and multiply it by the number of files within a particular database or instance (depending on whether it is SQL Server or Oracle) and by the number of backups taken between full backups to get to a particular state. Then the potential complexity of a restore can be seen.

So if complexity is introduced to the backup environment, already made more complex by the introduction of multiple media writers, why use data streams at all? Data stream backups are very useful for a number of reasons. Because the data stream only backs up the changed data since the last backup, the amount of data backed up can be significantly less that that generated by even an incremental backup of the files that contain the relevant data. This will significantly reduce the amount of data and the time required for backups overall and provide for a method of further shrinking the needed backup window. Additionally, the backup itself provides the ability to roll back to specific points in time, with remarkable accuracy. This can be important in situations where the accuracy of the point in time is of greater importance than the restorational complexity or additional application performance load places on the system.

One such application is Microsoft Exchange. Exchange can be backed up using either file or data stream–level backups for the protection of the contents of the e-mail system. There is a third type of backup that looks like a data stream backup but really is not: the mailbox- or "brick"-level backups. This is the ability of both NetBackup and CommVault to protect e-mail within Exchange at a mailbox-by-mailbox level, allowing the restoration of individual mail items and attachments directly back into original mailbox. This is not, however, a data stream backup of Exchange. The standard data stream backup reads the changes in the Exchange Jet database and stores those changes within regard to the actual structures that the data actually creates. Just as in the database example, the data stream backup of Exchange simply provides a set of blocks from which specific Storage Groups or Databases can be reconstructed.

The mailbox-level backup does something different—it scans each mailbox for changes at the mailbox level—new e-mail, attachments, and so on—and makes a copy of those changes into backup format that the backup software can track. Restores occur using a special interface into either NetBackup or CommVault that can identify the items that have been backed up and place them back into the appropriate mailbox. These processes, the backup more than the restore, place a very heavy load on the Exchange server. Look at the backup as an automated reading of every piece of e-mail within the Exchange server, at a rate that runs as fast as possible. This is equivalent to receiving and processing all the mail currently contained within the server, through the standard Exchange processing engine, during the period of the backup. Such a load will bring all other mail operations within the Exchange server to a virtual halt if applied to all mailboxes across the Exchange server(s) in question.

▓ **Note** If mailbox-level backups are to be applied at all in this type of environment, they should be limited to very specific mailboxes—those that contain mail that is business critical, of a sensitive nature, or has a legal or regulatory requirement to be backed up and stored for a specific period of time. All other mail should be backed up using the data stream method of protection.

But this is a discussion of multimedia writer servers. Why is it important to talk about data stream backups and Exchange mailbox backups when they don't seem to have a lot to do with the architecture of multimedia writer servers? The addition of multiple media writers to the environment represents a significant change in scale in the environment from even the single media writer one. These changes will generally only compound over time, requiring more media writers to be added to the environment to allow for data and more parallel backups to occur, meeting ever-tightening backup windows. This change in scale implies several items:

- *Organization size*: The size of the organization has generally grown in terms of people working for it. In general, the more data generated, the more people either generating the data or processing and analyzing the data. There is a particular impact in e-mail environments. The increase in users and the variety of user types within a multimedia writer environment will drive increased load on mail servers. This increased load will further drive what type of backups should happen and what the acceptable decrease in mail performance can be during the period of the backup.

- *Number of applications*: The number and complexity of the applications has changed. Single media writer environments are typified by single operating system environments with relatively low complexity. Once an additional media writer has to be added, it typically represents a growth in the number of different applications—many of which are now purpose built. Any application that is purpose built is by necessity more complex than those that are built for general usage as the application is geared to solving a very specific business problem, with very specific operation and design parameters. These parameters are unique to the application and are not accounted for in the standard backup application operation.

- *Number of operating system*: The number of different operating systems increases beyond one. In smaller environments, Microsoft Windows servers are the dominant server type. They are relatively simple to install and operate, and are similar enough to the common desktop (Windows 7/XP) that someone with a lower level of knowledge regarding running servers can support. The necessity of multiple media writers implies purpose-built applications. Purpose-built applications are not limited to a single operating system and are built on the operating system that makes sense to the developer to build it on. Therefore, there will generally be more than one operating system to support in the environment.

The addition of a second media writer is simply a starting point. The environment is scaled out to meet additional backup needs through the use of additional media writers, both general purpose and dedicated, depending on the backup problem that is being solved. Unless there are specialized needs, as will be discussed later, the environment grows so large that no amount of CPU/RAM/IO on the backup server will accommodate the metadata processing load, or there is enough of a physical risk to the environment that a warm/hot backup server disaster recovery (DR) strategy needs to be put into place if there is a requirement to add a second backup server. There are, however, some specialized considerations that add "variations to a theme" of the addition of media writers, and should be considered in conjunction with this environmental change.

Deduplication: When and Where?

The subject of deduplication has been touched on in several places throughout this book. But where and when do you implement it? Before we answer this question, a quick review of the types of deduplication is in order.

Deduplication comes in two flavors: source and target. In *source-based deduplication*, the client performs the initial block identification and deduplication function prior to transmitting the data to the media writer. Data is deduplicated globally across all clients that participate in the deduplication environment, with data deduplicated across a common deduplication media writer. Only the data that is unique and not already stored in the target media is sent over the network. This reduces the total amount of data transmitted by several orders of magnitude, at the expense of front-end processing overhead on the client to identify the blocks to process. The media writer is a special device that stores the data and maintains a repository of the data blocks stored by all clients, and a method of rebuilding the blocks into usable data once requested. As of the writing of this book, neither NetBackup or CommVault offered client-based deduplication strategies as a part of the native backup application.

Target Deduplication

Target-based deduplication, on the other hand, performs the deduplication after the data stream hits the media. Target-based deduplication can either be at the media writer level, as has been implemented in both NetBackup (PureDisk) and CommVault (SILO storage), or as an appliance acting as a media target, such as EMC DataDomain or Quantum DXi series disk targets. The target-based deduplication in these forms is also fully supported by both NetBackup and CommVault as either a DSU/DSSU (NetBackup) or as a standard MagLib (CommVault).

Deduplication in a target solution is also deduplicated across clients, but this deduplication does not occur until after the data is transmitted to the media writer or written to the deduplication media. However, since this occurs after the transmission of the data to either the media writer or to the media itself, the benefits of deduplication as it relates to the amount of data transmitted cannot be realized. However, the client does not have to do any more processing than with a normal client.

Source Deduplication

So when should you implement deduplication? Source-based deduplication is a good candidate for situations where there is a moderate amount of data, a low change rate, many files, or a bandwidth–constrained network connection. This form of deduplication, in most implementations, requires a large number of nodes processing data in a parallel stream in order to provide both the storage and throughput required to have backups run at acceptable rates. The number of nodes participating in the source-based deduplication gates both the throughput that can be archived as well as the amount of data that can be stored on the target. In order to avoid entire racks of nodes, the amount of data that is targeted at a source-based deduplication solution should be limited to specific situations, which will be described as follows.

Additionally, since the client performs the deduplication scans *prior* to sending the data, both the amount of data to scan and the amount of changed data should be limited. This gives the client time to process all changes and to reduce the overall load on the client when performing the backup. In particular, having high change rate data on clients significantly increases the load on the client as more data has to be scanned on the backup pass to check for deduplication commonality. Another side effect of high change rate data on source-based deduplication is that the amount of data transmitted and stored is also increased based both on the change rate (which will generate more data anyway) and the decrease in the deduplication ratio, due to an increased probability of unique data being generated as a result of the high change rate.

In situations such as a high density file system (HDFS) in which there are large numbers of files (the majority of which are static), source-based deduplication can shine. Since the deduplication client is only looking for changed blocks, and given that the majority of the files in the HDFS have not changed, once the initial metadata is generated, only the changed files need to be found and deduplication applied. But like anything else, this has limits. If the number of files is too large, even if the vast majority of the files are static, the scan can run out of time, run longer than the desired window, or simply not finish as a result of the client system limitations. Too many files are located within the file system to scan.

Source-based deduplication is also a great candidate for sites where the additional equipment should not or cannot be placed for the purposes of backup. Since source-based deduplication performs all deduplication on the client prior to sending data, it can be applied at a distance, in remote locations, without having to install any backup hardware—even a source deduplication target. Only the metadata and the unique data generated as a result of the client backups are sent to the central site, making source-based deduplication a great alternative to BaaS implementation for larger backup environments.

Deduplication for Virtual Machines (VMs)

While there is considerable debate about this, the use of source-based deduplication for virtual machine (VM) hypervisor backups is also very effective. Again since the deduplication of the data happens prior to the backup leaving the hypervisor, the amount of data required to represent entire sets of VMs can be very small. Why? Consider what a VM really is: a copy of an OS on which selected applications run. Since there are only a handful of operating systems that can run within a VM container and since a given hypervisor usually contains a single set of common operating systems, the probability of having like files, and therefore like sets of data blocks, is extremely high. This effect can be seen whether backing up the hypervisor directly or backing up each individual VM contained within the hypervisor. It is simply a decision about where to put the backup client.

So where is the debate on this? While the source-based deduplication for VMs is very effective, it still suffers from the same limitations as source-based deduplication does with standard clients: limited throughput, file counts, and data size. When applied at the hypervisor level, the number of files to scan is relatively low—on the order of a few hundred in a large implementation, but the amount of data to scan can be massive. This can limit the amount of time available to actually perform the backup of the collection of VMs. Additionally, since a hypervisor shares CPU and RAM between all VMs, any additionally load placed on the hypervisor side can have a negative impact on all VMs—especially a load induced by a backup client performing a scan of all the virtual disks for block-level analysis.

On the other hand, target-based deduplication is an excellent general-purpose solution to provide a storage solution that looks and feels like local disk but provides the benefits of deduplication. The deduplication is offloaded from the client and put onto the deduplication target, thus reducing the overall system impact caused by the backup. This is not without penalty as the data must first be transmitted to the deduplication target prior to deduplication, which does nothing to reduce the amount of data on the network. Given the ability to store large amounts of data quickly, as well as having the ability to maintain disk semantics to both the operating system and to the backup software (with some enhancements), target-based deduplication should be considered as the primary backup target for all new deployments of backup environments (including upgrades to existing ones). As has been explored previously, the replacement of traditional disk/tape solutions with deduplication targets has benefits that can outweigh the initial capital outlay over the medium term.

But which target deduplication solution to deploy? Both NetBackup and CommVault offer the ability to create target deduplication solutions using software on standard commodity hardware and operating systems. While this may have a smaller upfront cost, simply the cost of the server plus the licensing cost, the scalability limitations of the software-based solution limit their deployment to environments that may only require a single or two deduplication targets. This is to limit the amount of complex expansion and maintenance that is required on software-based solutions.

Purpose-built, appliance target-based deduplication solutions are the preferred method of deployment of deduplication as they provide the best flexibility of deployment and ease of management and expansion, especially when compared with the software solution. By using standard vendor-provided expansion systems, as well as having support models that cover both the hardware and software aspects of the appliance (something that the software solutions do not offer), the appliance solution has a superior support model. This further justifies the recommendation for its use as the primary media storage for backups.

Remote Office (RO) Deployments

One of the environments targeted for use by deduplication solutions is the situation that requires the deployment of backups to non-central or remote locations. There are three types of *remote office (RO)* deployments:

- Office

- Regional site

- Remote datacenter

The RO environment has a small number of servers to be protected, possibly even just desktops. No type of IT SME is locally available to troubleshoot any issues that occur in the environment. These environments most often do not have specialty server types, such as database or mail servers, and are most often populated by simple file servers. These types of environments are beginning to slightly shrink in numbers through the advent of cloud-based applications that require no local infrastructure. However, the RO will be still common in the traditional form for some time to come. There is most often only one type of operating system installed in the RO environment: Microsoft Windows.

The regional site (RS) environment is typified by the installation of specialty servers for specific business purposes, while still maintaining an overall small number of servers to be backed up—generally fewer than 30 servers total. There is usually a mail server in the environment as the number of people in the environment is often large enough to warrant the centralization of mail within the environment. An RS may also have one or more ROs operating from resources within the local environment, such as localized database or mail servers. An RS will have one or more IT SMEs available, possibly one that is familiar with backups. Other types of operating system platforms may be installed to serve specific business applications.

Finally, the remote datacenter (RDC) is a central site in microcosm. It will contain multiple application platform types, multiple operating system types, and most often more than one mail server. The server count is well over 30 servers, and depending on the definition, may approach the server count of the central site. The RDC will have multiple specialized IT SMEs available to manage the environment and to provide specialized support services. An RDC may have an RS using common resources or may simply have a larger number of ROs.

There are several common factors that resonate between all types of remotely managed backup sites:

- No local control of the backup environment

- Limited or shared network connectivity between sites

- Variations in operational skill level available for maintenance

Changes to the backup environment can occur without the backup administrator's knowledge, which can lead to unexpected and unpredictable backup performance and completion rates. In the RO and RS environment, this can be problematic as backup reliably is highly variable. However, in the RDC environment, this may lead to variations from standard practices established at the central site. While this in and of itself may not cause differences in completion rates, restores may be adversely affected as the deviations from standardize procedures may not allow for restores to happen in a predictable fashion from either central or RDC sites.

Limited or shared network connectivity will limit either the amount of data backed up from the remote site, the amount of data replicated from the remote site to the central site, or the window when backups and/or replication can occur. The data limits are most often felt in the RO to RS/RDC situation. ROs are generally only connected via low bandwidth links back to the central site or may only have Internet connectivity with no direct connectivity back to the central (or RO/RDC) site. However, in the RS/RDC situation, this effect is seen in the impact of replication traffic on other applications and data streams sharing the network that would connect the two sites. Application data streams are given higher business priority than backup streams in most environments, sometimes enforced by mechanisms such as Quality of Service (QoS) or network traffic shaping, forcing the backup stream to consume as little bandwidth as possible. Due to this common limitation, backups and/or replication can be limited in the hours that the operation can occur, or can be limited in throughput, thus extending the backup windows.

In the RO environment, even though there is not an SME to help maintain the environment, adverse changes can be introduced by end users making alterations to their systems, or inadvertently making hardware or network changes that have detrimental effects on the completion of the backups. In the RS environment, while there are SMEs available for general-purpose use, if there is not any backup expertise, changes intended to make issues better for the RS users may have the opposite effect on backups. Careful coordination between RS and central should be maintained in this situation to ensure that changes do not affect backups. The RDC environment is not necessarily affected in the same way as the other two by this factor, but as was discussed above, variations in operational procedures can have effects on backup and restore availability.

Remote Office (RO)

All three general types require a different approach from one another. The RO environment is obviously the simplest of the three. There are three different approaches that can be taken to back up a RO environment:

- Use source-based deduplication of the clients and pipe the backups from the RO to the central site

- Place a media writer locally at the RO, with a target-based deduplication device attached, perform backups locally, and replicate the result back to the central site.

- Use a BaaS solution to perform backups of the RO without any additional infrastructure.

All three have their applicability, based on the situation. The source-based deduplication solution provides a method that requires the least deployment of owned infrastructure, allows for remote storage of the backups (hence an automatic offsite capability), and provides backups that can be accomplished even over very small available bandwidth. No additional infrastructure is needed at the remote site to complete backups, and the benefits of the source-based deduplication can be realized across all remote sites—potentially reducing the amount of data that is required to be moved from each client to the central site. However, this method does require the potentially the largest outlay of both hardware and cost to implement. As has been previously discussed, a source-based deduplication infrastructure can require a significant investment of specialized nodes to provide the backup target for the client deduplication. In addition, when using either NetBackup or CommVault, this implementation of a source-based deduplication solution will require the implementation of a second backup environment as neither have a source solution at the time of this writing.

The second method to protect the data at an RO is to place a media writer locally at the site combined with a target-based deduplication solution, and remotely control the backups using the backup server at the central site. Offsite copies of the backups would be facilitated by target-based replication of the original backups from the RO to the central site. This method, while requiring deployment of infrastructure at the RO, also provides a method by which backups can be controlled through a common backup environment Both NetBackup and CommVault could be used: NetBackup controlling a Media Server, and CommVault running a MediaAgent. This makes the assumption that there is reliable connectivity between the central and remote sites—loss of connectivity means that no backups occur as the remote site is entirely dependent on the central site control to execute backups.

The target-based deduplication solution can be implemented in two different ways, depending on cost and complexity considerations: software or hardware. In the previous discussion, hardware- or appliance-based deduplication was listed as the preferred method of implementing target-based deduplication due to support and scalability considerations. However, for the RO situation, the software-based solution is entirely plausible as the scale of the solution to deploy is small enough that the other considerations can be outweighed by the ability to quickly deploy a solution using commodity hardware, given that the required performance specifications of the software are met. However, the issues with complexity, scalability, and complexity of implementation remain, and an appliance-based solution would still be preferred. But software-based solutions will warrant a serious look if the RO environment is small and relatively static in size.

The last solution is the newest solution, and one that was first discussed at the beginning of this chapter: BaaS (cloud) backups. The RO is a great candidate for a BaaS solution as it allows for the backup of the RO clients without the deployment of any additional hardware to support the backup. In particular, RO environments that have only Internet connectivity only have this option available to them; the other two methods require direct connectivity to operate. The downside, as previously discussed, is the requirement to manage a second backup solution and the potential ongoing costs associated with storing backups over time. But for many RO environments, this should be considered as the primary solution, given a cost analysis of the alternatives, even with the necessity to manage a second backup solution.

An exception to all the solutions listed here is in the case of very slow links back to the central site from the RO, links on the order of 256 k or slower, or simply unreliable links such as those that transit in or out of less advanced countries. In these cases, the link is likely too slow to support either source or target replication of any scale, and cloud-based backups cannot be affected due to the significant reduction in the speed of Internet connectivity. In this exception, the introduction of a small local backup server, of the same software type as the central site, with a small tape library will help alleviate the problem. Tape is used in this situation as the primary backup target because the potential number of clients will most likely be very low, and there will be requirement to get backups offsite—something that a local deduplication appliance will not be able to accomplish without connectivity.

Regional Site (RS)

The RS introduces complexities, many of which are not technical in nature. As previously discussed, the RS has many characteristics of an RDC—numbers of servers, specialty platforms, and even potentially differing operating systems. However, the RS does not have any specialized expertise in the areas of backups, a fact that complicates the management of backups from a central site. Network connectivity between the central site and the RS may have limitations, due both to technical and business needs, and the RS may be providing services to ROs in addition to providing local services.

The RS should be in the model of one or more media writers, managed by the central backup server, using target-based deduplication with offsite replication to a central site. It may seem odd that this is such a cut-and-dried solution. This general-case RS solution provides a way to scale the environment out horizontally to meet the local needs. This scalability is provided by the media writers, which can be deployed in either general-purpose mode or dedicated mode, as dictated by the requirements of the client.

If the RS also provides service to ROs, the model should be extended out. By extending out the architecture to the ROs in the form of media writers and deduplication targets, the overall cohesiveness of the backup environment can be maintained, backups can be scheduled from a central site, and replication can be controlled for the entire environment, from the RO up to the central site, from a single control point.

The central backup server provides the centralized controls needed to ensure a consistent environment, at least from the backup control perspective. Since there are no local backup personnel resources to run a backup environment, this particular aspect is important to ensure that backups are performed in a manner consistent with standards found in the central site, as well as to provide the ability to control the method and timing of both backups in the environment as a whole and the replication of backups offsite.

Target-based deduplication is used to provide a method to receive backup images from RO environments and to forward RS backups to the central site for offsite storage. If the RS is large enough, or represents good geographic disparity from the central site, the deduplication media device may also be able to act as the target of replication from the central site, as well as replicating the RS backups back to the central site to act as an offsite for the RS itself.

Source-based deduplication will most likely not be an option in an RS environment as the number and/or size of the environment will require a large deployment of a target source deduplication environment to absorb the backups for the environment. Since the plan is to replicate the backup offsite to the central site, an even bigger central source-based environment would need to be deployed to absorb all other RS environments into the central site. The area where source-based deduplication can be applied to the RS environment is as a target for RO backups and for special-purpose backups, such as HDFS file systems that may exist within the RS site.

As was mentioned previously, many of the complexities with management of the RS environment are not necessarily technical. Since the RS may not have specific specialties in the backup field, any support needed to ensure that the backups run correctly may not be forthcoming, or the support may be inaccurate. Additionally, since the individuals have specialties that are not focused on backups, there may be changes to the environment that although made to solve specific problems, may be detrimental to the overall completion of backups. The best way to solve this problem is through documentation. Setting up specific procedures and policies will help ensure that agents and media writers are set up in consistent ways. Additionally, the use of the central backup server to control the backup policies and schedule, thus isolating them from local control, will also help to solve some of the consistency issues.

There are some factors within specific environments that may force changes in this basic architecture. Security considerations, specifically the implementation of network firewall between sites, can drive changes. At a minimum, the introduction of a firewall will reduce the amount of data that can be moved on a given link because the firewall introduces a significant amount of overhead in processing the network traffic as it is passed through. This will slow other users of the firewall because it will be spending time passing the backup traffic, not that of other applications or connections.

The introduction of a firewall into the environment also poses a configuration challenge: individual network ports, or sets of ports, need to be allowed to pass through the firewall (*opened*) in order for the backups to work. If these ports are not opened correctly or are inadvertently closed, the backups will cease to function or will be extremely limited in the number of clients that can be processed in the environment.

Depending on the security, complexity, and reliability concerns a firewall imposes, it may be advisable in this situation to implement a second datazone/CommCell in the environment. The main consideration to think about when looking at this option is balancing the ability to remotely manage the environment versus the impact of the firewall against the centrally managed solution. While the bias should be toward having a central solution in the environment, if the backups prove to be unreliable due to issues with firewall performance or management, the risks of having a remotely managed solution are outweighed by the need to ensure reliable backups with consistent performance.

Regional Datacenter (RDC)

The next step in the sizing chain is the regional datacenter (RDC). The RDC can truly be thought of as a clone of the central site, both in terms of the relative number of servers, the operation complexities, and the amount of data that requires protection. RDCs may provide services to RS sites, RO environments, or combinations thereof. There are two basic approaches to having an effective backup environment in an RDC environment: establish a new datazone/CommCell or keep the central management model in place.

Extending the current central management model has definite advantages. All control of the backup environment remains in a single management point that simplifies the overall backup environment.

Central control ensures that backup policies are consistent, schedules for resources are coordinated, and all media are tracked from a single point. A centralized model also ensures that resources are utilized to the best possible level. Since the resources can be seen from a single point, any excess slack that is possible to distribute to other environments can be redirected. A central site also provides the simplest method of managing replication of backups from remote locations to more centrally located ones, whether this is an RO->RS, RS->RDC, or any other combination. The central site has tracked all backups and their image locations;

making copies becomes a trivial matter as the central system simply records a new location for the backup image.

However, the model begins to break down when dealing with very large numbers of servers in a distributed environment, on the order or 1000–2000 per backup server. While the backup data is all stored locally via the media writer, all metadata from every client is passed over the wide area network (WAN) connection to the central site. The metadata is very small relative to the data being backed up; however, when metadata streams are applied to WAN connections at scale, the WAN can be congested simply with the number of metadata streams that are generated as a result of clients performing backups in parallel. As has been discussed previously, if the metadata processing is slowed, regardless of the potential performance of the media writer or the client, the overall backup speed for clients is slowed by the proportional amount.

Wide Area Network (WAN) Connection Considerations

A related issue has to do with the number of WAN connections, or *hops*, that are made from the client to the backup server at the central site. Each of these WAN hops adds both reliability and latency issues. For instance, a client is located at an RO that is attached to an RS, and that RS is further connected to the central site where the backup server maintains the state of the environment as a whole. If the link between the RS and the central site is congested, then even if the link between the RS and the RO is not utilized, the backup of the client at the RO will be slowed down due to the congestion felt at the upper link.

Related to an upstream congestion issue is that of combined latency on the WAN links. Remember that *latency* is the time, measured in milliseconds (ms), required to transit a single packet on a link from transmitter to receiver. Latency is governed by a number of issues, such as switch/router performance, quality of the transmission media, and so on, but is primarily affected on WAN links by the physical distance between sites. This effect is cumulative over the number of links, so if I have 1 link that has 10 ms latency between physical sites A and B, and I have a second link that has 15 ms latency between sites B and C, the latency between sites A and C is no less than 25 ms (10 ms + 15 ms). Latency affects performance by limiting the amount of data a single stream can transmit in a period of time, thus effectively reducing net throughput of single streams. When applied to backups, the longer the latency, the slower the transmission of the metadata and the performance of the backup.

WAN links are also susceptible to outages: fires, floods, and earthquakes can disrupt the connection. Outages on the WAN link in this type of configuration represent outages in the backup. Without the central site, the remote sites do not have any way to start backups running.

Another issue faced when dealing with a decision regarding the maintenance of centralized control is that of reliability and backup server protection. The backup server effectively represents a single point of failure in the environment; if the backup server goes down, backups do not run. In many environments, if backups do not complete for a short period of time due to issues with the backup server, as long as the server is restored within one or two missed backup sessions (either incremental or full backups), it is not a big deal. However, in larger environments, particularly in environments that have evolved to the point of having the Central->RDC->RS->RO relationships, the failure of the backup server represents a real problem because the amount of time required to catch up the multiple environments with failed backups would be greater that the time available to complete the catch-up operation. An additional effect is that missed backups also miss capturing transient and potentially important data.

While this can be somewhat alleviated through clustering and protecting the backup server in other ways, the net effect is that an outage by a single central server ingests an adverse situation that is not acceptable to the organization. The continued expansion of the backup environment to support more and more clients with a reliance on a single server, even with a modicum of protection offered by clustering and WAN redundancy, will render the central solution unacceptable.

The centralized management of backups is the preferred configuration. However, centralization simply for its own sake or to maintain a single model for the environment will produce environments at a larger scale that simply cannot keep up or introduce too much risk into the environment. This is why a second datazone/CommCell should be strongly considered in RDC environments. This seems like a contradiction to the theme of the rest of this book: "Centralized management is good." However, like everything else, it is has limits.

Consider our first statement regarding the RDC: it is essentially a central site in microcosm. As such, the RDC should have all the resources to function as an independent unit. It may be generally impractical to try to manage an RDC from a central site as the sheer number of clients, policies/storage policies, and resulting metadata traffic will overwhelm the network and back up server resources at the central site.

Adding a Second Datazone in the RDC

In order to avoid these issues, a second datazone/CommCell should be considered to be built in the RDC. The second datazone will help to ensure that backups of the RDC and any related sites are successful by providing a "localized" backup resource that can be fully utilized for the needs of the particular site. Additionally, one of the gating factors for growing backup servers is the number of clients that can be processed because of limitations with the CPU/RAM/disk that ultimately prevent client metadata from being processed in a timely manner. The addition of a second datazone in an RDC provides an effective doubling of the total number of clients that can be backed up within the enterprise as a whole.

The second datazone in the RDC will also function as a "central" site for any ancillary RS or RO sites that can be routed to them. The RDC can also be used as a DR site for remote sites, as long as the infrastructure is in place to support the additional load generated by DR activities. The second datazone in the RDC is primarily in place to alleviate the load from the central site, allowing it to process backups faster, as well as removing any nondirect traffic that previously had to pass through the RDC to the central site as part of the replication process.

Backup policies can also be tailored to meet the specific needs of the environment. In previous discussions, the divergence of backup policies from a centralized standard was discouraged as it could lead to situations where backups were not consistently completed due to policy or resource conflict, or other issues that would affect the environment. However, in the second datazone model, given that there are resources available that can affect directed changes to the backup environment, as long as the changes are

- Consistent with the general design of backup policies for the enterprise.

- Have been assessed as truly needed to meet specific issues found within the RDC datazone scope.

These changes can be need-based items such as the following:

- Staffing levels at the RDC site: May require changes to ensure effective backup support coverage.

- Time/Timezone related: RDCs may exist within different time zones or have differing production schedules that require major portions of the backup schedule to change to meet these needs. The effect of the time zone may also be felt in the reduction in maintenance windows due to centralized management.

- Process related: The RDC may contain specialized applications that require backup processes different from those found at the central site.

While the last two points can also apply to changes within a datazone at any site, including the central site, changes within existing datazones can be carried forward and managed within a single point. When applied to multiple datazones, the number of differences between management points becomes important to reduce the operational complexity of the environment by having as many common backup schedules, processes, and methods as possible. If these guidelines are followed, the new datazone can be effectively integrated and managed as an overall part of the enterprise backup structure.

DR Potential of RDCs

An interesting side effect of a second datazone is the ability to begin to provide a level of disaster protection for the central site, as long as the media and operating system are compatible. Again, since the RDC is substantial in size, there is a level of infrastructure, both from a physical and personnel perspective that can be utilized for other purposes. One of these purposes could be the protection of backup environment at the central site from events that could lead to its loss—both physical and logical threats. This can be accomplished by providing a "warm" standby set of backup servers that contain the catalogs/databases necessary to restart/restore the backup environment in the central site.

NetBackup DR

When using NetBackup, this is done through the replication of both the catalog and the EMM databases. These two elements make up the core of the backup environment: the catalog with the information regarding the backup images and their retention, and the EMM database containing the information regarding the associated media locations on which the images are stored and their current locations. The simplest method of ensuring a quick turnaround in a DR backup restart is to provide an array-based replication of the catalog backup image, the actual catalog, and the EMM databases. The array-based replication allows the catalog to be directly restored into the warm copy of the backup server, providing a virtually instantaneous method getting the catalog information back. The EMM database should be able to be restored in a similar way, but since it uses a database backend, it may not be in a usable state (depending on the state of the backup during the replication). If this is the case, the catalog backup contains a point-in-time copy of both the catalog and the EMM database that can be restored. However, the catalog backup only contains backup information up to the time of the last time the catalog was protected—any backups made past that point will need to be imported (a painful process for a large number of backup images) or will simply not exist from the perspective of the backup server. Alternatively, to store the catalog backup on an array with replication capabilities (and assuming that a replicated deduplication solution is in place), the catalog backup can be placed on that backup target, stored efficiently (allowing for more copies to be maintained), and replicated along with all the backups that it is covering. The storage of the catalog on the deduplication device is simply to leverage an existing form of replication, not for the storage efficiency of the storage media.

CommVault DR

CommVault provides a slightly different solution. Since a CommCell depends entirely on a SQL database and the individual MediaAgents are primarily responsible for maintaining a large amount of metadata regarding the backups that it makes, array-based replication may only solve part of the problem. First, the CommServe (more specifically, the SQL Server database that the CommServe uses) must be replicated to the secondary site. This can be done in several ways, depending on the speed and type of recovery required. The first way is to simply direct DR backups that are completed on a periodic basis to a remote destination versus a local one. This allows the CommServe to simply restore the DR backup and move forward. However, this solution required additional licensing—specifically a Dual IP license to allow the install of the CommServe and the import of the DR backup onto a server that is different from the generating server. This method of protection only offers the ability to track backups as far forward as the last DR backup time—potentially leading to the need to import media or else lose a small subset of backups as a result of the disaster event.

The second method is to simply implement SQL log shipping to send the transaction logs from the primary database to a standby database. This method provides a more robust method of protecting the CommCell as each transaction into the SQL Server is replicated—effectively creating a near real-time method of tracking backups into a DR environment as they are completed. This implementation, however, can be resource intensive, particularly on the LAN/WAN because it requires a low-level, but almost constant stream of SQL transaction logs from the source CommServe to the target.

While the two products may use different methods of recovering their metadata, when implementing a DR environment in a central<->RDC relationship, it is more important to have an effective means of replicating the backups themselves. Without them, there is no point to the metadata replication. While tape can provide this mechanism by shipping the cartridges directly from the central to the RDC, we already have a solution that performs this task more efficiently: deduplication appliances.

Using Deduplication for DR

By using a deduplication appliance on both the central site and the RDC, there is the ability to perform cross-replication between the two sites: the central site replicates to the RDC, and the RDC replicates to the central site. This provides offsite capability for the backups of both sites, as well as providing a level of DR, protecting the backups in case of a site failure. If the catalog backups are included as part of this replication, there is now a combined backup/catalog set offsite without shipping a single tape.

There is one other target that can also function as a replication point as well for longer-term backups, further eliminating tape: cloud storage. For backups that are stored long term (longer than 1–2 years), tape was traditionally the answer: create a copy of the backup on a tape, ship the tape to an offsite vault, and wait. However, with the advent of cloud storage, longer-term storage of backups is possible, simply by making a copy of the backup to a cloud storage device, either via software (CommVault) or via an appliance. Although the retrieval time can be longer, this will allow a "resourceless" storage of the backup in an offsite location. However, based on current cost models, it can be expensive, so it is important to assess the cost of traditional tape, plus long-term offsite storage, versus the monthly costs of storing backups in a cloud target. It is also important to consider the other challenges of cloud storage in its current incarnation as well as prior to implementation.

The introduction of a second datazone into an RDC does pose some challenges that need to be considered prior to making the plunge. The introduction of a second datazone also introduces a second point of management into the enterprise as a whole. Now, instead of having to manage one set of schedules, polices, and backups, there are two. This simply means that more care needs to be taken when administering the datazone servers to ensure that all policies are consistent—as much as the environment allows. But given the limitations of scale that began to be seen in the RDC environment, a second datazone is definitely the recommendation when populating or growing an existing environment into an RDC posture.

Remote Office Wrap-Up

The RO environment poses differing challenges and design elements as the overall environment grows. In the RO environment, it is a decision between maintaining infrastructure (deployment of media writers/targets) and purchasing services (BaaS). When moving to larger environments, such as the RS and RDC, efficiencies and issues of scale must be considered for all aspects of the backup environment: servers, network, and storage. The growth of backups into environments requires a complex calculus of balancing the needs of the backup versus the capabilities of the clients, which has no one way in which to work. But there are common threads to observe and ways to approach the design of the environments that make this calculus simpler than it may seem.

Long-Distance Backups

One of the topics touched on in the previous discussion regarding remote backups is the impact of WAN and distance on assessing the elements of design to include within a backup environment. The effects of latency and available bandwidth become very noticeable quickly as limiting factors in completing backups, even when only the metadata of the backups is traversing the link. But why?

Long-distance backups are defined as backups over a distance with a network length of more than 200 miles, or more than 20 ms of one way latency. The distance is defined in either terms of actual distance or latency distance because of a central problem: the speed of light. Any signal is inherently limited by the amount of time that light can travel from point A to point B. This is a "laws-of-physics" limitation—one that cannot be overcome. A 200-mile signal has approximately 10 ms of latency built in simply by the speed of light. This means that when running a synchronous protocol, such as TCP (which most backup software uses for transport), each packet of information requires a *round trip* delay of no less than 20 ms.

The actual time of transport will be much greater, however, as there are other elements that affect this latency. Network switching/routing, inline error correction, and line noise all add latency to the signal, increasing the average round trip time between points, and reducing the overall single stream throughput of a particular network connection. This network latency has profound effect on both direct backups as well as metadata, as it limits the amount of data that can be transported in a given unit of time, thus limiting either the amount of data that can be moved for a single backup stream or the amount of metadata that can be moved, increasing processing time and reducing the overall backup throughput at the originating site.

A related problem is that of bandwidth. Remember that speed and bandwidth are two separate but related measurements: speed is the amount of data that any particular connection can send per unit time between points, and bandwidth represents the total amount of "lanes" available, depending on connection speed (see Figure 9–14).

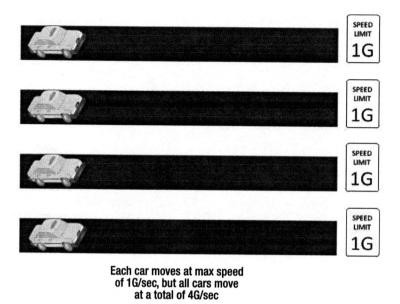

Each car moves at max speed
of 1G/sec, but all cars move
at a total of 4G/sec

Figure 9–14. Speed versus bandwidth

Bandwidth over distance may be limited by effects technology, available connectivity between sites, or cost. Bandwidth is particularly limiting for backups over distance because each distinct backup stream will generate its own connection at a particular rate, consuming the overall bandwidth available. A low bandwidth connection may be able to handle a larger number of streams at a lower transmission rate, or a smaller number of streams at a higher transmission rate. This balance between streams and bandwidth affects backups that are made directly across the connection and metadata. But metadata is not as affected as the amount of data, and the required transport rate tends to be lower than that of a standard backup stream.

Bandwidth over distance also can be very expensive. This is why it is typically a shared resource between differing types of users. Backups are generally only one user type among many competing users—one that can consume entire connections without planning. When looking at backup over distance, a consideration must be made about ways to limit the amount of bandwidth that the backup uses to allow other business as much access as possible so that these activities can continue to run.

So how can the impact of latency and bandwidth be reduced? There are several strategies, many of which have already been covered:

- Avoid WAN-based backups of data.

- Set up remote resources to act as local targets.

- Replicate efficiently, using compression or deduplication.

- Look at the use of WAN optimizing devices to reduce the amount of data actually transmitted over the WAN.

- Make backups as short as possible, potentially extending times between full backups to minimize the day-to-day impact of the backup traffic.

- Use synthetic full backup methods to make full backups at the central site from replicated incremental backups.

- Use alternate technologies, such as source-based deduplication, to keep traffic at a bare minimum.

- As a last resort, place local datazones in remote locations to fully run backups locally, only passing reporting and management information over the connection.

The use of these different strategies will optimize as much as possible the utilization of the WAN network connection.

Transnational Backups

Backups within a particular country, regardless of whether it is an RO, RS, RDC, or combination thereof, will usually present issues of distance and management, as discussed previously. However, backups that are managed across national borders have both technical and legal implications. From a technical standpoint, transnational backups should be treated as individual RDCs. This is due to general limitations in WAN connectivity that will prevent many of the backup methods that use distance management, such as remote media writers, from working effectively, due to the network distance limitations discussed above.

Aside from the technical issues, there are legal issues as well. Many countries have restrictions on the type and content of data that can leave their borders—backups included. Replications of backups may violate the laws of one or more countries as what is deemed "controlled" or "sensitive" information is transported across borders as a result of the replication process. The problem is compounded if the replication link traverses a number of countries in transit between the originating and target sites as the simple act of moving the data across the borders may result in violations in multiple jurisdictions at once.

For this reason it is important to do two things when working with trans-national backups:

- Consult with legal counsel to determine what the regulations are in the particular jurisdiction with regard to information transport.

- Treat the site as a separate "central" site to minimize the risk and exposure to these legal issues.

Only legal counsel can advise the backup administrator on what can and cannot be moved across borders. Not consulting some type of counsel on these matters can open the organization up to many different types of legal challenges that can be detrimental to the operation. So in order to avoid these issues as much as possible, simply treat the site as a new central site. Keeping backups and the management of the backups within the border of the jurisdiction should help reduce any issues that may arise.

Summary

Assembling all the elements of a backup environment is a complex task. Even from the simplest environments, the decisions that are made will have a profound effect as the environment grows and more data is backed up. Issues such as client performance, network congestion, and even legal issues must be considered when looking at backup environments to ensure that backups both provide the correct level of data protection and impact the organizational operation a little as possible.

This chapter provided a framework from which to consider all the different elements in order to create or modify a design for the backup environment that is appropriate to your environment.

CHAPTER 10

Monitoring and Reporting

Throughout this book, we have discussed various aspects of the backup environment: network utilization, server load, and so on, but have not discussed how you gather this information or what items are needed to be observed within the environment in order to determine its health. A good monitoring and reporting package is critical in gathering the needed data and presenting the information in a format that makes sense. Without such a package, it is virtually impossible to know when your environment needs to grow, or even to know why backups have their current performance characteristics—good or bad. This chapter is intended to provide an overview of the following:

- How to monitor backups
- What is necessary to monitor
- What metrics should be reported on

Monitoring and reporting are actually two separate items, but are generally grouped together. *Monitoring is focused around gathering data with the intent of performing some action based on the data.*

Monitoring can be either *real time*, in which case there is someone who can act on events produced by the monitor as they happen; or *periodic*, which will only provide the ability to react to events that have happened in the past. Monitoring is typically focused around tactical items such as individual image or subclient success, connection ability, and so on (items that need to be acted upon in a timely manner).

Reporting, on the other hand is used to determine items such as the higher-level success or failure of backups in the environment, the health of the environment, and strategic items such as the growth rates of the backups. *Reporting is an after-the-fact action: once all backups are complete, what is the ultimate result?*

Reporting is also used for other more strategic items such as capacity analysis, cost recovery and reporting, and so on, and provides standardized formats in which data is manipulated to meet the needs of the report consumers. Reporting may be a required feature within the environment, providing evidence of meeting regulatory requirements around the protection of sensitive or business critical data. More often, reporting is needed to demonstrate that data is being protected and to instill confidence in the ability to recover data as needed. This is particularly true for environments that use outsourcing to manage the backups—achievement of SLAs cannot be proven without accurate reporting of the metrics that make up the agreed-upon service level. However, reporting cannot happen without monitoring—while monitoring packages produce reports, reporting packages are useless without the data provided by the monitor.

When the term *package* is discussed, it simply means a collected method of gathering and reporting the data. There are a number of ways to perform the monitoring function, and any number of separate reporting packages can be used to manipulate the resulting data. But for the purposes of this chapter, only packages that include both a monitoring and reporting capability specifically targeted around the backup environment will be discussed.

A monitoring/reporting package can be one that is developed by the backup software provider, such as OpsCenter from Symantec (geared around NetBackup), or Simpana Monitor from CommVault, a third-party monitoring package such as EMC Data Protection Advisor or the APTARE suite of products, or even in-house data gathering, such as the use of shell scripts, written in languages such as Perl or Powershell, to query the backup software directly and send the results.

All these methods have their advantages and disadvantages, as shown in Table 10–1.

Table 10–1. Comparing Methods of Building or Acquiring Reporting Tools

Method	Advantages	Disadvantages
Backup software produced	<ul><li>Tight integration with backup software.</li><li>Provides solid reporting on all aspects the backup environment that is managed by the software.</li><li>Well-understood methods of monitoring more than one backup environment.</li><li>Reports provided are good reports, but limited in scope.</li><li>Automation built in for report distribution.</li></ul>	<ul><li>Does not gather data about items outside of the backup software, but relevant to health, such as network or operating system (OS)–level information</li><li>Reports have limited or no customizing ability—what you see is what you get.</li><li>Cannot monitor more than a single vendor of backup software.</li></ul>
Third party	<ul><li>Good integration with backup software.</li><li>Provides views into aspects of the backup environment that are not simply backup software–related such as network, OS, and other hardware.</li><li>Reporting is robust and highly customizable.</li><li>Can report on multiple backup software vendors in a single view.</li><li>Report automation is built in for distribution.</li><li>Can report on more esoteric storage media such as cloud providers.</li></ul>	<ul><li>Requires either installation of separate agent on backup server(s) and/or clients to be monitored, installation of backup software on reporting server, or both.</li><li>Requires access to multiple management domains (network, server, storage area network (SAN), and so on) in order to gather non-backup–related information.</li><li>Agents can add additional load on backup servers/clients.</li><li>Can be version-sensitive—only specific software versions may be supported.</li><li>Cost can be significant.</li></ul>

Method	Advantages	Disadvantages
In-house data gathering	• Tight integration with backup software as it is queried directly. • Targeted information gathering—only the information needed is provided. • Does not rely on additional servers to store data unless desired to have longer term storage. • Troubleshooting can be fast—knowledge is in-house. • Low capital cost of entry.	• Maintenance and support is completely in-house. If your developer leaves, who can write additional code? • No reporting capability other than simple statistics or status reports. Any reporting would also have to be developed. • Difficult to adjust existing reports to meet new criteria. • Does not keep data inherently—no way to query historical data without manual maintenance of data store. • Can also be *very* version-dependent. • Does not provide any capability to gather information about other aspects of the environment to provide correlation.

So which parts of the backup environment should you gather data from? There are three areas from which data should be collected for analysis as part of a monitoring and reporting package:

- Backup software

- Backup servers

- Backup media utilization

This represents the minimum amount of data that should be collected. If at all possible, data should also be gathered on the following sections of a backup environment:

- Client health

- Network (LAN/WAN)

- SAN (if used)

- Deduplication ratios (if using deduplication)

This optional data, even if only parts of it can be gathered, will provide a more complete view of the backup environment and allow for better analysis and troubleshooting.

Backup Software

Backup software is the source of the vast majority of data necessary to analyze the environment. Without the data provided by backup software, even simple items such as "how well is my backup system running?" will be impossible to assess. Fortunately, this type of data is also the easiest to gather as it is provided in any number of ways from the backup software. At a minimum, the following data points should be gathered from the backup software on a daily basis:

- Number of failed/successful backups

- Backup speed of clients protected

- Failure codes from incomplete backups

- Amount of data protected

- Amount of disk storage capacity used for backup targets

- Number of free/consumed media under management (tape backup only)

- Location of current catalog backup

Both combined and separate, this data provides all the basic information that is needed to completely manage and assess the health of the backups that are occurring (or not).

Success/Failure

The rationale behind measuring the number of failed backups is fairly obvious, but why measure the number of successful backups? It provides a measure of scale and effectiveness of the backup environment when comparing the number of failures with the number of successes. If an environment were to have 100 failed backups per night, that would sound like a large number. However, if the number of successful backups is 800, the number of failed backups in relation to the number of successful backups is much better to assess (although, 100 failures would not be a number to strive for). However, trying to achieve a 100 percent success rate is unrealistic as well—there will always be some percentage of clients that fail for reasons outside of the control of the backup software. Good backup success rates range between 95–99 percent from backup window to window.

Failure Codes

In addition to gathering simple statistics regarding the number of success and failures, it is also important to gather a list of the failure codes that are generated when the backups do fail. This enables two critical functions. The first is obviously troubleshooting failed backups in order to ensure that they run correctly in the future. However, a secondary (and in some ways more important) function is the assessment of failure trends within the backup environment. Clusters of the same type of backup failures within the environment as a whole, or even within a group of clients, can point to overall structural problems within the environment that can possibly lead to bigger problems. Even sets of related failures can point to specific issues within the environment that may eventually lead to systemic failure.

Client Backup Speed

In a number of previous discussions, the ability of the client to send data to the backup media was the main gating factor in determining the ability of a particular client to be able to be backed up in a timely manner. Additionally, the client backup speeds, in aggregate and as compared to the available amount of backup windows and media resources, also determine the number of backups that can be completed by the environment as a whole. This measure also provides a method by which problem clients can be identified, as slow backups may be an indication of other issues that the backup client may be having in general.

Amount of Data Protected

The amount of data is critical in determining the overall growth rate of the environment and is needed to identify both how much data is protected, but also allows the ability to project when the environment will run out of capacity. The current size provides another measure of scope when assessing the overall backup environment. The health of a backup environment that backs up 100 TB in 12 hours is vastly different from one that backs up 10 TB in 12 hours with the same hardware and configuration! The amount of data backed up also is needed to simply determine how much capacity is left in the environment, how fast it is consumed and project when more capacity will need to be added for backup storage.

Count of Current Tape Media

Related to the amount of data backed up within the environment is the measurement of the media count or storage capacity of the backup media. Media count measurements are utilized for tape-based environments and are useful in determining the size of libraries needed, maintaining expected inventory of backup tapes, and tracking the number of tapes consumed over a given period of time. These types of interpretations of this data allows the assessment of both the available and projected capacity of tape, as well as projecting costs associated with additional tape purchases to support both normal operations as well as environmental growth.

Disk Storage Capacity

Storage capacity is a measurement used for disk-based backup environments. The measurement of the amount of data backed up is not useful, particularly in a disk-based environment, without a benchmark of comparison. The storage capacity measurement should be taken in two different manners: based on individual DSU/MagLib units and as a measurement of the capacity of the environment as a whole. The individual units are important to measure to ensure that there is capacity for use in the next round of backups—a tactical measure. However, the environment capacity is a more strategic measure. This determines the overall potential capacity of the environment and can help pinpoint specific disk units that are being overloaded, making the environment as a whole look fuller than it really is. For instance, if a given environment has 100 TB of capacity, and backups are failing on four 10 TB media writers due to full targets, but the remainder of the backups are successful, it may indicate that the particular media writers have too much data pointed at them. In this case, a study should be undertaken to determine free space is available to distribute the load, thus making better use of the total capacity of the environment.

Location of Last Catalog Backup

The last (and possibly most important) critical element that should be reported on is maintaining the report on the location and viability of the last catalog backup. In the event of a catastrophic loss of the backup server, whether related to physical disaster or to simple failure, quickly locating the last catalog backup will be critical to bringing the environment back online. Without this report, and especially in an environment where there are a large number of backup images (either tape or disk), simply determining the location and image identifier of the last good catalog backup may be impossible, as there is not any unique identifier that targets a particular backup image as a catalog backup. A unique requirement of this particular element is that the information should be stored in a format and a location that can be available in the event that electronic access to the backup is not possible. Without knowing the location and identity of the last catalog backup, it is virtually impossible to rebuild the backup environment in the event of a disaster, as the catalog contains all information the backup software needs to restore data to the clients.

This represents a minimum listing of the elements within the backup software that should be monitored and reported on during the regular daily backup cycle. The data that is gathered as a result of these monitoring reports can be combined with other data to produce other types of analysis that may be useful to the environment as a whole.

Backup Servers

The data gathered from the backup software is only part of the answer. As has been discussed in previous chapters, while the performance of the backup is largely gated by how fast the backup client can move data, the total potential ability of the backup environment to gather data in aggregate is gated by the ability of the backup servers to process data, in the case of the backup servers, and by the ability of the media writers to move the data. The data that needs to be gathered and reported upon are the usual suspects:

- CPU utilization

- Memory utilization

- Network utilization

CPU Utilization

CPU utilization applies primarily to the backup servers, such as the Master server or CommServe. The utilization of the CPU determines the ability of the backup server to process the backup metadata as it is being received. As CPU utilization climbs, the ability to process metadata begins to decrease as the processor can take on less and less work. This does not apply much to media writers as their CPU requirements are largely irrelevant to the ability to move data to the media. CPU utilization is generally measured in units of percent utilized.

Memory Utilization

Memory utilization does affect both backup servers and media writers. System RAM is used for several items and determines both how much data can be cached for writing to media, as well as the number of backups that can be run. RAM is used to provide caching areas for the backup media in order to regulate the data stream that is written to the device and smooth out the data being received from the client. The smoothing process optimizes the data flow to the device to maximize the throughput. The caching process also allows multiplexing to work by interleaving blocks from the cache as they are received. If RAM is in short supply, cache cannot be allocated and, in some cases, the processes that receive the backup stream may not start.

A lack of RAM also can limit the number of backups that can run for the same reason. Each backup consumes some amount of system memory on both the backup server and the media writer; on the backup server for connections to the catalog metadata processing; and connections to processes to actually write the data to the backup media on the media writer. These connections may be manifested in creating cache areas, starting additional processes, or both. Either way, additional RAM is consumed per backup started. The amount of RAM can provide a simple gate to the number of processes that can start—and therefore the number of backups.

Network Utilization

The backup data must make it to the backup servers before either of these two factors can even come into account. Network utilization provides a measure of the amount of throughput that can get to the servers. Network utilization can be measured from a number of different locations, depending on the amount of instrumentation that is available and the capabilities of the monitoring and reporting package used. However, the simplest measure is the network utilization of the backup server (and media writer) network connection. This will provide a basic measure of the performance and limitations of the local connections—a measure of how much data can *potentially* be received at the server side.

But what to measure? There are many different points of measurement that are built into the operating system. Just a basic view is shown in Figure 10–1 of some of the many different types of data that can be gathered to determine performance.

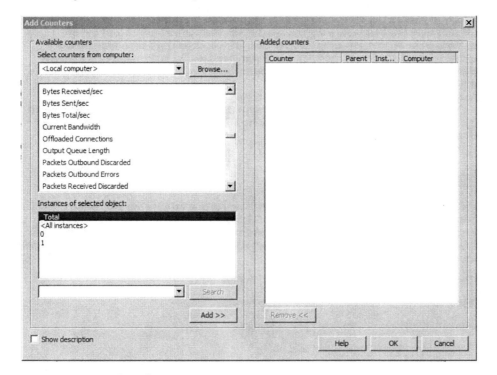

Figure 10–1. *Network performance counters*

So which ones are needed from a backup server perspective? While all the elements provide useful information and can be used to drill down into specific issues, the two general elements that are most useful to gather data on are the total number of bytes per second and the number of packets per second that pass through the interface. Of this, since this is a backup server (or media writer), the vast majority of data throughput that is relevant to monitor is the "read" or "received" component of these measures. Since the backup server is generally receiving data to write to other media, there should not be much data being written back out the network interface.

The exception to this is when using NAS-based media, such as a CIFS share or a deduplication appliance as the media target. When using these types of devices, the media writer in particular simply acts as a pass-through device, taking backup data streams in and redirecting them back out to a secondary target. This consumes both received and sent sides of the network interface.

The two types of data describe two different aspects of the network that affect the performance of backups. The measurement of the amount of bytes per second through the network interface allows for the determination of the percentage of available bandwidth that has been consumed during the point of backups. Once the total amount of bytes per second begins to approach the total amount of bandwidth available, the overall throughput of the system will start to decline, assuming that the network is the limiting factor for the backup. This applies to both backup servers and media writers, but more so to the media writers as there is more data to move, and the impact of slower throughput is more pronounced. However, this can apply to backup servers in the processing of metadata. If the throughput of the metadata is slowed due to the consumption of bandwidth by other uses, the overall throughput of the environment will be reduced. This is particularly noticeable when using a single server as both the backup server and media writer since the network interface is doing double duty.

The measurement of packets per second represents the number of connections that are possible on a given interface. With a network interface of a given bandwidth, there are a limited number of individual packets that can be processed in that bandwidth. This essentially places a limit on the number of connections that can be introduced to a particular interface. As more packets are passed through the interface, the number that can be processed is reduced, and the overall ability to have clients back up in parallel is reduced.

Taken together, the combination of the bytes and packets per second provide a picture into the network health of the backup environment. Reporting on one section only provides half of the picture. Both items need to be taken into consideration when looking at how the network impacts the overall backup environment.

Backup Media Utilization

The last backup software component that needs to be monitored is that around the utilization of backup media in the environment. Backup media is the ultimate determinant of the holding capacity of the environment as a whole, without information regarding how much of the media holding capacity is in use, or how much is available for use. When managing backup environments that use tape as the backup media, it is important to track the following data:

- Total number of tapes in the environment and the identities

- Number and identities of tapes in scratch

- Number and identities of tapes used and still onsite

- Number and identities of tapes used and offsite

For environments that use disk as the storage media, obviously different data needs to be gathered on the capacity of the environment:

- Total capacity

- Capacity per media writer

- Remaining capacity per media writer

Tape environments require detailed tracking of the media in order to ensure that media is available for the next backup cycle, that the correct media is used, and that media that has not reached scheduled expiration is not used and correctly stored. Capacity within tape environments is entirely driven by the number of cartridges that are available. The total number of tapes in the environment provides the potential backup capacity. This statistic is used as the baseline for other measurements.

Optional Elements

The preceding items represent the critical items that should be monitored and reported upon in order to keep a minimum of a healthy environment. There are several other areas that should also be monitored to get a better picture of the overall environment:

- Client performance

- Network performance

- SAN/Disk performance

- Deduplication ratios

Client Performance

Client performance has been listed multiple times as a gating factor on the performance of individual backups. But if this is the case, why not monitor the performance at the client level (CPU, RAM, network, I/O) for all clients, all the time? There are several reasons. First, the quantity of data that would be gathered, even from a small environment, would be large and not have a lot of value. The vast majority of clients within the backup environment will not have issues—gathering information of this type regarding clients is only useful when identifying problems. There is a case to be made around performing predictive analysis of key clients—gather data full time, and use this data to ensure that performance is always at peak—however, this is generally accomplished for application purposes, not for backup purposes.

CPU/RAM Utilization

Measuring the CPU and RAM utilization is useful in determining client performance for the same reasons as they are valuable in determining server performance—they gate the number and speed with which processes can run at any particular time. If backup processes either cannot run, are queued for running, or run at a lower priority, they will run slower on a given CPU. Likewise, if there is not enough RAM to completely run the backup process, it will be "swapped" between memory and disk, thus slowing the overall process (and therefore backup) performance. Looking at these utilization factors can identify if this is an issue during the backup process that is affecting the overall performance. Looking at the data over a period of time may identify particular time periods where this utilization is at a minimum and guide the backup to be performed during these points.

I/O Utilization

I/O utilization of the client also has an impact on the client performance. If the client is running an I/O-intensive process, such as a database, during the backup, the backup process is competing for the I/O available on the particular device. This can be especially pronounced on database stream backups, using functionality similar to either VDI or RMAN, as discussed previously. Since the database is active during the backup, any backup activity competes with that generated by the database itself. Previously this was discussed in the context of the backup affecting the application performance. However, this data can help suggest periods in which the backup speed can be maximized by running the backup during periods of lower I/O—thus providing the backup client with maximum available bandwidth to move the backup data. The same methodology can be applied to any other type of application as well—simply look for the dip in I/O and apply the backup there.

Client Network Utilization

Client network utilization also can have a significant impact on the backup performance. Just as with client CPU and memory, if the client is generating a quantity of network traffic that is not related to the backup, the backup has to compete with this traffic for transmission time. The good news is that there can be a correlation between network and I/O traffic—if an application is generating I/O, the data has to be coming from/going to some source. However, this is not always the case—data may be being processed for local storage or use by another piece of the application. However, there is enough of a correlation in general to warrant the observation of both to determine if simply putting the backup during the point of low I/O will solve the issue.

If this is not the case, the same method can be used to identify points at which the backup throughput can be maximized: look for lulls in the throughput and apply the backup at that point. But there are cases where there is either not a lull or the lull is not significant enough to make an overall difference in the backup throughput. This is where the network data from the client can lead to a decision regarding the conversion of the backup client into a dedicated media writer—a Dedicated Media Server in the case of NetBackup, or a Dedicated MediaAgent for a CommVault environment. If the network will no longer support the transmission of the backup in a timely manner, and the data set is much larger than the size of the network connection (a minimum of 200 GB for Gigabit Ethernet, for instance), this is the time when the media writer conversion should be considered. However, the point of this discussion is not to provide a solution to this particular problem. This discussion is intended to highlight the purpose of monitoring and reporting: to provide information that is needed to make decisions regarding any changes that may be necessary for the backup environment, and point the administrator in the right direction.

Network Performance

When looking at network performance, the network measured at the client and at the server are not the only points of potential performance or reliability issues. When dealing with either LAN or WAN connections, there is an entire infrastructure that lies between the connection points that can introduce issues into the environment. In gathering data regarding network issues, the view at the transporting infrastructure level is also instructive—both the client and the servers may have plenty of available network bandwidth, but the backups across the connection are still slow.

A couple of simple tests can check to see if the transport itself is the issue. Results from ping tests—issuing the 'ping' command on the backup client, targeting the server, reversing the process, and observing the latency results—can expose networks that have latency issues that may be affecting the performance of the network. Using a separate, simple transport mechanism such as FTP to test the transfer rates between points can give a basis of comparison that can be used against the backup transport rates. If the rates are roughly the same order of magnitude, the transport itself can be identified as a potential problem.

It is not recommended that data be gathered directly from the network infrastructure by the backup administrators, unless a) they are qualified or responsible for the network infrastructure, and b) they have an understanding of the data that is gathered. The data that is and can be gathered on LAN and/or WAN networks is very complex and has a great deal of interdependency on the topology of the network from which the data is gathered. If a network issue is suspected, perform the basic tests that were suggested previously and work with the network administrators to identify any issues that may exist between the client and the servers involved. Taking this approach removes the backup software from the analysis and either isolates the issue to the network or will eliminate the network as the source of the performance problem. In some cases, you may be simply identifying what are known as "law of physics" issues—performance problems that are caused by factors that cannot be changed due to items such as route processing time, distance-based latency issues, available bandwidth, and so on. However, without qualified review of these data points, correct interpretation of issues will be impossible.

SAN/Disk Performance

SAN environments present similar issues. While not as complex as LAN/WAN environments, they have their own performance characteristics and issues that require qualified analysis, but there are some simple tests that can be run to determine whether there are issues with the transport itself. Disk performance in general, and by extension the gross level performance of the SAN, can be measured with tools that are built into the OS. However, just as with the LAN measurement tools, disk performance measurement tools have many different points of measurement (see Figure 10–2).

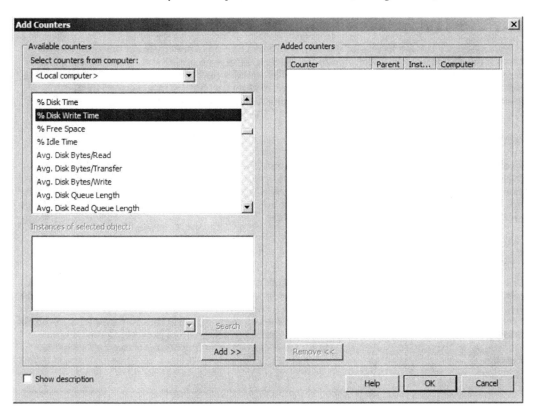

Figure 10–2. *Disk performance counters*

Again, just as with the network counters, the disk counters have a number of different data points that can be captured, each measuring a different aspect of disk performance. Unfortunately, unlike the network components, the critical disk measurements of IOPS and latency can only be inferred from these measures since they are variable in nature and have a dependency on the individual block of data being transferred at any period of time. Additionally, latency in particular and transfer rates in general can be affected by the underlying SAN fabric that extends between the physical disk and the client/server using the storage. Also, in most disk arrays attached to SAN fabrics, there are significant amounts of cache, with particular "staging" methods that also affect the performance of storage and I/O rates that are achievable with a particular set of physical disks. None of the data regarding these aspects of a SAN is directly observable from the OS—it requires specialized tools to gather and analyze the data to determine problem areas.

So what can be done to help determine if there is an I/O issue? Watch three elements over time to determine *trends* in the data:

- Disk idle percentage
- Bytes moved per time
- Disk queue depth

Disk Idle Percentage

Disk idle percentage will expose how busy the disk is without having to specify exact metrics on what busy means. If the disk is 0 percent idle, that indicates that there is no additional "time" for the disk to accomplish any other tasks, and that there may be a disk transfer problem. If the disk is 50 percent idle, there is still potential for transfer, but other issues may be blocking. Both Windows and UNIX environments can measure this metric using the various tools that are included with the OS.

Bytes Moved Per Time

Bytes moved per time is simply a measurement of bandwidth. By looking at the amount of data that is transmitted and comparing it with the "theoretical" bandwidth available on a connection (or set of connections), a gross determination can be made to see whether the data is being moved at a rate to the disk drives that is within the order of magnitude expected by the connection speed. If it is not within the expected limits, a disk issue may be causing the problem.

Disk Queue Depth

Finally, the *disk queue depth* measures the outstanding activity that remains unprocessed and queued for transfer from the OS to disk. The disk queue is related to the disk idle time and largely correlates how busy a disk is to how fast it takes the disk, from the OS perspective, to accept the transfer and move to the next transfer. The queue length can be artificially limited, depending on the characteristics of the OS and the storage subsystem to prevent the queue from getting too large, thus preventing the I/O from never catching up to the workload. Again, both Windows and UNIX environments can measure this queue directly.

■ **Note** In both the LAN and SAN sections, external experts are recommended to be consulted when looking at performance issues. However, do *not* simply state the problem as "My [LAN|SAN] is slow." That type of problem definition does not help in identifying any issues that may be occurring. Slow is a subjective measure and has no relevance unless compared to a previous state. Bring data that supports a problem definition of "I have noticed a slowdown in my backups. I think it may because of the [network|disk] and here is the data I have that shows what I think to be the issue." This approach will be much more useful as the specialist will have some baseline data to interpret and consider, rather than just a general statement, and will speed resolution/explanation.

Deduplication Ratios

The previous measurements of client, network, and SAN data were centered on primarily performance data; the measurement of the *deduplication ratio* is a capacity-centric measurement. In the previous discussions about deduplication, the type of data stored had a very large determinate factoring on the efficiency of the deduplication process and subsequently the amount of data actually stored. The measurement of the data actually stored to the data transferred is the deduplication ratio. In order to capacity plan for a deduplication environment, it is important to understand both the day-to-day deduplication ratios as well as long-term deduplication.

The day-to-day deduplication ratio is important to understand in order to gauge efficiency of the deduplication process and to identify the daily growth rate of the appliance. This measure will help identify trends from a daily perspective and allow the ability to project the growth of the data within the appliance. This will help prevent the appliance from filling up and ensure that space is available for daily backups by providing an estimated space requirement for that day, based on the historical deduplication rates for that cycle.

Deduplication rates should be measured between cycles and not between days. Why? When performing backups, there tends to be patterns that emerge between specific days of the backup cycle, more so than from day to day. Think of it this way: if on every Monday a processing task is performed, on Tuesday a read-only analysis of the task is performed, and Wednesday through Friday new data is generated, the type and quantity of data will vary from day to day. But if looked at between subsequent Monday backups, for instance, the same type of activity occurs, generating similar patterns of data storage and access, and providing a general pattern of access that can affect deduplication. Looking at the deduplication ratio between cycles will help to identify the patterns that can be used to ensure that for a particular day, storage is available for use and that subsequent growth of a particular day will not attempt to overfill the appliance and subsequently fail the backup cycle.

The long-term deduplication rate is useful in projecting capacity needs for the environment as a whole. While the deduplication rate from day to day will vary, the long-term deduplication rate determines the overall effectiveness of the storage, which allows for the projection of needs for future deduplication appliances, as well as assess the overall effectiveness of the appliance as it applies to the environment. If the overall deduplication of the environment declines as new data types are added, it may indicate that the effectiveness deduplication may not warrant the use of the appliance for that data type.

Summary

Monitoring and reporting is a critical component of the backup environment. Without any type of reporting mechanism, it is impossible to determine if the environment is healthy, or even if backups are completing successfully. There are several items that should be monitored within the environment to provide basic health and success statistics, with several others that can help with both troubleshooting and the long-term health of the environment as a whole. Monitoring provides the backup administrator with critical information in a timely manner to ensure that backups run as reliably as possible. Reporting serves an equally critical role in providing structured information that can be used to ensure that items such as agreed-upon Service Level Agreements (SLAs) are met and that management is aware of backup successes and business value.

■ ■ ■

CHAPTER 11

Summary

This book has covered a great number of technical details regarding how to think about designing and maintaining backup and recovery environments. This chapter is dedicated to summarizing some final thoughts about backup and recovery in general.

Good Backup Is Important!

In most environments, backups are treated as an afterthought, insurance against something that will "never" happen, or as an annoyance that must be completed. However, this is far from the truth. Good backups provide protection to any organization. In this day and age, information is king—the better your information, the better the organization can perform and compete. Given this emphasis on data, it should be treated just as you would treat physical inventory—securing, preventing loss, and having additional stock on hand if the original stock is lost. Backups provide a means by which all these functions can be completed, thus protecting critical assets within the organization.

More and more, data backups are required to meet organizational, legal, or regulatory requirements. Organizations, particularly large organizations or publicly traded companies, are required by various regulatory agency and/or by Sarbanes-Oxley (commonly known as SOX) to maintain data backups of business critical data for specified periods of time. Businesses and organizations that fall under the requirements of SOX must maintain records related to specific financial and other types of transactions, as well as other types of business records for a period of no shorter than five years after the conclusion of the "audit period"—typically the end of the fiscal year. The records must be protected in such a way to be retrievable for "future use"—essentially the records must be backed up so they will be unaffected by changes or deprecation of technology. Businesses and organizations that do not comply with these requirements can be subjected to heavy fines and perhaps other penalties. Backups represent the only acceptable way to meet many of these requirements and should be treated with the appropriate level of importance.

Backups also provide productivity benefits by protecting data. Without a backup, data that is lost represents lost productivity in either re-creating or regenerating the information for the organization. If this is critical information for the business to run, it may also represent income lost because the data may affect business decisions or operations. Additional productivity can also be realized from backups through the use of them as a data replication mechanism. While there are more efficient methods of data replication, there are certain situations in which backups can provide a secure method of replicating entire images of data to remote locations, where they can be restored and used either as primary data sources, reporting sources, or simply as copies of live data for application or other types of development.

The bottom line—backups protect the business. Yes, it is like buying insurance—nobody likes to pay for something that may or may not happen, costs a lot of money, and does not obviously contribute to the bottom line. However, unlike insurance, backups are used more frequently than is realized by those holding the money, something a good reporting structure can help illustrate.

Reporting does more than simply provide information to manage the environment. A good reporting infrastructure allows the backup administrator to provide information about the usefulness of a backup to the organization. Backup reports can show the frequency of restores, which represent the value of not losing data to the organization. Backup success rates show the overall value of cost avoidance and/or productivity loss by protecting critical data sets.

Defending Costs

Backup costs money. Sometimes a lot of money. But as we have discussed previously, there is value in that expenditure in protecting the business. There are some strategies that can be used to defend what seems to the business to be a never-ending outflow of cash against something that does not seem to add any tangible value to the business.

First, there are business costs to not having backups. As was discussed above, the cost of losing data has some value to the business. Compare the loss of this business data, in terms of revenue and productivity lost, against the cost of the backup environment. In most, if not all cases, the cost of losing the data far outweighs the cost of the backup.

Second, there are increasing regulatory requirements to maintain backup copies of data that is deemed critical to business operations. Data such as e-mail, product designs, source code, and so on are business assets and may be required to be protected under any number of regulatory codes. Something as simple as log files detailing transactions that are executed by key business members can be required to be maintained for extended periods of time. If these data types are not maintained, the impact to the business may be large fines, censure, or restriction of business operations; and in extreme cases (or Sarbanes-Oxley compliance cases), the potential of criminal and/or civil penalties. These all represent large potential costs on the business that can be levied if data is not protected. Performing backups represent a small cost against these types of impacts.

The last type of impact was referenced above: legal. In an increasing number of cases, businesses are being litigated against based on their intentions, not necessarily their actions. These intentions are being illustrated using electronic evidence such as e-mail, documents, and electronic financial records. In some cases, these pieces of evidence may be taken out of context to illustrate a particular point of view. Typically the only defense is to show the full context of what was intended. If that context is not available because there were no backups of that data taken, there is nothing to provide a defense against such accusations. While the converse argument—the historical data can be as damning as the presented evidence—can be made, backups of data are probably your best defense.

Be sure to consult your legal advisors for their interpretation of the best strategy! They are the experts in the legal field, so structure your backups according to their best estimate of the risk. In any case, the cost of not having backups at all in the case of ligation can be as great as, if not greater than, the regulatory risk listed previously, and will also outweigh the cost of the infrastructure.

Taken as a whole—business, regulatory, and legal—the cost avoidance that is afforded by having a strong backup infrastructure is a small price to pay. Even if none of these is ever realized, it typically only takes one case to sink a business. A statistic that is often quoted is that 70 percent of the businesses without a strong backup and recovery infrastructure that were affected by 9/11 never reopened. Of the remaining 30 percent, almost 90 percent of them failed within 6 months. While we all hope that 9/11 was a one-time event, there are any number of catastrophes (fires, floods, tornadoes, and so on) that can have similar impacts from a business perspective. It is a small cost to the business and the people that are employed there to simply have good backups.

One Size Does *Not* Fit All...

Within this book, a number of different environment sizes, configurations and options have been discussed. However, they all represent starting points, or points along a continuum of backup infrastructure. The size and configuration of backup environments is as varied as the organizations, departments and divisions which they support. There is no one formula that can be applied to backup environments—they are entities unto themselves that cannot be defined precisely ahead of time, nor predicted in their growth. While this seems to be an obvious fact, there is always pressure to define what an environment will look like in some period of time in the future. While general cases can be made, as we have seen, any number of variations in the data, business, and organization structure can radically alter the direction of the environment.

One analogy I like to use is that a piece of backup software is an operating system unto itself. It has a core structure, relationships to other clients, and communication methods, and it is heavily reliant on the underlying hardware to perform very low-level tasks—all basic items that an operating system has to undertake. It is an operating system that must successfully complete the most complex of tasks—taking all types of disparate data and combining them into a single managed data stream that can be interpreted at some time in the future. The fact that it can be accomplished at all is amazing in itself. The fact that people, as the readers of this book, can comprehend such complexity and succeed in the face of such adversity, often in nameless anonymity, is even more extraordinary. Hopefully what has been written here will provide assistance in creating solutions that solve the ever-growing and more complex problem of protecting critical business data through backups for organizations of all sizes.

Index

■ ■ ■

W, X

Y

Z

Breinigsville, PA USA
28 February 2011
256442BV00004B/1/P

05500747